HER FINEST HOUR

HER FINEST HOUR

THE HEROIC LIFE OF DIANA ROWDEN, WARTIME SECRET AGENT

GABRIELLE McDONALD-ROTHWELL

AMBERLEY

First published 2017

Amberley Publishing
The Hill, Stroud
Gloucestershire, GL5 4EP

www.amberley-books.com

British Library Cataloguing in Publication Data.
A catalogue record for this book is available from the British Library.

ISBN 978 1 4456 6164 3 (hardback)
ISBN 978 1 4456 6165 0 (ebook)

Typesetting and Origination by Amberley Publishing.
Printed in the UK.

But the souls of the righteous are in the hand of God,
and there shall no torment touch them ...

- The Book of Wisdom

To Geoffrey

And to all the men and women, the brave *résistants* who fought
in the Jura in the Second World War

Contents

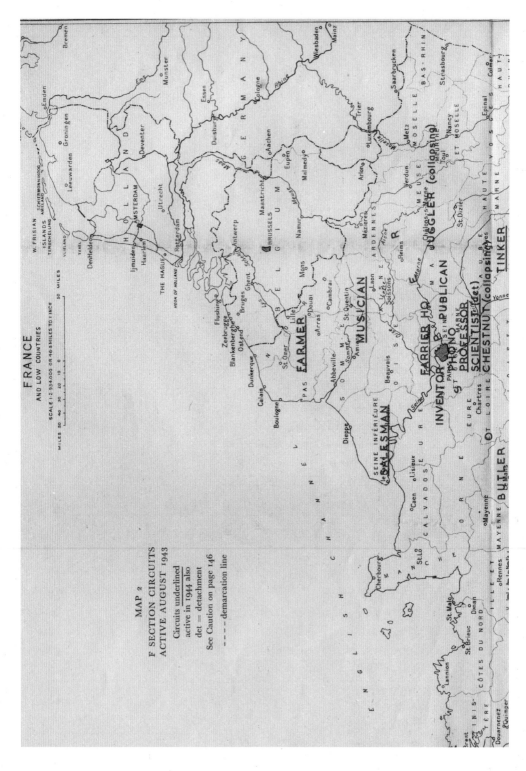

FRANCE
AND LOW COUNTRIES

SCALE 1:2,934,000 OR 46·5 MILES TO 1 INCH

MILES 50 40 30 20 10 0 50 MILES

MAP 2

F SECTION CIRCUITS
ACTIVE AUGUST 1943

Circuits underlined
active in 1944 also
det = detachment
See Caution on page 146
---- demarcation line

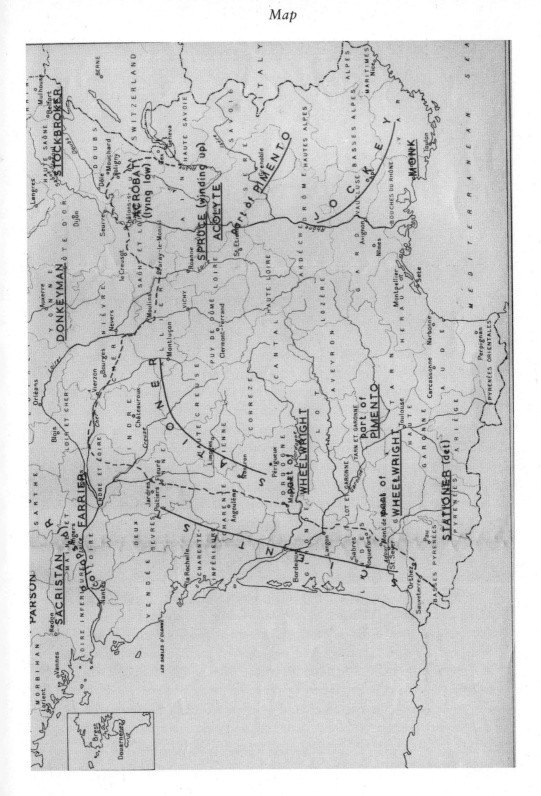

Foreword

This book reveals a story of heroism, betrayal, despair, inhumanity and execution.

I am delighted and I feel very honoured to be invited to write this foreword. I have studied the members of the Special Operations Executive (SOE) French Section for nearly thirty years. My interest began after family visits to France in the 1980s when I was intrigued by memorials that are not seen in Britain, simply because we were not occupied. These memorials are to people who died in the war after deportation to the concentration camps or as hostages who were summarily shot. Consequently, I decided to learn more about the brave people of the French Resistance and it soon became very clear to me that the British were greatly involved. It is comforting to note that the French are belatedly becoming increasingly aware of the part played by the SOE in training, arming and coordinating sabotage and an armed insurgency. Eisenhower claimed that the effectiveness of the French Resistance shortened the war by nine months.

In May 1940, around the time of Dunkirk, Winston Churchill was appointed as Prime Minister. Shortly afterwards, France was defeated. For the first time in British history, we could not land troops onto mainland Europe. Churchill had experienced warfare several times and realised the value of fighting the enemy from within. The SOE was formed to harass the enemy, to sabotage factories and infrastructure and to eventually prepare for the day when we could finally invade and liberate Europe. SOE operated in all occupied countries – though France was arguably the most important as it was the location of the landings on D-Day.

Churchill famously wanted to 'Set Europe Ablaze', but who was going to strike the matches? The task was given to the SOE to train and then transport agents behind enemy lines. Agents trained as Organisers, recruited and then trained French volunteers, arranged parachute drops of the necessary arms and explosives, and coordinated attacks. Wireless Operators were vital to send and receive coded signals to arrange supply drops for the planned missions. Couriers, mainly women, carried messages between the Wireless Operator and the Organiser. In 1942, Churchill gave permission for women to be recruited by SOE. For the first time in warfare, women would be treated in the same way as men and expected to attack the enemy and face similar dangers.

But who were the SOE agents? The main requirement was to have excellent language skills, to be resourceful, brave and dedicated. One such person was Diana Rowden, a British subject, and who was one of the thirty-nine women agents who volunteered to serve her country with the aim of liberating France – the country she loved and had adopted. Unlike most British recruits, Diana had experienced life under the Nazis before managing to escape from France via Spain to England in 1941. Consequently, she knew exactly what to expect – and yet despite this, Diana bravely volunteered to return as an SOE courier.

Diana Rowden is listed on my website as one of the 425 agents of the SOE French Section that operated in occupied France during the Second World War. Her story is just one of many that could, and perhaps should, be told. Each one on the list was an ordinary person who when the need arose put their hand up and offered to perform some extraordinary deeds. Diana's story illustrates the power of the human spirit to fight for what she believed to be right.

Gabrielle Rothwell has written an inspirational account of human endeavour, devotion and sacrifice. She has thoroughly researched her subject by the use of all the available books, records and reports. She has discovered new information through interviews and has made use of her access to private family papers. The writer describes in detail the selection and training of SOE agents and sets the scene of occupied France into which her subject was landed. Diana Rowden's arrest has been thoroughly examined and remains an intriguing event in the history of SOE in France. The post-war trial and punishment of Diana's captors and executioners makes grim reading but makes one proud of the way the SOE and some brave French citizens stood up to their evil enemy. Through the efforts of people like Diana Rowden, Nazi Germany was defeated and we, the fortunate ones, benefit today from that fight and sacrifice. May we remember Diana Rowden and all that she and her comrades endured. This book describes her finest hour so that she should never be forgotten.

David M. Harrison
Lytham St Anne's, UK
www.soe-french.co.uk

Preface

May, 2005: I am sitting in a very old church in Ottrott-le-Haut, high in the Vosges Mountains in eastern France, many thousands of miles from my home in New Zealand. The church is small and beautiful and I drink in its cool, dark atmosphere. Candles glow beneath the statues of St Mary and St Joseph. There is a mixture of smells – incense and history down the years. It is here that I seek escape from the day's images: the camp at Natzweiler, a young English woman in WAAF uniform, a white monument pointing to the sky, a green guard tower, steps leading down to a crematorium with an oven so small I cannot envisage how it contained a human body, a chimney, dirty cells with scratch marks on the walls, as if the occupants have tried desperately to claw their way out, a plaque outside the crematorium with the names of four women: Andrée Borrel, Vera Leigh, Diana Rowden and Sonia Olschanesky.

What has brought me here to this place so far from my home? This is a question I have often been asked, from hoteliers, from people I have asked directions, and even from my own family. All are incredulous that I would undertake such a journey. In my heart I know the answer. My mission is to research the life of one of these women, Diana Rowden, an agent for a top-secret wartime organisation, the Special Operations Executive (SOE), and the only English girl in the party of four women who were executed in a concentration camp virtually unknown, Natzweiler, the only camp on French soil – a place of horror and death.

Diana had been working as a courier in the Jura – a particularly dangerous area in France as the Germans knew English agents were in the zone, and with the Allies on the offensive that the end of the war was in sight. The Jura was an area riddled with Nazis, double and even triple agents, spies in the pay of the German Gestapo, thieves and murderers – people only too happy to throw in their lot with the occupying forces.

The story of Diana Hope Rowden has never been told in full, and, in the words of Maurice Buckmaster, head of the French Section of SOE, 'The stories of some of Diana's contempories have to a large extent eclipsed her magnificent record.'

For many years in my capacity as a journalist and war historian I had studied the Second World War, in particular the Special Operations Executive and the Royal Air Force. I had heard and read much about women agents such as Odette Churchill and Violette Szabo, but it was not until 2004 that the idea of writing Diana's biography first germinated. A friend of mine and my mother's who lived close to me in Auckland, Don Miles, himself a former SOE agent who had been inserted into France before D-Day to fight behind enemy lines, would often talk about SOE and would bring up Diana's name. We knew very little about her ... what had become of her, what was her mission in France, and why was there so little written about her? All we knew was that she had died in a concentration camp, probably in Germany.

From then on her name kept cropping up in conversations and so I researched her on my computer. I learned she had been executed together with three other agents in a concentration camp called Natzweiler and that they had met a horrific death. As I read I suddenly remembered a documentary I had seen some time in the 1980s: four women, or maybe three, walking down some steps, one wearing a fur coat, two with dark hair, one with dyed blond hair, and another with a ribbon in her hair – the camera following them – walking up the steps, then walking back down – a low building surrounded by tall trees in the distance – the name Borrel spoken by a Frenchman – curls of smoke rising from a chimney – a man with dark hair with long fingers, like those of an artist, telling the interviewer what he had seen. For some reason this documentary had always stayed in my mind.

Had this documentary been about Diana? Over the next few months I found two books, *Death Be Not Proud* by Elizabeth Nicholas, who had gone to school with Diana, and *Flames in the Field* by Rita Kramer. Both books concentrated on the women who had died in Natzweiler and included others who had served with the French Section of the Special Operations Executive.

But it was Diana who kept me awake at night. It was her story which gripped me like nothing else I had read, and which still haunts me to this day.

So in 2005 I visited the camp at Natzweiler, a place well off the beaten track, roughly a forty-minute drive from Ottrott-le-Haut. The journey to the camp took me up into the mountains through beautiful pine forests with views of alpine villages far below. As we climbed I thought of the four doomed women taking this same journey and what their thoughts must have been. A museum was under construction the day we were there and as we entered through the gates I was struck not only by the beauty of the surroundings but the silence. There was no wildlife, no birds, just an eerie and deathly silence that hung over the camp. A huge monument to the fallen stands near the entrance, while steps lead down to the buildings used to house the prisoners far below. Everything is as it was: the crematorium, the prisoners' cells, the guard houses. A lone shoe lay at the entrance, old and shabby as if somebody had carelessly thrown it to one side. The oven was so small I wondered how a human body was able to fit in to its narrow cavity. I walked outside into the fresh air and read the inscription on the plaque dedicated to the four SOE agents.

Near the bottom of the camp people had laid wreaths to the fallen. I knelt down and read some of the cards; most from the families of the dead prisoners. I gazed around, trying to seek answers as to why this had happened, why so many people had died in this camp, among them the four women with their lives before them. And I was aware of a peculiar dragging sensation, which did not leave me until I was back at the Hostellerie at Ottrott.

Later, inside the church, far away from the horror and death I had seen that day, I prayed for the souls of all those who died in the camp. I thought about Diana. I resolved that when I returned to New Zealand I would write her full story so the world would know what happened to a young Englishwoman of the finest character who died in barbaric circumstances in a concentration camp high up in the Vosges Mountains in 1944.

Don Miles died in 2009 and I was able to tell him that I would write Diana's biography and keep her memory alive.

Gabrielle McDonald-Rothwell,
Auckland, New Zealand

Author's Note

Various scenes regarding Diana depicted throughout the book have been reconstructed using the following files, documentations, family letters and interviews with numerous people:

Author Rita Kramer made available all her files.

Harry Rée's personal records of his time in the Jura.

Professor Michael Foot has written extensively on SOE in France and these are readily available from libraries and the National Archives at Kew.

The Janier-Dubry family and Yvonne Clerc spoke to me about Diana and readily made available to me documents and letters never before published.

For Diana's early life I had access to Elizabeth Nicholas's notes and files and her book *Death Be Not Proud*. Also Mrs Rowden's personal letters and reminiscences from Victoria Boyle, cousin of Diana.

Max Hastings, Nigel West, Selwyn Jepson and E. K. Cookridge have all written about the Secret War and SOE.

Squadron Leader William Simpson wrote about his friendship with Diana before she went to France.

Bob Maloubier in conversation with me conveyed his recollections of Diana during training and also in London, as did Noreen Riols and Helen Rolfe in conversations at Valençay.

Acknowledgements

Professor Michael Foot makes a valid point about writing history: 'The first rule of a historian is that if there are two explanations, one simple and one complicated, go with the simpler one.' I have tried to do this throughout the writing of this biography.

So many people have helped me in my research and I wish to thank them all for bringing this work to fruition. There have been difficulties writing from New Zealand, and without the help from the following people it would have been an impossible task. Over the last three years there have been many sleepless nights when the going was tough, times when I failed to find answers, especially regarding Diana's early years. But somehow in those grey hours, somebody would cheer me up and I was able to return to the task again.

People have been so generous with their time and patience. Firstly, in England there was Gavin Rowden, the Rowden family archivist, who found John Rowden, the son of Christian Rowden's brother-in-law, in Melbourne. John was in possession of vital Rowden papers including letters from Mrs Rowden to his father after the war, and these he gave to Gavin to give to me when he came to Auckland two years ago. Since that time Gavin has been unceasing in his help, sending valuable citations, family documents and photographs.

Robert Body put me in touch with the SOE Forum, a wonderful group of historians and writers whose help has been invaluable. Writers like Paul McCue, Dr David Harrison and Steven Kippax immediately offered help. They sent contacts, photos, sites to explore, documents, etc. They were unstinting with their help. Questions I asked came back with immediate answers and never failed to attach relevant documents. David came up with the impossible – finding people like Victoria Boyle, Diana's cousin, when I had all but given up hope of finding any remaining Rowden family members. And many thanks go to David for writing the Foreword.

It was through the SOE Forum that I met Elspeth Forbes-Robertson. What can I say about Elspeth? Her knowledge of SOE is formidable, her razor-sharp mind never missing a beat. She took me under her wing immediately, pointing me in the right direction, introducing me to many people, and in 2015 when I went to France for the Memorial service at Valençay, she took me back to England to stay with her in Hampshire. In those few days Elspeth was tireless, taking me up to London to introduce me to the Special Forces Club, finding Diana's pied-à-terre in Knightsbridge, then to Beaulieu, to Boarmans, to the Tangmere Museum. An amazing woman.

Zelie Hilton went to the National Archives in London and sent me Diana's and Brian Stonehouse's personal files and liased with Carolyn Griffith of the Special Forces Club. My thanks go to Zelie and Carolyn for their invaluable help. Also Claire Rivers, Headmistress of St Mark's School in Limpsfield, Surrey, for her advice and permission to reproduce various publications; Lyn Croucher for the history of Hadlow Down and the Rowden family in Tilford; the late Bob Maloubier, who shared his memories of Diana; and Anna Menzies-Caldwell, who also shared memories of her father, Jean Mennesson.

I also wish to thank Susan Tomkins, archivist at Beaulieu, who generously gave me an afternoon in which she discussed Diana's Beaulieu report and the woman agents of SOE who had been through the school; John Sissons, who journeyed to Karlsruhe for photographs of the prison; Martyn Cox, who was very generous with his time; Pierre Treville, Derek Parker, Fred Judge, Bernard O'Connor, Nick Fox, Rolf Dahlo, Lynn Hodgson, Helen Rolfe, sister of Lilian, Francis Suttill, Steve Tyas, Malcolm Poole, Ron Navicki, Gordon Stevens, Judith Hiller, Phil Tomaseli, Mark Yeats, Rick Stroud, Stella Marsh, Rick Newton, Philip Stoner, Mr and Mrs Charles Chamberlain, owners of Boarmans estate, Elizabeth Carteret, daughter of Yvonne Clerc, the UK Law Society and the Military Intelligence Museum who provided valuable data.

Noreen Riols on more than one occasion patiently and generously gave her time, both in France and in England, sharing her thoughts and reminiscences of the people of SOE. Thank you Noreen. Philip Athill in London put me in touch with Mrs Ida Stonehouse in New York, for which my grateful thanks, and to Mrs Stonehouse for giving permission to reproduce Brian Stonehouse's sketch of the four SOE women in Natzweiler.

To Victoria Boyle, cousin of Diana, with whom I have had the greatest pleasure in meeting and discussing the lives of Diana and her mother. I have been most fortunate in finding you, and my love and thanks for your generosity in sharing with me those personal memories that have added so much value to Diana's biography.

In France, thanks to my dear friends Christiane Voha and Claude Janier-Dubry. From when we first made contact you took me under your wing, generously offering me a base in Clairvaux-le-Lacs from which to work and pursue my story about a young English woman they knew a long time ago and someone they never ever forgot. You were patient with me, a woman who had little French, and tireless in your devotion to see this book to print, never sparing of your time and support. We spent countless hours poring over letters and documents, you answering my numerous questions, and driving me to places I would otherwise not have been able to get to; I thank you unreservedly.

The late Yvonne Clerc and her daughter Elizabeth Carteret gave me a memorable afternoon with Claude and Christiane in beautiful St Amour. Yvonne's help was invaluable as she, too, right from the beginning sent me documents and letters that were essential to this biography. I thank her from the bottom of my heart.

Lastly in New Zealand to my dear friend Corinne Deluzin Mendez, my amazing *Professeur de Français*. Corinne patiently schooled me in essential French phraseology, spending hours translating numerous documents, and gave me so much of her time and energy. *Tu es formidable ... oui?*

To Claudine and Amy at the Browns Bay Photographic shop, thank you for all your amazing reproductions. To the Mairangi Bay Writers' Group, all of whom helped, supported and listened to my readings at each of our meetings. *Merci, mes amis chéris.*

To my dear friend Annette, who has been there for me for all of my books, and who read the drafts of this one, the longest and hardest to write of them all, my love and thanks always for your support and listening patiently when I was at my wit's end.

To my editor, Aaron Meek, for his sound knowledge and advice; my four children, Paul, and daughter-in-law Cate, who helped me many times when technology failed; and Laurence, Fleur and Luke, who continually supported when I was overtired and overwrought, my love always. And to Geoffrey Bear, who helped with the writing of all the flying scenes, read through various drafts, offered support and encouragement, and who had to put up with a part-time wife for more than three years, my love and gratitude always.

If I have left anybody out, my apologies.

What I owe all of you is beyond evaluation.

PART ONE

Prologue

'*Men whose wisdom and courage make them worthy of heaven are called heroes.*'

- Bishop Isidore of Seville in the sixth century

On the morning of 18 November 1943 a dark-skinned, dark-eyed man with slicked-back greasy hair arrives in Clairvaux-le-lacs in the region of the Jura on the border of France and Switzerland. This small, cobblestoned village nestling quietly in the Franche-Comté is an area of blue slate-grey lakes and purple mountains, woods and valleys and dark green forests.

The stranger takes no notice of the beauty of the countryside and the village. He has other things on his mind. And the villagers take little notice of him. Great gusts of freezing wind keep the people inside. Above the village the purple hills of the Jura are just visible through grey, damp mist. One day in the future one of the residents of Clairvaux would remember how she had looked up at the grey sky on that cold November day and shivered.

As a watery sun begins to appear at last through the mist, Aimee Janier-Dubry, a young mother of two children, peers through thick curtains. The days are short at this time of year. Soon the snows will come. Last year they had been snowed in and had to be dug out by the snow ploughs. Just a few more weeks and then Christmas. In the meantime, there is food to prepare – a big feast to welcome *Benoit*, the new agent whom they have been expecting for weeks. He will be taking the place of the wireless operator, John Young, code named *Gabriel*, who is returning to England.

A short time later a taxi draws up outside. Aimee recognises the driver – he will have come from Lons. Lons-le Saunier is the largest town in the Jura and seventeen kilometres from Clairvaux. She goes back to her work. Aimee's husband Raoul hears the loud knock on the door of the bureau, his office, where he has been busy in his wood-cutting factory, a big building isolated in the middle of the woods adjacent to the house. The factory employs twenty or so men and is worked as a family concern. There is Raoul, his brother Armand, and two sisters, Edith, married to Gaston Juif, and Ida, married to Henri Poli. All the family is active in the Resistance.

The stranger is brought into Raoul's office and the man goes straight up to him. '*Bonjour, je suis Benoit*. I am Gabriel's replacement.'

'*Ah ... vous êtes Benoit?*' replies Raoul. '*Nous avons attendu longtemp pour vous.*' We have been waiting a long time for you. You have the password? He waits for an answer. But the man says nothing. Instead he fidgets in his pocket and looks around as if searching for somebody or something. Then he produces a letter. 'Here is a letter written by the wife of *Gabriel.*'

It is proof enough and Janier-Dubry takes him through the factory and into the house of his sister Ida. He introduces the new agent to her and *Benoit* produces the proper credentials; instructions written on thin paper concealed in a match box and the letter from *Gabriel's* wife. There is no reason to doubt. They strike up a conversation: 'Have you news of London?' asks Raoul. *Benoit* is slightly evasive, and looks around the factory, finally answering: '*Bien sur*' ... the invasion can't be too long ... surely?'

Raoul remarks it was just as well *Benoit* is wearing a *Canadienne*, the thick fur-lined jacket worn in the Jura. It is going to be a long winter.

Two British secret agents from the Special Operations Executive in London, *Gabriel* and *Paulette*, are lodged on the ground floor of the building adjacent to the factory. They are working for the *Acrobat* and *Stockbroker réseaux* of the Resistance, the security and safety of which has never been compromised.

That morning *Paulette*, sheltering behind the window curtains, watches as the man gets out of the taxi and walks into the factory. 'That must be him, it must surely be him,' she murmurs to *Gabriel*.

They go down to meet the new agent and Raoul makes the introductions. *Gabriel* is very pleased to see *Benoit*. He shakes his hand.

'How is SOE? There is always trouble with that organisation. Always there is delay in the dispatch of arms and explosives I ask for. What do they think of me in London?'

But *Benoit* is vague, making only cursory comments and a small flicker of doubt creases *Gabriel's* brow. He must have some instinct of danger because he spends all day in the Juif house and does not go out.

Some hours later ... by now the mist has cleared and stars glow white in the now blackening sky. Having shut out the cold of the night Aimee goes back to her cooking, preparing the evening's dinner, caring for the children. She hardly hears the five Citroën cars and the black saloon come to a halt outside the house. Boots crunch on the drive. *Feldengarmerie* troops, *Soldaten* ... armed with German Karabiner rifles, Lugers, machine pistols, Walthers in their hands ... run up the drive leading to the front door. They kick it open then spill into the warmth of the kitchen.

'*Hande hoch! Schnell! Schnell! Sie* ... against the wall!'

They wave the guns around, threatening, then one or two of the men open fire and bullets spray the kitchen ceiling. The children scream and Aimee runs to them, putting her arms around them, hugging them to her.

Raoul Janier-Dubry has been visiting his sick mother in the house next door and is about to go into his house. The air is very cold and he pulls his jacket up around his ears. Suddenly he stops dead in his tracks. What is happening? *Mon dieu* ... why is the house surrounded by cars? Surely not what he has been dreading?

With a sickening jab a gun is thrust against his back and he feels the metal hit his ribs. In German: 'Just walk into the house ... very slowly.'

'*Fais pas le con!*' Don't be stupid! He says this in a joking way because he is very afraid. Then quickly: '*Oh pardon!*'

Not daring to turn around, Raoul walks forward slowly, carefully, as a blind man would do. He is aware of the loud beating of his heart, the door opening, and the gun jabbing viciously now into his neck as the voice says: 'Inside! *Vite!*' Roughly he is shoved into the kitchen, the warmth rising up to meet him.

He notices all these things: drops of sweat trickling down his back, two men wearing glasses in round tortoiseshell frames, *Feldgendarmerie*, German military police, the family lined up against the wall, shouting, the children crying, cowering under their mother's skirts, guns being waved around, people everywhere, Gestapo dressed in civilian clothes and shoes, good quality yellow leather.

All these things and the feeling of being in a dream.

In the house next door Raoul's brother-in-law Henri Juif, *Gabriel, Paulette* and the rest of the Juif family are pushed up against a wall. The man called *Benoit* waves a gun at them. *Ce n'est pas possible!* What has happened? Just that afternoon this man and *Paulette* had been sitting in a café sipping coffee, talking with other *résistants*.

Paulette gathers her thoughts as best she can and, outwardly very calm, stands against the kitchen wall near the woodbox and holds behind her back a framed photo of *Gabriel* which is to be used for his new *carte d'identité*. She has collected this from Lons earlier the same day. At Beaulieu they had given her the nickname *Sans Peur*. Without fear.

Remember your training ... never show you're afraid.

Very quietly, slowly, she removes the photo from the frame and drops it into the woodbox behind her.

The Germans do not notice this. Instead they wave the guns threateningly in the faces of the prisoners. 'Answer! Where is the radio transmitter? Answer! *Wo ist es?*'

The radio transmitter is not found and unceremoniously they are shoved next door – the Juifs, Polis, *Gabriel, Paulette* into the Janier-Dubry house. Now they are all together with the man they know as *Benoit,* the man who is waving a gun at them, the new radio operator from London, the man in whose honour Aimee Janier-Dubry had been cooking a celebration dinner.

No pretence now is necessary from this man they thought was their friend. His voice is harsh as he shouts at them: 'We are going to find the transmitter and the crystals, that is for certain, but if you want to stay alive you will tell us where it is, and quickly!'

Raoul, manhandled by two strong Gestapo men makes a move towards the false *Benoit*. '*Salopard!*' You bastard! And he spits in *Benoit's* face. '*Tu n'es qu'un merde méprisable!* You contemptible filth! We Janier-Dubrys have long memories. *Pas de souci.* Don't worry. We'll find you.'

The false agent laughs. 'You won't be around much longer to make false promises, *n'est ce pas.*'

One of the Gestapo men pokes a gun into Raoul's stomach. 'Enough! For the last time, where is the transmitter?'

One by one, sometimes all together, they reply: '*Je ne sais pas.* I do not know.'

'I swear on my daughter's life ... I have never seen it,' says Ida Poli and prays that God will forgive her.

Madame Juif, backed against the wall, also denies she knows anything as bullets go *thump thump* into the dresser.

The Germans search frantically. They look in a portmanteau and in all the rooms. They ransack the house ... it is a desperate search ... everything is taken out of drawers, cupboards are tipped upside down ... crockery broken ... pandemonium ...

In the confusion, Madame Juif finally remembers with a sickening jolt: '*Mon dieu* ... the raincoat ... don't let them go near the coat stand.'

She murmurs quietly in the hope that no one will hear or notice: 'I have to cover my baby ... he is cold and frightened.'

So intent are the Germans on searching for the radio crystals they do not hear these words or notice her slight movements as she edges closer to the coatstand by the door.

There is the coat rack ... just one touch away ... feeling behind her she quietly takes the crystals from the coat and puts them under the mattress of her two-year-old son.

Safety of sorts ... for all of them. Death has been averted ... for now.

Click! The light is turned off and the room plunges into darkness. One of the Germans covering the two English agents immediately fires and a bullet hits the blackness of the ceiling. A child lets out a high-pitched scream. Ida's son, his face white with fright, dives under the table, his body shaking. The smell of cordite mixed with that of cooking bites into the warm air. Another shot is fired at the floor, the bullet ricocheting and passing through the kitchen table where it misses by centimetres the four-year-old boy.

M. Vincent, an active member of the Resistance, is also now in the kitchen having been arrested outside on the road. He is carrying a bag filled with black-market butter wrapped in greaseproof paper.

'Empty! *Vite!*' shouts one of the Germans.

M. Vincent, his hands shaking, his face a picture of fear and confusion, tips the butter out on to the table... then puts it back in the bag. He places it on to the table again, his hands trembling. And so it goes on ... in ... out ... in ... out.

Prologue

Raoul is leaning against his bedroom door when a German pushes past him, opens the door, looks inside, then as if he has changed his mind, goes back into the kitchen, leaving the bedroom door open.

Aimee quietly mouths to her husband: 'Run for it!'

But Raoul does not want to leave his family. He shakes his head. Almost impatiently Aimee sidles quietly through the door and opens the window: 'Hop it!'

Raoul looks back at her one last time and jumps from the window. Shouting breaks out and a gunshot explodes into the cold night air.[1]

1

Early Days

'Wherever and for as long as freedom flourishes on the earth, the men and women who possess it will thank them and will say they did not die in vain.'

- HRH Queen Elizabeth II, Runnymede, 1953

The Second World War produced people of the finest character, none more so than a twenty-nine-year-old English girl, Diana Rowden, who paid the ultimate sacrifice. Within sight of liberation, she would perish just after the Allies had landed on the French coast on D Day, 6 June 1944. Among the heroes and heroines of the Rowden Scottish clan none have enriched its heritage more than Diana, who at the end of the Second World War was posthumously awarded the MBE, the French *Croix de Guerre* and Mentioned in Dispatches.

The name Diana has been a name sprinkled throughout history. In a biblical sense it means luminous, perfect. Diana was a Roman goddess of hunting and the moon. The French derivation of the name is *Diane,* and it is interesting that Diana Rowden's parents named her thus as she was to grow up loving France and all things French.

Diana Hope Rowden was born on Sunday, 31 January, 1915 at 15 Halsey Street in the northern part of Chelsea, London. The four-storey terraced house in the West End is typical of that part of London. She was born into a world of turmoil – England was at war with Germany. The 'war to end all wars', was scarcely more then a few months old. On that Sunday, the day of her birth, the first poison gas attack by the Germans against the Russians was launched.

Diana was born into an illustrious and extended family of Army officers, clerics and lawyers, including a King's Counsel on her father's side. In official documents they are described variously as Chaplain, Vicar, Clergyman and Lawyer. They were educated at the top universities and colleges of the day. A number of ancestors had attended Winchester College and gone on to Oxford. Diana's Rowden family has been traced back to the early 1500s and there exists a pedigree which shows it can be traced back as far as the twelfth century.

The Rowden family originated at Rowden in Herefordshire where they owned a manor, Rowden Manor, an area of some 250 acres a few miles out of Bromyard. The family took the name Rowden when one of their forbears named Thomas Townley acquired the manor in 1360 until 1800 when it was sold. Three houses all bore the name Rowden – Rowden Abbey, Rowden House and Rowden Mill. From Herefordshire the family drifted across to Gloucestershire then to Oxfordshire.

Diana started life with a strong spiritual heritage. Her great-great-grandfather, Edward Rowden, who lived to the age of eighty-eight, had been the vicar of Highworth in Wiltshire for a remarkable sixty-five years. It would seem he had great influence in the market town, and one suspects that his ten children made the vicarage a very busy, and at times, noisy place. His own father, Francis Rowden, lived to be almost a hundred years old and had been preaching chaplain in Whitehall, London, no doubt with a congregation including George III. And Diana's great-grandfather, the Reverend George Croke Rowden, (1820–1863), Clerk in Holy Orders and Precentor of Chichester Cathedral, and third son of Edward, had his portrait painted by Herbert Draper and displayed in the National Portrait Gallery in London.

Diana's paternal grandfather, Aldred William Rowden (1849–1919) was a barrister. By the age of fifty he had 'taken silk' to become a King's Counsel – the mark of a lawyer of outstanding ability.

In 1919 her father, Aldred Clement Rowden, became Registrar of the Corporation of the Sons of the Clergy in Bloomsbury, a position he occupied from when he was demobbed until he died. Born in 1888, he had served as a subaltern in the 5th Battalion of the Queen's (Royal West Surrey) Regiment, a territorial unit based in Guildford, Surrey. After the outbreak of the First World War he was posted to the Royal Sussex Regiment as a lieutenant, later acting major, with the 4th Battalion in Horsham, and then with the 72nd Provisional Battalion based at Lessness Heath in Kent. He was serving as the battalion's adjutant when his daughter was born.

Diana's mother, Muriel Maitland-Makgill-Crichton, was born at Marylebone, Middlesex in 1892 and came from a long line of Scottish thoroughbreds. Muriel, whose second name was appropriately Christian, had as her great-grandfather David Maitland-Makgill-Crichton of Rankeillour, Fife, Scotland who was heir to the line of James Crichton, 1st Viscount Frendraught. He had been a pillar of the Scottish Kirk. He had twenty-two grandchildren. He also had a remarkable military connection, for all six uncles on Diana's mother's side were in the services, and so too were the three male Maitland-Makgill-Crichton cousins. Diana's grandfather Andrew Maitland-Makgill-Crichton carried on the tradition of large families, having twelve children. Diana, the first-born of Muriel Christian, the youngest daughter of Andrew Maitland-Makgill-Crichton's twelve children, was the youngest grandchild of Andrew Maitland-Makgill-Crichton's impressive family.

The Maitland family's motto, 'By Wisdom and Courage', is surely a fitting tribute to one of its most courageous daughters.

It was a natural progression perhaps, with such a formidable background, together with a deep love of France and a vehement hatred of the Germans, that Diana was drawn swiftly into the fight for the country she loved.

The marriage between twenty-four-year old Aldred Clement Rowden and twenty-one-year-old Muriel Christian Maitland-Makgill-Crichton took place at the Church of St Mark (Church of England) in North Audley Street, London. The marriage certificate states the groom's profession as 'Gentleman' of 28 Green Street, West, and the bride's address is noted as 17A Great Cumberland Place, West. The witnesses were Aldred William Rowden, the groom's father, Kings Counsel, Andrew Maitland-Makgill-Crichton, cousin of the bride, and Cecil A. Empson, uncle of the bridegroom.

An excerpt from the *Dundee Courier* on 17 July 1913 paints a typical picture prior to a pre-war society wedding of the times:

The bride who was given away by her father ... carried a sheaf of lilli. She wore a gorgeous gown of rich white liberty satin draped with beautiful old Limerick lace, and trimmed with diamante embroidery, while the skirt was caught with an ornament of the same … her tulle veil draped gracefully over a spray of orange blossom and she carried a sheaf of lilies. Her present from the bridegroom was pearl and diamond ear-rings.

The bride's going-away outfit was a dress made of mushroom shot satin and her hat was black velvet with a black tulle brim with black tulle butterfly wings. The bride and groom honeymooned in Devonshire.

Diana's birth was followed by her brothers, Maurice Edward Aldred and Cecil William Aldred, in 1918 and 1921 respectively, by which time the family home was at 2 Bloomsbury Place, London WC1.

However, the marriage was not happy, and not long after the birth of Cecil, Diana's parents separated, leaving Christian to bring up their three children. She was a strong, independent woman fortunate enough to be unencumbered with a regular job. Like many other British people of means in the years between the two world wars, she knew that a small income would go further in France than in England because the value of the British currency was high at that time. Mrs Rowden had holidayed in the south of France before her marriage and saw it as a wonderfully multicultural place to bring up the children, to say nothing of the favourable climate. In the early 1920s, after packing essentials and putting some of the furniture into storage, the family sailed from the Tilbury docks for the French Riviera. They rented villas in St Jean Cap Ferrat and Menton on the Italian/French border in the Provence-Alpes-Cote d'Azur region in the south-east, which they used as a base; part of the year was spent in both places. Menton, known as *la Perle de la France* (the pearl of France) had always been a popular destination for wealthy English and Russian aristocrats, who built many luxurious hotels and villas, some of which were used as hospitals during the First World War for injured troops to convalesce in the warmth.

The Rowdens lived in the south of France for some years. Diana later told friends that she was about seven at the time they left England and that from the very start she was sublimely happy. Shortly after their arrival Mrs Rowden quickly befriended and hired an Italian, Vincenzo, as companion and servant and bought an old yacht, which they aptly named the *Sans Peur*.

They anchored at St Jean Cap Ferrat and drifted along the Italian Riviera, living on the sea and pausing a while near Menton. Years later Mrs Rowden would speak to author Elizabeth Nicholas of those halcyon days: 'Diana sleeping on deck with a line tied round her big toe to wake her should it be jerked by a fish ... cheerfully gutting fish and skilfully sailing a small boat with reckless skill.'[1]

For Diana, who had been born under the sign of Aquarius, the water sign, the move to a land of sun and sea where she and her brothers spent much time on the beach, fishing, boating and swimming was unbelievably happy. It was a carefree life on the peninsula of Cape Ferrat, mostly unencumbered by the restrictions of school and rules. The rest of the year they drifted along the French and Italian coast, cared for by Vincenzo.

At this time in her life she was a small, red-haired, sweet-natured girl with freckles and very sporty. The children attended school rarely and only in the winter months at St George's in St Remo, just over the border in Italy, and the Cours Maintenon in Cannes. They became trilingual, speaking English, French, and Italian, with a good smattering of Spanish. Mrs Rowden seems to have been an eccentric woman and the locals picked this up, calling her 'the mad Englishwoman'. The children attracted attention, especially on Sundays when they attended Mass wearing their kilts. Diana was always very proud of her Scottish origins.

A cousin of Diana's, Mark Chetwynd-Stapylton, the son of Mrs Rowden's sister Vera, remembered times when he and the Rowden cousins played games together as children when they were in England, which was rare,

> ... like hide and seek in the garden, riding bicycles on Berkhamsted Common in Hertfordshire, and eying each other across the table at meal times. Diana's mother, whom we always called Aunt Chris, and my mother were very close, Chris being older than my mother. When my parents, my two sisters, and my brother and I lived at Berkhamsted as we did for some twenty years, our cousins, the Rowdens, stayed on occasions with us during the school holidays. We were told to 'be nice to your cousins' whom we really did not know that well. Chris's husband or ex-husband, was always vaguely referred to as 'Uncle Buddy' but we, the children, never met him. We never thought of him. Of Maurice

I have no clear picture; Kit, I visualize as rather tall and gangly and 'wet' for his age, and Diana as a bit of a tomboy. But there was something about her which was essentially French although she looked very English. It showed in the soft lilt of her English accent, her gestures like the shrug of her shoulders, and the way she used her hands when she talked. Diana was red-haired, freckled, with slightly protruding teeth and very clear reflective blue-grey eyes, As she grew older I could see that one day she would be very good looking. She spoke and laughed a lot, which she did often, wishing to get on with her cousins, I suppose.[2]

Clara Harper, who would become one of Diana's school friends, remembers a wet Sunday in 1923 in Menton when 'a nice looking young woman came into the row in front of me in St John's Church with three children in kilts'. She recognised them as the inhabitants of a villa nearby, towards the Italian frontier close to the sea.

But the idyll could not last, and in the late 1920s Mrs Rowden, mindful of her responsibility as a parent, realised it was time for her children to be 'properly' educated: the only place for that was England. Accordingly, after many years of sun and sea, they packed up once again and sailed for England. The children, still without a father figure but benefiting from their mother's strong character, had failed to persuade a determined Mrs Rowden to remain in France. Returning in the latter part of 1929 to a country cold, grey and damp, on the verge of an economic depression, was a shock to the children, especially Diana. They settled in Hadlow Down, a beautiful village near Mayfield in East Sussex, and it was here that Diana became friendly with a family named Phelps whose daughter Bridget attended the Manor House School in Surrey. Upon their recommendation Mrs Rowden decided to send Diana there in 1930 as a boarder. Built in 1896, the small, three-storey, red-brick Georgian school was set beneath a long, low line of hills in the village of Limpsfield, a short distance from Croydon Aerodrome. It was rumoured to be haunted, although that fact did not seem to faze Diana. The principal of the school was Miss Fellows, who was respected by everybody. Two daughters of Winston Churchill, Sarah and later Mary, attended the Manor House; Mary, who lived not far away at Chartwell, would ride her horse to school each day.

Diana at this time missed everything about France and found it difficult to adjust to the restraints of the country of her birth, a place she could barely remember. The gay, outgoing child became shy, withdrawn and introverted. She hated the rigidity of a boarding school with its rules and regulations, its confining spaces that always seemed bleak and cold. She missed very much her brothers (who also were at boarding school), the warmth of the sun, the sea and her carefree previous life. Often she could be found sitting quietly in her study looking out the window across to the playing fields or walking in the grounds by herself.

Diana found it difficult to make friends but eventually became close to one particular girl, with whom she shared a small, wooden-floored dormitory with just two beds, each with a regulation white cover. Her new and perhaps her only close friend at the Manor House was Elizabeth Nicholas, who in the 1950s would write a book entitled *Death Be Not Proud* in which she described her school days with Diana at the Manor House. Elizabeth wrote about the smell of

> ... ink and chalk dust, the lazy droning of bees around the flower beds in summer, the goal posts pointing white and bleak towards a winter sky. Diana was of it, but not part of it. She was too mature for us. We were very much schoolgirls in grubby white blouses, only concerned with games and feuds, midnight feasts and ha-ha jokes. She was already adult and withdrawn from our diversions. I don't think any of us really knew her.

Eventually Diana told Elizabeth something of her former life in France, describing the Mediterranean sun on the white-hot vines, the purple bougainvillea climbing the walls of their villa, and the extraordinary turquoise-coloured sea; the sensitive Elisabeth glimpsed for the first time the reason for Diana's remoteness. She saw how a child who had been brought up with sun and sea and freedom in a country such as France would find it difficult to fit in with the restraints of a boarding school under grey English skies.

The Manor House was a typical small boarding school for young ladies aged between fourteen and eighteen of good families. It had been opened in 1897 with just a handful of pupils but by 1920 the roll had grown to over forty. The teaching was limited and the old house was in a bad state of disrepair with questionable sanitary facilities.

However, about the time Diana was to leave the Manor House a further wing was added to cope with extra pupils, and tennis courts, a gym and a small swimming pool had been built. There was also a laboratory well equipped for science lessons.

It was a genteel education for young ladies of good breeding. Pupils were taught to eat asparagus daintily with their fingers – the only proper way to eat asparagus – and never to cut a roll of bread with a knife (one breaks it with one's hands). They rode bareback and played lacrosse and tennis. Hockey was deemed inappropriate because it would make the young ladies round-shouldered. Each morning the maid, dressed in cap and apron, would wake Diana by announcing 'Miss Rowden, your bath is ready'. It was always cold. Physical discomfort was always associated with the traditional stiff upper lip and not complaining. The school was small, nine girls to a class, and there were many international students.

One student described the food as terrible. Once a month the girls attned on the headmistress for a formal meal. Nobody was allowed to ask for anything, including the salt and pepper, and they would always be polite to the person on either side of them. 'For the rest of my life I never had to worry about the proper way to behave, thanks to that early school training.'[3]

In *Three Houses, Many Lives,* Gillian Tindall writes about Diana.

> It would have been good to have known about Diana Rowden while struggling to grow up within the Manor House's stunting confines, with its nunnery feuds, its endless petty and punitive rules and its restricted syllabus. That might have bestowed some confidence that there was a wider world out there. But although the much-publicised story of another wartime heroine, Odette Hallowes, was well known by the 1950s, no one ever mentioned Diana Rowden to us. Instead, the chosen Model Old Girl was the youngest daughter of Winston Churchill, the one who, as Lady Soames, went on to lead a scandal-free life, unlike her two sisters.[4]

It is then understandable that Diana, who had spent her happy childhood years living an unrestrained and carefree life in the south of France, should find the Manor House restricting and confining, and that her days there would be unhappy. After having talked with

Mrs Rowden during the 1950s, Elizabeth Nicholas thought Diana something of a paradox – it was almost as if she had shown two faces to the world: one of a sunny-natured child in France, and the other of a quiet, shy and withdrawn teenager at a private school in England. However, she gave no sign of her unhappiness to her fellow peers. Instead, she remained remote. Years later Elizabeth Nicholls was amazed when Diana's mother spoke of her daughter as a turbulent tomboy, living a beach-combing life along the Mediterranean coast, a passionate devotee of boats and fishing and the sea. The Diana of the Cote d'Azur, the sea urchin of whom Mrs Rowden spoke, bore not the slightest resemblance to the Diana Elizabeth had known at school: 'From what Mrs Rowden told me I could not believe we were talking about the same person. I had shared a bedroom with a poised, sophisticated young woman, and I could not even now visualise her as anything other.'

One of Diana's teachers at the Manor House was Mlle Mathieu, who taught French. A tall woman who wore glasses with a grey streak in her dark hair which was drawn back into an untidy bun, she was rumoured to have a heart problem. She was very strict and determined her students were going to learn and speak French with the correct accent. The girls would sometimes make fun of her behind her back and tease the woman, too old to be a mademoiselle, who, hot and flustered with the effort of keeping an unruly class in order, most of whom did not want to be taught, would stand in front of the blackboard, long pointer in one hand, and bellow out '*ah – quel saleté*' or '*créatures grossières*' – 'what coarse creatures' – two of her favourite terms of abuse when faced with bad grammar and inadequate translation.

The girls would dread French lessons and cower before her lashing tongue as the teacher vented her rage. Diana, who spoke fluent French, was spared the worst of Mademoiselle's whip-cracking, but like the rest of them trembled before her all-encompassing rage. The elderly teacher, whom Elizabeth Nicholas referred to as 'the tyrant of our school days', had been born in the Vosges and retired there at the beginning of the Second World War. Strangely, this was close to the area where Diana was to end her life. At war's end Mlle Mathieu crossed the Channel to visit England once again, but her heart gave out and she died within sight of the white cliffs of Dover.

War Comes to France

'Without victory there is no survival'

- Winston Churchill

At the end of 1932, when she was seventeen, Diana left the Manor House School. Whilst there she had obtained her advanced Certificate for Italian Grammar and Literature. At this time she was an attractive woman of average height (about five feet four inches), slender but strongly built, with fair reddish hair. This was a time of new beginnings and endings. Naturally thoughts of returning to France were predominant. Mrs Rowden thought it necessary for her daughter to be 'finished', as many young people of aristocratic lineage were in those days. Some of Diana's peers from the Manor House were going to Switzerland but there was only one thought for her – to return to France as soon as possible and study at the Sorbonne in Paris. She decided to apply for a scholarship and was thrilled when she achieved this aim. It would enable her to study in-depth those languages – French, Italian and Spanish – for which she had a natural aptitude. The world at that time was still in the grip of an economic depression. However, France, whose economic position differed considerably from that of Britain, where unemployment had soared to over three million, was much less dependent on foreign trade and therefore largely sheltered from the worst effects of the Depression. It was also self-sufficient in food and had kept its currency on the gold standard, which gave it a very high exchange rate when Britain and the United States devalued in 1931 and 1933. The worst effects of the Depression were to strike later in France than other countries. It would be a good time for Diana and her mother to be returning. At this time Diana's brothers, Maurice and Cecil (always called 'Kit'), were boarding at Lancing, the public school in Sussex, and doing very well, particularly Maurice, who became House Captain in 1936 and who had a talent for sports, mainly swimming; he was the holder of four school swimming records as well as captain of the team. He attended Lancing until July 1937, at which time, like his father and grandfather, he went up to New College, Oxford.

Leaving Maurice and Cecil at school, Diana and her mother returned to France and settled in Paris. Because of her scholarship to the Sorbonne, Diana had no difficulty in being accepted onto the appropriate language courses. In letters to her brothers she wrote about how happy she was to be living in the beautiful City of Light, with its rich culture and *joie de vivre*. However tensions were building up in Germany and she viewed with growing alarm the reports almost on a daily basis in newspapers of the growth of the National Socialist Party, the Nazi Party, under the leadership of Adolf Hitler, who was steadily growing in popularity. Unknown to most of the rest of the world Germany had been surreptitiously rearming for some time. At this time the Nazis had 230 seats in the Reichstag. However, the thuggery of the SA (the Stormtroopers or 'Brownshirts' as they were known) towards the Jews was slowly indoctrinating the public into accepting or at least tolerating a dangerous attitude of racial hatred. Diana had very clear ideas of right and wrong. Like some people (but by no means all) she viewed the Nazis as crude and brutal and their behaviour was anathema to her. The French and the English perpetually had their daggers drawn, with England favouring the Germans, and Diana could not help but worry about what was going to happen. The British were slow to realise just how far-reaching Hitler's ambitions actually were. At this time in England oje of the very few politicians who spoke out about the danger of Hitler and Hitlerism was Winston Churchill, First Lord of the Admiralty, who had no compunction about expressing his feelings:

When we watch with distress the tumultuous insurgence of ferocity and war spirit, the pitiless ill-treatment of minorities, the denial of the normal protections of civilised society, the persecution of large numbers of individuals solely on the ground of race ... one cannot help feeling glad that the fierce passions that are raging in Germany have not yet found any other outlet but upon themselves.

Few people took any notice of those chilling words.

On 30 January 1933 Hitler took office as Chancellor of Germany. As the 1930s progressed the dark shadows spreading across Europe finally turned into rumblings of war. In a speech to Parliament Churchill warned about the deadly peril that was closing in upon them: 'The French must be greatly concerned at what is taking place in Germany. There are a good many people who have been saying for several years, "Thank God for the French Army".'

Having completed her education and qualifying with high marks as a member of the Institute of Linguists, Diana began work as a translator and freelance journalist in Paris. This was work she enjoyed. She was a brilliant linguist, by this time being fluent in English, French, Italian and Spanish with a smattering of Portugeuse, and quickly found steady work writing articles for newspapers including *The European Herald* (based in the south of France), student newspapers and periodicals.

On 30 December 1935, while Diana was working in the French capital, her father died. Aldred Rowden was only forty-seven. His occupation is given as 'Major Retired' on his death certificate; the cause of death was given as coronary embolism and arteriosclerosis. There appears to be no reason for Mr Rowden's heart attack, but in a later letter to a cousin Mrs Rowden wrote that his death was from 'war-related injuries'. There are no records available to show anything which might relate to this condition, but Mrs Rowden must be believed. It is always possible that his ill health may have come about from his service in the Great War. From available documentation, Mr Rowden had been living in Squire's Hill, Tilford, a small village close to where his former wife had bought Lowicks House. Diana's grandfather, Aldred William Rowden, who had died in 1919 at Holybourne Vicarage, Hampshire, had also lived at Squire's Hill. It seems that Diana's parents, living reasonably close to each other, would have kept in touch as there is no evidence to suggest the marital breakup had been acrimonious. After all, there was a family connection. Today there is a gravestone inscribed with the names of Diana, her parents and grandparents in the parish church in the adjacent village of Holybourne.

Mr Rowden's place of death is given as Little Eatendon, which is a small part of the hamlet of Stonegate, itself part of Ticehurst, then a rural setting with very few buildings of any note. It remains unchanged today. The death certificate also notes 'informant at death' as 'inmate', which seems to imply that Mr Rowden had been living in an institution. A photograph taken of Diana and her two brothers in 1935 shows his three children; Diana, aged twenty, is standing between her two brothers and they are all wearing clothes typical of the 1930s. Diana, a hat perched on one side of her head, is wearing a long skirt and warm jacket, her hands out of sight; her hair is short and curly, crimped perhaps, in the 1930s style. Her brother Kit, standing on her right, has the same long thin upper lip. Diana's eyes are closed, either because she is shy at having her photo taken, or perhaps the sun is in her eyes. It must be winter because they are muffled up in winter clothes with what seems to be the docks in the background, which could suggest they were awaiting passage – either to or from England – perhaps for their father's funeral. The date and the season certainly fit in with the time of their father's death.

Passenger lists on vessels between England and France in the latter half of the 1930s show that Diana, her mother and brothers made several journeys between the two countries. Between the months of June and September 1936 Maurice, aged eighteen and now at Oxford, and Cecil, fifteen and still at Lancing, travelled by sea on the *Marnix Van Sint Aldegonde* from Villefranche to Southampton. Their address is noted as 32 Albion St, Hyde Park, W2. In the same year between June and November Mrs Rowden, aged forty-three and living at 5 Selbourne Rd, Littlehampton, made two sea voyages on the *Ormonde* and the *Orsova* between Tilbury docks in London and Toulon, ostensibly to keep an eye on her two sons. She appears to have had two addresses at that time, Selbourne Road and the Albion Street address.

In 1936, while Diana was busy enjoying her work as a freelance journalist in France, civil war broke out in Spain. The conflict was to rage throughout the country for almost three years, Francisco Franco later becoming dictator in 1939. In the same year Hitler and the dictator of Italy, Benito Mussolini, became military and political allies when they signed a 'Pact of Steel'– an alliance that committed one partner to help the other should his country be involved in a war. In 1938, as the rest of the world looked on helplessly, Hitler marched into Austria in just a few days. Later in the same year he annexed the Sudetenland – a part of Czechoslovakia. At this point Neville Chamberlain, Prime Minister of Great Britain, flew to Germany in an attempt to stop Hitler. On 29 September Chamberlain, the French Premier Edouard Daladier, Hitler and Mussolini signed the Munich Agreement, which allowed Nazi Germany's annexation of Czechoslovakia. Tension and fear reached fever pitch, and almost overnight the face of France seemed to change, as though the mask of hope had been roughly pulled off. Since the end of the First World War the country had been bitterly divided and fragmented. According to Denis Brogan (later Sir), Scottish historian and an authority on modern France, in some ways the country had the psychology of a defeated nation. Many French bourgeois in the 1930s feared fascism far less than communism.

The perceptibly aged Neville Chamberlain returned to England from visiting Hitler in his mountain retreat at Berchtesgaden high in the Bavarian Alps. He had been unable to dissuade Hitler from his warmongering. Immediately, two-and-a-half million fit men under sixty in Britain were mobilised. But Chamberlain decided to try one last time. On his return, facing a battery of press cameras and journalists and a jubilant crowd only too willing to believe in peace, he triumphantly waved a piece of paper signed by Hitler proclaiming the so-called Peace Agreement: 'Peace in our time.' It wasn't worth the paper it was written on.

In 1939 the English writer Nancy Mitford went to Perpignan to join her husband Peter Rodd, who was a relief worker for the Spanish refugees who were crowding into France. In England the Mitford family had been famously politically divided, with half of them favouring the policies of Nazi Germany. In a letter written by Nancy to her mother, she seems to grasp the situation: 'Darling Muv, if you could have a look, as I have, at some of the less agreeable results of fascism in a country ... you would be less anxious for the swastika to become a flag on which the sun never sets.' (Her mother and her sister Unity had taken tea with Hitler – 'such a nice man' – not long before.)[1]

In the meantime the summer of 1939 ran its course; day after day the sun shone down out of a cloudless sky, lulling for a moment the threat of war. In her memoir *The Past is Myself* Christabel Bielenberg, an Englishwoman married to a German lawyer but who travelled regularly between the two countries to visit her parents in England, wrote:

> Crossing the border into Germany was enough to be caught up immediately in a horrifying atmosphere fraught with impending catastrophe. The strident voice of the propaganda machine was screeching out its abuse of Poland. Partial mobilization was in full swing, and no trained army personnel could leave the country without permission from his unit. War in the east was planned to start in a matter of weeks and von Ribbentrop [Foreign Minister of Nazi Germany] had successfully persuaded Hitler that neither England nor France would join in.

In August Great Britain and France announced that they would guarantee Poland's frontiers, promising to go to war if Germany attacked. But Hitler forged ahead regardless, invading Poland in a ferocious blitzkreig. At 11.00 a.m. on 3 September 1939, a warm and sunny Sunday, all over Great Britain people listened to the words of Prime Minister Chamberlain proclaiming that 'consequently we are now at war with Germany'. It was the second time in twenty-five years that war was declared between Britain and Germany. Following the announcement the sirens sounded, sending people hurrying to the nearest air-raid shelters. A blackout was enforced in the days following and people drove with dim, hooded lights at night. For the rest of her life Christabel Bielenberg would remember every detail of the night that war broke out:

> The ticking of the clock in the hall, her husband's even breathing, the thin chime from the Dahlem church steeple which sounded every hour, the occasional creaking from upstairs as the children moved in their bunks, and then just before dawn, the muted stirrings and the sudden burst of song from a nightingale in the silver birch tree.[2]

Over the next days and weeks Diana listened to the radio describing the horrific Polish blitzkrieg, knowing without a doubt that invasion was inevitable. She read the British newspapers, which described everything in detail: gas-masks were to be carried in cardboard cases that could also be used as handbags for ration books; everybody had to have identity cards; petrol and food were to be heavily rationed. Over one million children with their names written on labels were to be evacuated from the major cities. All windows had to have curtains made from heavy, dark material for the 'blackout', and windows were to be sealed with sticky tape to prevent flying glass. Wardens patrolled the streets, banging on doors and shouting, 'Put that light out!' and everybody sang 'Run, Rabbit, Run'.

In Paris there were constant rumours of corruption and subversion amongst the politicians and vague talk of an accommodation with the Germans. It was a strange mixture of panic and euphoria – a fear of what was going to happen and relief that the uncertainty, the wondering, was soon to be resolved one way or another. The blitzkrieg, or 'lightning war', moved to its inevitable conclusion. European countries fell like dominoes. Russia, in alliance with Germany, seized part of Poland and marched into Finland. A British Expeditionary Force and some squadrons of the Royal Air Force were sent to France, and on 10 September Hitler swore that 'Germany would fight to the bitter end'. Britain had a tremendous battle on its hands, and Winston Churchill, now the new leader of the British people, addressed the nation in an inspirational speech: 'You ask what is our aim? I can answer in one word: Victory – Victory at all costs, victory in spite of all terrors; victory, however hard and long the road may be; for without victory there is no survival.' However, there were some people who had little faith in Britain's strength and its ability to defend itself. One of these was the American aviator Charles Lindbergh, who wrote in his diary that 'the country has neither the spirit nor the ability needed for a modern war ... It is not only in aviation that they are behind ... the people show little sign of changing. They need an entirely new spirit, if British greatness is to endure.'

Then came the period of the *drole de guerre*, 'the phoney war', when there was little or no action and people began to relax. Maybe all would be well? In Paris the cafés were still crowded, and Charles Trenet sang *'Boum!'*. *Goodbye Mr Chips* and *The Wizard of Oz* played to cinemas packed with people almost as if the war would never happen; people even queued to book for *Gone with the Wind* which wasn't due to open until December. Despite Hitler's chilling words, 'I place a low value on the French army's will to fight. Every army is a mirror of its people,' the French felt certain that the country was impenetrable, safely behind the defences of the Maginot Line. Major

Barlone wrote in *A French Officer's Diary*, an account of the war in Northern France, that 'we are convinced that Hitler will not attack before the spring ... we know that our land is safe from invasion, thanks to the Maginot Line'. The huge and expensive Maginot Line was the longest and most complex system of fortifications ever built – an area of eighty-seven miles of defensive steel and concrete forts along the Franco-German frontier. The French were so certain of its impregnability that some Parisian women had suggested planting roses along it to cheer up the soldiers. After all, their army had defeated the Germans once before, *n'est ce pas?* It would not – could not – happen again. Surely the combined Allied forces – French, British, Dutch and Belgian – were numerically superior to the Germans? But in the early hours of Friday, 10 May 1940 some 135 German divisions, having already invaded Holland, Belgium and Luxembourg, made their move straight for France. On 15 May Paul Reynaud, the French Prime Minister, telephoned Winston Churchill and said, 'We have been defeated. We are beaten.'

'Surely it can't have happened so soon?' Churchill replied.

'The front is broken near Sedan; they are pouring through in great numbers with tanks and armoured cars,' replied Reynaud.

The period of the phoney war had now come to an end and the battle for France had begun. As German tanks rolled towards Paris and it became obvious that soon the enemy would be at the door, food became scarce. Those who did not flee immediately stockpiled food and soon there was little to buy. Going out to buy bread one day Diana noticed a crowd gathered around a notice near the boulangerie: 'Take your children out of Paris' it read. Most people obeyed, seeing no other option. But weeks passed and nothing happened, and eventually the people went home again.

On 21 May Allied troops who had gone to the aid of France, including the British Expeditionary Force, were trapped in an area along the northern coast of France. A miracle was needed and it came in the way of a small beach named Dunkirk. The following operation became known as the 'Miracle of Dunkirk', code-named Operation Dynamo, so named because the British Navy, supported by a fleet of small boats manned by able-bodied men not already in the armed forces, evacuated and saved the lives of thousands of Allied soldiers trapped on the beaches and harbour of Dunkirk between 27 May and 4 June 1940. The figures of this magnificent feat are thought to total around 198,000 British and 140,000 French and Belgian troops. After the fall of Dunkirk, thousands of British and French soldiers as well as Belgian, Dutch and Polish airmen who were unable to be evacuated all headed south, hoping to cross the Pyrenees into Spain and Gibraltar.

Very soon escape lines were set up. False identity cards with official stamps were printed by people in charge of the lines, and Allied airmen and soldiers who had fought at Dunkirk were helped to escape through France into Spain and Portugal. The Spanish had been amongst the first to establish escape routes across the Pyrenees, the nearly five-hundred-kilometre mountain range, which was one of the few places not controlled by the Axis powers.

One of the most famous escape lines was known as the 'Pat Line', so called after Albert Guerisse, a Belgian doctor known as Patrick O'Leary who did wonderful work in setting up escape routes over the Pyrenees. O'Leary was later captured and imprisoned. Some years in the future his name would always be connected with Diana Rowden. The 'Pat Line' was run by Ian Garrow, a captain in the Highland Light Infantry who had managed to evade capture. In this he was helped by the intrepid Nancy Wake, a former New Zealander married to a wealthy French industrialist and who was living in the south of France before the war. Nancy Wake and Garrow quickly set about organising escorts to bring escapers down from the German Occupied Zone and setting up guides to take them over the Pyrenees. Some of these escorts were women, one of whom, Dedee de Jong, did tireless work before being denounced and imprisoned in Ravensbrück Concentration Camp for women. Nancy Wake would become known to the Germans as 'the White Mouse' and eventually join the Special Operations Executive.

Not all of the servicemen-evaders were lucky enough to have freshly printed identity cards, and many were wounded and lacking not only documents but money for food or any means to exchange their uniforms for civilian clothes. Few had more than the rudiments of schoolboy French. Although the British still had a diplomatic presence in Spain, with an ambassador in Madrid and a consulate in the big cities, British escapees who succeeded in getting to Spain were first interned in the concentration camp of Miranda, notorious for treating prisoners inhumanely. When they were finally released they were sent on their way to Gibraltar. However, by the autumn of 1940 escape was already becoming much more dangerous and security in the internment camps was tightened.

By early June General Erwin Rommel's 7th Panzer Division had thrust through the French front between Abbeville and Amiens and reached the outskirts of Rouen. English newspapers reported that 'the French are fighting with tenacity, but they are outnumbered two to one'. Churchill told the British people that a 'tremendous battle is raging in France'.

André Morize wrote that France was confused, 'tangled up like an immense skein of wool being manipulated by a superhuman, evil power'. In the ensuing days panic reigned, with thousands of refugees crowding the roads in cars, many on foot, others pushing loaded carts. The beautiful French countryside was littered with detritus – paper, bottles, punctured tyres, straw mattresses and broken-down cars – all of which had been abandoned when the petrol inevitably had run out. People had no option but to relieve themselves on the side of the road. The smell of dead bodies (some people had dropped down dead during their flight) – animals as well as people – the thirst, hunger, weariness, fear and frustration and, in many cases, hysteria, was the terrible ambience of this new war.

Diana, who by this time had joined the Red Cross, firstly as a volunteer nurse and later in Janury 1940 as an ambulance driver in northern France despite the fact she never managed to acquire a driver's licence, was determined to do her bit to help the sick, the wounded and the dying. She was one of many British and American volunteers, some of whom were already in France, like Nancy Wake, who by now had also joined a volunteer ambulance corp as a driver. She had borrowed an old truck, on the point of falling apart, but which somehow managed to keep going on long journeys between the North and the South. Like Diana, her nursing was of some help on all the ambulance journeys in cases like trying to stem the flow of blood, but often there was little else she could do; there were few supplies and often patients died before they could reach a hospital.

'It was a very difficult time,' Nancy remembered, 'as it was my first experience of war, and though I did have some medical background, I'd never seen injuries like those.'[3]

There is no record to suggest that Nancy and Diana met up during this chaotic and perilous time, but they had two things in common: an intense hatred of Germans and a deep love for France, their adopted country. Both immensely brave, they would undertake dangerous work on escape lines for Allied soldiers and end up joining the same organisation, the Special Operations Executive – albeit at different times, Diana leaving England to return to France in June 1943 and Nancy in March 1944.

Mrs Rowden, realising that France, unprepared and vulnerable, was teetering on the verge of defeat and that before long German troops would invade Paris, was worried about her daughter, who was not only helping at the *Croix Rouge* but also with the escape routes over the Pyrenees. She also knew that the people at the first sign of war with the *Allemands* had started to leave France in droves. At first, in a spirited attempt to shake her fist at Hitler, she had dug in her heels with a 'Hitler be damned!' attitude. 'Why should we flee from that little upstart?' she said to Diana.'We British have never been the underdog and I don't intend to start now.'

In a letter written to her brother-in-law in 1949 Mrs Rowden described their sentiments at that perilous time.[4] What were they going to do? Should they stay in France or should they go? These thoughts raced through their minds. Other British people were leaving – some had already left. 'I knew Diana did not want to leave France,' wrote Mrs Rowden. '"Come what may, I want to stay," she said. "This is my country as much as England. But maybe you should go, Mama." War. *War!* We would gaze down into the street below as figures rushed here and there. She told me about a story she had read by Maupassant. A story of war – a war between France and Germany in which innocent people were shot. She had read it in her last year at school. Leave France! No, she would never do that. Not ever. "France would be more than a match for the Boche," she said. And if the worst happened ... well, she would stay and fight.'[5]

As expected the Germans headed towards Paris. In eloquent prose, journalist Noel Barber, who at the time was working for the *Continental Daily Mail* in Paris, wrote that the city had the appearance of a stage set:

On this Monday, 10 June the pavement cafés on the boulevards are as crowded as ever, a kaleidoscope of gaily flowered dresses, of men fighting for places at the minuscule tables, ordering a vin rouge or a bière de pression, yet the roads are so empty that they give the city a nostalgic turn-of-the-century character like an old sepia postcard unearthed from a dusty drawer. A dull rumble can be heard north-east of Paris, the rumble of heavy guns. The broken glass from Paris's first air raid four days ago still tinkles under the feet of the refugees moving east along the boulevards. The restaurants are empty, the Ritz deserted. For the third time in a lifetime, Paris prepares for a siege.[6]

Paris in June 1940 was a city in mourning, described by Marie-Madeleine Fourcade in *L'Arche de Noé*: 'Thick clouds of soot from the burning petrol reserves masked brilliant sunshine ... In this sad frenzy of departure people rescued whatever possessions they could save ... Weeping women pushed old people who had been squashed into prams; their children followed behind, overpowered by the heat.'

Paris, a city on the point of being invaded by the Germans, was not a city which pulled together. The unpredictable French people, rather than pulling together as the citizens of Warsaw did, seem to have done just the opposite. In her historical novel *Suite Française* Irene Nemirovsky described the fear and desperation, the poor stealing from the rich – and the other way round:

One could smell it in the heat of that hot day of the 9 June. Footpaths and pavements along the chestnut-lined avenues were crammed with crowds and as the day turned into evening the sky was dotted with stars, people looking up, their grey faces shadowed with fear. Many put their heads to one side, their hands over one ear. Was that droning noise high above them, the noise of aircraft? Was it friend ... or foe? What should they do? Were they going to be bombed? Where could they run to?

Back in Paris Diana and her mother listened to Churchill broadcasting on the BBC with his usual splendid rhetoric that 'nothing will alter our feelings towards the gallant French people who have fallen into this terrible misfortune ... the genius of France will rise again'. And on 14 June – when newspapers reported that German panzers were racing across France and that in the ensuing panic twelve million people, including many Britons, were fleeing from the German army that was ostensibly outside the gates of Paris – Mrs Rowden finally conceded the worst had happened. Neighbours told her to flee. The enemy was coming. *'Vous devez aller, Madame, vous et votre fille.'* You must go, Madam, you and your daughter, before it's too late.

Already they had left it very late. If they were caught they would be put into camps for the duration of the war, the fate of many Britons who were unable to get away. Mrs Rowden tried to persuade Diana that now it was time to depart. But she reckoned without the implacability of her daughter, even more stubborn and determined than she. All the pleading in the world would not persuade Diana to return to England. Mrs Rowden looked at her daughter, her face in shadow, the light of the lamp casting soft lights on her auburn hair. All her fears came to the surface and the room grew dark very suddenly. In a letter written in 1949 to her cousin, she wrote: 'We were in France when it fell in 1940. Diana was adamant that she would not leave. She said: "I know it's a very bad show but don't worry Mama. We will win in the end. I'm not afraid. God is on our side."'[7]

But France was a beaten nation. Three million Parisians had now fled the city. Shopkeepers had boarded up their shops and everybody had stockpiled food. No one could be reached on the telephone as wires had been cut. Roads outside of the city were blocked with the cars of those lucky people who had petrol, with people on foot, many of whom pushed carts loaded with their meagre belongings, their children, the elderly and their pets. To make matters worse, people were strafed indiscriminately by low-flying German Stuka aircraft that dive-bombed families crouching in terror in the sultry June heat. Leon Werth in *33 Days* described that time as being filled with emotion: 'In wartime God exists ... History is being made without us. The road is weeping ... I am weeping for France.'

Novelist Irene Nemirovsky wrote that Paris had the strangest smell:

It was a combination of chestnut trees in bloom and of petrol with a few grains of dust that cracked under your teeth like pepper ... you could smell the suffering in the air, in the silence. Everyone looked at their house and thought, 'Tomorrow it will be in ruins, tomorrow I'll have nothing left. We haven't hurt anyone. Why?'[8]

On 11 June the French military governor of Paris, General Pierre Hering, declared Paris an open city to save it from military bombardment – a final warning to its British population to escape from an increasingly untenable situation. The BBC reported that 'German troops marched into Paris in the early hours of this morning as French and allied forces retreated. French troops withdrew to avoid a violent battle and total destruction of Paris. They are believed to have taken a new line of defence south of the city.' British war correspondent Alexander Worth wrote that 'France is a mass of troops, tired, demoralized-looking, all without rifles, drifting into Paris ... which in its anguish is strangely calm and beautiful.' The *Sydney Morning Herald* reported that 'One of the lights of civilization has been extinguished.'

To the horror of those remaining Parisians and the rest of the world which had stood helplessly by, the Germans, many on horseback, others on foot, strutted down the Champs-Élysées and occupied the most beautiful city in the world. In newsreels and in newspapers, a red-faced man, tears streaming down his face, his fist pumping the air shouted: *'Merde aux* Boches! *Vive la France!'* It was over. The swastika was hoisted on to the Eiffel Tower and German headquarters were quickly established in one of the city's most luxurious hotels, the George V.

Diana now knew she would have to get her mother on a boat for England as soon as possible, as it was obvious Mrs Rowden wouldn't leave without her. Everybody seemed to be making for Bordeaux, but it would be a hazardous journey. Not only were the roads more choked than ever but, to make matters worse, there was heavy rain, making Alexander Worth comment: 'It just would rain for the refugees, when it didn't rain for Hitler's invasion.' None who made that terrible journey would ever forget it.

By 22 June 1940 the war in France was finally over. France and Germany signed an armistice, the Germans famously insisting that the ceremony should take place in the railway carriage near Compiègne where Germany had been forced to accept defeat at the end of the First World War – an event that had been described as 'the deepest humiliation of all time'.

Under the terms of the armistice Marshal Philippe Petain, a First World War hero, was appointed to head the government, the headquarters of which were to be at the spa town of Vichy. The eighty-six-year-old Marechal was proud of his appearance, especially his flowing white moustache. His watery eyes, the colour a startling blue, were always known as the *'bons yeux bleus du Marechal'*.

One of the most sinister terms of the armistice stipulated that people were obliged to 'surrender on demand' anyone whom the

Gestapo wished to interrogate, imprison, intern in concentration camps or return to Germany for trial. The country was divided between the German Occupied Zone (the Channel and Atlantic coasts, together with most of the north of France, including Paris) and the so-called Free Zone, south of a line running west from the Franco-Swiss border near Geneva and then south from near the city of Tours to the Spanish border; under a separate agreement Italy was to occupy a small corner of south-east France. The armistice also stated that 'Germany must be offered full security for the continuation of the war with England into which she has been forced'. The collaboration between the *Marechal* with the hated *Allemands* brought to an end a period in France's history never before experienced.

The French made no secret of the fact that England would be next in line. French General Weygand's famous words, 'In three weeks' time England's neck will be wrung like a chicken's', took pride of place among the many prophecies flying around Bordeaux. Churchill when he heard this prediction was reported as saying some time later, 'some chicken, some neck'.

Charles de Gaulle, a little-known general at the time who had gone to London to carry on the fight from there, rallied the French people, speaking to them on the BBC service:

People of France ... our country is in mortal peril. Let us all fight to save her. Come what may, the flame of French resistance must not die ... I urge all Frenchmen who would remain free to hear me and follow me. Somewhere there must shine and burn the flame of French resistance. France has lost a battle ... she has not lost the war.

On the strength of this speech the *Marechal* sentenced de Gaulle to death for treason. On 28 June, Churchill, who was not well-disposed towards de Gaulle at all – a reciprocal feeling – accepted him as leader of '*France Libre*', the Free French, and gave him financial and military backing.

It is generally recognised that if Churchill had not become Prime Minister in May 1940 in succession to Chamberlain, Britain would have either been defeated or would have been forced to reach a humiliating settlement. The outcome of the war could have been very different. The Foreign Secretary, Lord Halifax, together with other members of the Cabinet felt resistance to Hitler was futile, especially with France and the Low Countries on the verge of collapse. Negotiations of peace should therefore be put into action. It took all of Churchill's persuasiveness and determination to make the government continue the fight. He refused to listen to defeatist talk, his brilliant rhetoric delivered in his unique bulldog growl coming to the fore at a crucial meeting of government ministers when they were wavering over peace settlements: 'If this long island story of ours is to end at last, let it end only when each one of us lies choking in his own blood upon the ground.'

Without a doubt Churchill's indefatigable spirit spread right across Britain, the nation feeding off his indominability. Sir Norman Brook, senior civil servant, summed it up perfectly: 'He was the beam of a searchlight ceaselessly swinging around and penetrating the remote recesses of his administration.'

The French government had moved to Bordeaux on 13 June on the last stage of its retreat. It was a city in a state of chaos resulting from both panic and apathy. Those with influence had commandeered rooms in the Hotel Splendide, the Hotel Normandie or the Hotel Montre. German aircraft had dropped magnetic mines in the Gironde estuary, effectively sealing off the port.

It is unclear what date exactly Diana and her mother left Paris for Bordeaux, but just before the city was taken they joined the mass of people desperately trying to make their escape through streets blocked for hundreds of yards. Leaving behind most of their possessions, they each took one small suitcase, a rolled-up rug and sandwiches. June of that year was exceptionally hot. At the railway stations where the gates were closed and guarded by soldiers, thousands of people including children, some with no possessions or just a few, and all packed in like sardines, jammed the stations trying to get water. Some tried to clamber over the rails for non-existent trains. Crowds hanging on to the gates shook them and shouted at the soldiers, imploring them to let them through.

The large, dismal Gare Montparnasse was a scene of horror: grandmothers held dead babies in their arms, mothers mad with grief who had lost their children, their husbands, and all reason for living. Filth, stench and misery filled the station. The Gare d'Austerlitz near the River Seine had a direct south-bound line.

An ominous sign read 'Rendezvous for lost people'. Somehow Mrs Rowden and Diana managed to get seats in an overcrowded, ancient carriage. It was to be a long journey as some of the lines heading south had been bombed by the Germans. Five thousand refugees from Belgium and Holland, many of whom were wounded, were arriving at the station. It was a hopeless situation as there were just twenty volunteer nurses to look after them. People fainted and children were trampled underfoot. In one carriage a woman gave birth. Some of these people had been locked in the railway carriages, furnaces in the suffocating heat, for fourteen hours or more. American writer Clare Boothe, who had arrived from Belgium, wrote, 'They came off the trains with their bewildered faces, white faces, faces beaten out of shape by the Niagara of human tears that flowed down them.'

Some years later Mrs Rowden recalled the nightmare of that trip, and the bravery and unselfishness of her daughter who comforted the sick, the elderly, the frightened children, and was the first to jump up at the innumerable stops to go in search of food and water for the sick. It was hazardous to leave the carriage, for at each stop hundreds of people were ready to fight for her seat. Further south, when the train was forced to stop while bomb damage was cleared, Red Cross nurses came round with watery powdered milk and Diana again left the train to help the nurses. Mrs Rowden was always fearful lest she was unable to get back on board. Her worst fears were realised when at one of these stops Diana did not return. Anxiously she scoured the platform through grimy windows, an almost impossible task as the platform was filled with hostile, panic-stricken crowds. She confided her fears to a priest sitting opposite her squashed up against the wall of the carriage. He told her he would try and save her seat if she wanted to leave the train to search.

Mrs Rowden did not waste a second. Fear for her daughter gave her the strength to push her way through the throng standing near the exit: 'I have to find my daughter!' she cried, calling out Diana's name and trying to make her voice heard above the heaving, desperate crowd. It was hopeless. All she could do was hope that somehow Diana had managed to get into another carriage, and with that thought she fought her way back to her seat. The *pere* had not been able to keep it and he too had been forced to give his seat to a woman who looked as though she was going to faint. Not a moment too soon. The overloaded train started to move, and as it rumbled slowly out of the station Diana's mother started to pray.

Little did she know that Diana was in fact not far away. With a tin of condensed milk in her hand she had been trying to force her way back through the crowd when she saw the train leaving the station. She had no hope now of getting on another train. But there might just be a chance of getting to Tours, which was roughly midway between Bordeaux and Brittany.

Finally Mrs Rowden reached Bordeaux, a city crammed to overflowing with refugees unable to find shelter. Many slept in their cars, others on park benches or on the floor of the big hotels. For those lucky enough to obtain Spanish or Portuguese visas there was hope, but for hundreds of thousands it was the end of the road. Nothing could throw off the stupor which blanketed the city or the ugly mood that the citizens, who resented the unwelcome invasion, could no longer disguise. Outside the Portuguese consulate riots followed as men and women queued for visas. Many of these were Jews, Poles, Czechs, German and Austrian refugees – those marked for concentration camps.

Somehow Mrs Rowden, by now bone-tired and desperately worried for the safety of her daughter, managed to find the British consulate, located near the Hotel Splendide. Some hours later it was here that she had a joyful reunion with Diana, who had been very lucky. Somehow she had been able to get a lift to the port with two American Red Cross nurses who were going to Bordeaux to help with the injured refugees. As America was not involved in the war at that stage, she felt she had some protection as the ambulances were clearly marked with the neutral American flag.

Most people like Mrs Rowden, one of two thousand Britons in Bordeaux, hoped to be evacuated by sea, but the mined Gironde River presented a danger. Expecting Diana to go with her to England, Mrs Rowden now queued for a passage. Pandemonium raged everywhere in that beautiful city. Percy Philip of the *New York Times* described 'the fatigue, the danger from bombing, the nerve-racking strain that was nothing compared to the terrible sickness of heart. France had lost'. It would seem that all of Paris was jam-packed into this city of indecision.

Noel Barber wrote that it was sadness more than fear which was the dominant emotion among the hundreds of Britons crowding around the consulate steps in Bordeaux. Many were tortured by the same thoughts as Alexander Werth that 'this lovely, gentle land of France which we had all loved, was rapidly disintegrating'.

Already Diana, an exceptionally clear-thinking, courageous and selfless woman, felt it was her duty to continue with her work. She had first-hand experience of sending wounded soldiers through escape lines, and had seen and experienced much through her Red Cross work in the long months and weeks leading up to France's defeat. This had made her determined to stay behind, whether it be nursing the wounded, helping escapees, or in whatever way she could. It was a determination made up firstly of a fierce love for France and a hatred of Germany and all that it stood for, that it had dared to violate French soil. It was therefore a blending of two very powerful emotions, love and hate. A quote by Antoine de Saint-Exupéry perhaps expresses Diana's feelings for France: 'France is the flesh that sustains me, a network of connections that rules me, a collection of axes that are the foundation of my affections.'

Mrs Rowden takes up the story:

We reached Bordeaux but my daughter would not come home. She insisted on staying behind to look after the wounded. Diana had joined the French Red Cross and in the desperate weeks of 1940 I became separated from her ... She had stayed behind, of her own choice, believing it was her duty to continue with her work.[9]

She queued for a ticket and as she did so she couldn't help overhearing an English voice saying, 'We're probably leaving one melting pot for another ... we're likely to be sunk by a bloody torpedo half-way across.' Alexander Worth was on the docks and as he waited for a launch to ferry him to his ship he noticed people around him weeping: 'To leave France, and to leave it like this, is hard.'

Mrs Rowden must have had similar thoughts because Diana reassured her, telling her not to worry, that all being well she would eventually see her back in London. Then, suddenly, her mother was safely on the coal boat – one of the last boats to leave Bordeaux, which would take her to England. Mrs Rowden would have had much on her mind. Not only did she worry about Diana in a country now at war, but Maurice and Cecil too were about to go to war. Maurice had left

New College, Oxford to go into the Oxford and Bucks Light Infantry. He subsequently got a commission in the 60th King's Royal Rifle Corps. He would end up fighting at Alamein and Tunis and would be invalided home just after Diana, then a trained agent, was flown into France. Cecil at nineteen would join a Yorkshire Regiment and, like Maurice, also get a commission in the 60th King's Royal Rifle Corps.

One can imagine Diana's thoughts as she stood on the quay, bidding her mother farewell as the boat steamed out of Bordeaux harbour.

Escaping from France

Vivre dans la defaite c'est mourir tous les jours
(To live in defeat is to die every day)

- Napoleon

While Diana was making her perilous journey from Bordeaux back to northern France, the Battle of Britain was being waged across the Channel. Britain stood alone, vulnerably alone. Day after day across the blue summer skies war was defiantly fought by the young men of the Royal Air Force in their Spitfires and Hurricanes, who risked life and limb to defend their small island. Just these pilots and the persuasive eloquence of Churchill were to hold the tiny country together. Never had victory seemed more remote than during that summer of 1940. A grim cartoon by David Low in the *Daily Herald* showed a British Tommy, rifle in hand, standing defiantly on the Kent coast looking towards mainland Europe. The caption said simply: 'Very well – Alone!'

Once back in northern France Diana set about returning to nursing wounded British soldiers. She was popular with both patients and staff. A gentle, caring and considerate young woman, she inspired her patients with confidence, putting them immediately at ease.

By now the streets of Paris were full of Germans in uniform. Officers drove in confiscated Citroëns and Peugeots; guards, some in the hated black SS uniforms, occupied buildings or strutted around the streets. Signposts were erected in German and notices in German were plastered everywhere, directing people to the various military barracks and hospitals and to the *Kommandatur* in the Place de l'Opéra. Those on leave wandered around in groups, visiting the Eiffel Tower and the Louvre, having their photos taken sitting on the steps of the beautiful Sacre Coeur, and even having their portraits painted as if they were ordinary tourists and eating in the expensive restaurants, like Maxim's. But they weren't tourists and Parisians were afraid. It showed in the way they would cross the street quickly to avoid the enemy; they looked pale, tired and cowed.

Behind the Germans' backs the Parisians would spit on the pavement the enemy had walked on. They had taken over their beautiful city and now every day was a battle to get through, to stay alive and to feed their children.

Diana spent the next year witnessing the occupation's devastating effects on the country she loved. After the collapse of France there was a real shortage of food in the cities, with only basics like cheese, dry grey bread, boiled eggs (if you could get them), rough red wine and foul ersatz coffee (made mainly from acorns). However, it was always better in the country as there was milk, meat and vegetables, and apples and other fruit when in season. If one had money then one could obtain food on the black market. Even in the hospitals, which were full of wounded, the food situation was bad. Suffering and turmoil were widespread. In the north, towns and villages were in ruins and the countryside was packed with half-starved and homeless refugees. More than two million French soldiers were now prisoners-of-war, and a new hatred for the Boche had been born that would last until the final days of the war and beyond. This devastation, in which families had been torn apart, affected Diana very deeply. She felt their pain, their desolation and resolved that if she had to go back to England she would do her utmost to carry on the fight for the liberation of the country she loved.

In September, Jews, Africans and Algerians who had originally fled Paris were barred from returning and their property confiscated. By the end of September 1940 the hospitals were not even safe and the American Volunteer Ambulance Corps, a non-denominational unit, was forced out of service.

However, life had to go on. For France to have been defeated and occupied by the Germans seemed incredible and obscene. Ted Allebury wrote in *A Time Without Shadows* that it didn't make much difference whether you were French or German, the same indignities and human virtues and vices still applied: 'Occupiers and occupied are just men and women, like the marriage service – for better or worse, richer or poorer, in sickness and in health.'

By the middle of June 1941, a year after the fall of Paris, resistance was growing increasingly in France. English newspapers reported that small acts of defiance like placing flowers at the Arc de Triomphe or tearing up German posters were common, despite arrests, torture and deportation awaiting the resisters.

Once settled back into nursing, Diana made contact with the Resistance groups and helped once more with the escape routes. The free zone in south-west France amounted to approximately 45 per cent of the total area of France, with 33 per cent of the French labour force. In order to cross the demarcation zone (*the ligne de démarcation*) from one zone to the other one had to produce the correct authority, and this came in the form of an *Ausweis,* a pass, usually reserved for people in certain occupations. This was difficult but not impossible to acquire. The experience of helping with the escape lines proved invaluable to Diana as she would eventually take the same route when it was time for her to leave.

She listened to radio broadcasts by de Gaulle, who was safely in London and determined to rally the French people. He reiterated that nothing was lost for France and invited all French officers and soldiers who were in Britain to get in touch with him: 'Whatever happens, the flame of resistance must not die and will not die.'

Although it was dangerous for Diana, a British citizen, to stay in occupied France, she was determined to remain as long as she could. The German army was everywhere and she tried to move from place to place as often as she could when she was not staying in the hospital. Her total lack of fear and flawless French would not be enough to save her if she was arrested; anyone looking at Diana with her freckled skin, deep blue eyes and a tartan ribbon in her reddish-fair hair could not help but wonder if she was English.

As one of her friends was to say in the future, 'She even walked like an Englishwoman.'[1] The uniform of the French Red Cross afforded her some protection and she managed somehow to avoid any confrontation with the enemy.

Around this time it was rumoured that all Britons were going to be rounded up and sent to prison camps but even this did not deter her. It would take time for the Germans to round up several thousand Britons who were still in the country. Some had tried to escape but were unable to for various reasons; others, many of whom were elderly, were determined to stay, come what may.

Diana now witnessed the complete upheaval and subjugation of her adopted country. France was a country divided, not only geographically. Some people ignored the Germans and got on with their lives as best they could, others actively collaborated. As far as the prospect of liberation was concerned, for the majority it was not taken seriously: that would mean the country at war again with Frenchmen killed and families destroyed. There were however small pockets of resistance cropping up everywhere, men and women working together with one common aim, to get rid of the hated Boche. These were patriots who put this aim above everything else and who hoped that England at some time would come to their aid.

On 14 July the Vichy government duly ordered the internment of all British servicemen in the seventeenth-century Fort St Jean at Marseilles. British escapers and evaders were greeted with the message: 'You have asked for death and we shall give it to you.'

And in Paris on the 25th the ever-present rumours regarding Britons still remaining in France came to a head when the German-controlled radio announced that the Vichy government would deport all British subjects from its territory; British expatriates on the Cote d'Azur had been told to leave a month previous. Many of them were elderly and had been cut off from their incomes by the speed of the French collapse the previous year.

Diana now knew she had no choice. She would have to leave, but it was not until mid-1941, when her position as a British citizen became increasingly untenable, that she now had no choice but to return to England. No doubt she had often thought of her brothers who were on active service, and of her mother and whether she had returned safely to England, a country under attack almost nightly from Goering's Luftwaffe.

There is no official documentation which gives the date that she left France, but it has been established that she arrived in England in the summer of 1941. With the help of a burgeoning Resistance movement she made her way back through Spain and Portugal by circuitous routes. Diana had the correct papers and special passes for her long journey to the Spanish border. She would have gone by train to a certain point – the closest to the Spanish border being Grenoble in south-eastern France at the foot of the French Alps. It was a journey

Diana would remember for the next few years: the sadness at having to leave France and the friends she had made, the thought that she might never return, the inevitable feelings about England again and what she would be able to do for the war effort.

At Grenoble she changed to a *wagon-lits* train which took her down to the Spanish frontier by way of the Rhone valley. The train rapidly sped on towards the Franco-Spanish border, nearer and nearer to England and home. It was a long, tiring journey but as the train passed through Narbonne, Perpignan and Cerbère, the last French town on the Mediterranean coast before the frontier, the scenery, with its golden-brown countryside stretching for miles and rows and rows of plane trees, changed to the azure blue of the Mediteranean sparkling in the heat of the mid-day sun. At the border all passengers had to get out and go through French customs, showing their correct papers and passports, ration cards and any unused coupons. Their luggage was examined and eventually they were allowed back on the train for the short journey to Port Bou, the nearest Spanish town on the other side of the frontier. Their passports were examined once again in a small, dirty room with officials sitting behind a long counter. For those whose papers did not pass muster, a dark cell awaited them for the night until such time as they were allowed to go. All went well. Diana stood patiently in line while her papers were examined. It was fortunate that not only did she speak the language but she knew the procedure for crossing from France into Spain. Her command of Spanish was an asset and whenever she was questioned she would answer politely and clearly. She had the correct amount of money with her – five hundred French francs – the limit one was allowed to bring into the country. All baggage was examined minutely, but here once again there were no problems owing to her knowledge of the Spanish customs and railway authorities. Soon she was sitting in the train that was to take her to Barcelona and on to Portugal. It passed through neglected and drab towns. Spain, a neutral country in the present war, had been ravaged by civil war and was in a state of poverty and misery.

Finally they arrived in Barcelona and immediately Diana went to the British Consulate, which was situated in an opulent part of the city. It was an attractive building screened by tall trees lining the side of a busy boulevard. A Union Jack hung from a flagstaff from the balcony of a bay window. She was directed to a hotel where she was able to have a meal and a much-needed bath. Barcelona, compared with other parts of the country where she had seen real poverty, seemed to be affluent. So on to Lisbon by train the next day. The country, full of refugees, was a clearing house for British, Germans and Americans and had a strict policy of neutrality. Most Portugeuse were wholly pro-British and pro-American and admired Churchill and Roosevelt. From the British Overseas Airways office Diana collected her ticket, and the following day she boarded an aircraft for England – bound for home.

Home! It had been more than a year since she had last seen her mother. As they flew over the coast Portugal lay below, a patchwork quilt of green fields, golden-brown hills, and yellow sands. Around seven hours later they landed in England.

The flight from Lisbon/Gibraltar landed at Andover. There would have been many emotions at the sight of the green fields and country lanes of Hampshire: sadness certainly at having to leave her beloved France, and thankfulness that she had reached England where she would soon join her mother; and always the thought of what lay ahead.

SOE agent George Millar, who would drop into France just after D–Day and returned to England at the cessation of war in 1945 after fighting with the Resistance in the company of Christabel Beilenberg and her three young sons, was affected very deeply at his first sight of England. He could not take his eyes 'off the funny higgledy-piggledy country that lay below. I had never been more glad than to come home.'

Diana had escaped from occupied France just in time. Resistance activity was running rife by the end of the year. For Parisians it meant body searches, queues and the continual demand for *papiers*. Vichy had decided to deport British subjects 'to regulate the position of Britons in France'. Paris Radio reported: 'After getting rid of the Free French parasite and the enemies of France as well as the Communists and the Jews, it is now the turn of the British.'

4

The Special Operations Executive

Une guerre obscure et meritoire
(An obscure war and meritorious)
- Professor Michael Foot, SOE in France

When you are fighting for your life against a ruthless opponent you cannot be governed by Queensberry rules. This government [Neville Chamberlain's] would rather lose the war under Queensberry rules than do anything unbecoming to an absolutely perfect gentleman. That kind of thing will not do.
- Commander R. T. Bower, 8 May 1940, two days before
Winston Churchill became Prime Minister

While Diana had been working in France, a top-secret special organisation, one which would encourage sabotage and subversion behind enemy lines, was being set up in England. Some aspects of war have at certain times and in certan circumstances been considered less than respectable. In the state subversion that generally accompanies a war effort, those involved are motivated by patriotism with the means justified by the end. In 1940 there were no hard and fast rules. In England no organisation existed for conducting irregular warfare, and even if there were, there were no trained operators. The First World War was long over and those soldiers who had conducted irregular warfare, like Lawrence of Arabia, who had died in 1935, were past the recruitment age. It was obvious that there would be opposition from the Chamberlain government, the Prime Minister being a stickler for traditions such as the King's Regulations, but with the advent of Winston Churchill as Prime Minister all this was about to change.

With the country at its lowest ebb, the Battle of Britain about to begin and England on the verge of invasion, something had to be done. The city of London was in darkness. As Herman Goering's bombers pounded the city night after night, Londoners, gritting their teeth, called it 'the little Blitz' and returned to the grind of daily life, going out in the evening and dining with friends.

In May 1940 the newly elected Churchill had formed his coalition government and, angry, defiant and utterly resolved, urged the people to never give in. It was simply a matter of survival and he rallied the people to fight on in the beaches, in the streets and in the hills: 'We shall defend our island, whatever the cost will be ... We shall never surrender.' He instinctively knew that the best way to survive was to try and throw the enemy on to the backfoot and to call on all those Frenchmen who were in the French Empire and in the 'so-called Unoccupied France' to take action.

As early as 25 May, the Chiefs of Staff had forseen that France might collapse, and that if she did 'the creation of widespread revolt in Germany's conquered territories would become a major British strategic objective'.[1] For this a special organisation would be needed, and in their view it would need to be set up promptly.[2]

On 1 July several government ministers including Dr Hugh Dalton, Minister of Economic Warfare, Secretary of the War Cabinet, Lord Hankey, the Colonial Secretary, Lord Lloyd, an old friend of T. E. Lawrence's and Colonel (later Major-General) Sir Stewart Menzies, 'C' of SIS, gathered in the Foreign Office. The meeting was chaired by Lord Halifax (Viscount Halifax from 1934–1944) and senior British Conservative politicians. At this meeting it was unilaterally decided that some form of undercover operation must be organised in enemy-occupied territories, and the following day Dalton wrote to Halifax:

What is needed is a new organisation to co-ordinate, inspire, control and assist the nationals of the oppressed countries who must themselves be the direct participants. It should be comparable to the Sinn Fein movement in Ireland, to the Chinese Guerillas now operating against Japan, to the Spanish Irregulars who played a notable part in Wellington's campaign or ... to the organisations which the Nazis themselves have developed so

44

remarkably in almost every country in the world. An organisation on this scale and of this character is not something which can be handled by the ordinary departmental machinery of either the British Civil Service or the British military machine. We need absolute secrecy, a certain fanatical enthusiasm, willingness to work with people of different nationalities, complete political reliability ... But the organisation in my view should be entirely independent of the War Office machine.

This often-quoted letter influenced a good deal of SOE's early thinking on the problems of strategy.

Halifax took the meeting's conclusions to Churchill, who in a memo to his personal representative to the Chiefs of Staff wrote: 'How wonderful it would be if the Germans could be made to wonder where they were going to be struck next, instead of forcing us to try to wall in the island and roof it over!'[3]

On 16 July Churchill sent for Dalton, an Eton-educated, left-wing socialist, and invited him to take charge of the new secret organisation and 'to set Europe ablaze'. At first Dalton was to remark that regular soldiers were not men to stir up revolution, but history would prove him to be a staunch protagonist of Churchill's war strategy. Under his direction the ideal of sacrificing oneself for one's country – the sentiment of *dulce et decorum est pro patria mori* – was highly developed to a marked degree amongst patriots of many foreign nations whose countries had been overrun by the Axis powers.

It is thought by some that Churchill had first engineered the idea of infiltrating covert operatives into enemy-occupied territories through reading John Steinbeck's novel *The Moon is Down,* a powerful tale of resistance about an occupation force in the Second World War in an undisclosed country, possibly Norway. The occupiers, who initially behave impeccably, revert to type and in time become objects of intense hatred, the moral being there is no happiness for a body of troops in a conquered country with a hostile population. As the book was published in 1942, the suggestion that it provoked Churchill into a clandestine war is surely incorrect, as by that stage SOE was established and up and running. Much more likely is that, having read the book and being a fan of Steinbeck, Churchill may have been reassured that the idea of inserting well-trained infiltrators into enemy-occupied territories to ultimately shorten the war was a good one.

The Prime Minister had long been keen on guerrilla tactics since he had observed them first-hand as a young officer in Cuba and South Africa, where the Boers had used these to great effect:

Following the fall of France in June 1940, for almost four years Winston Churchill waged war with the conviction that Britain, even after the accession of Russia and the US as fellow-foes of Hitler, lacked power to confront the Nazis' military might on the Continent. This made it essential to challenge the enemy by other means – the strategic bomber offensive against Germany and guerrilla campaigns in the occupied countries. Churchill feared that if the peoples of occupied Europe were left to their own devices they would remain sunk in passivity, acquiescence and collaboration – and he was probably right.[4]

Daily newspapers reported the creation of the new secret organisation:

The war cabinet today approved a draft document signed on 19 July by Neville Chamberlain. Its aim, in Churchill's words, is to 'set Europe ablaze.' Labour MP Hugh Dalton was asked to head the planned organisation. Both MI6, which has its own sabotage department and the army have expressed opposition because it intrudes into their territory, but Dalton is determined it will succeed.

However, Hugh Dalton would be replaced as Minister of Economic Warfare in early 1942 by Lord Selbourne, a close friend of Churchill. It has been reported that there were sighs of relief all around. Because of the abrasive personality of Dalton, a top British official observed that SOE 'sometimes came nearer to setting Whitehall ablaze'. One of Dalton's political rivals described him as 'the biggest bloodiest shit I've ever met'. Churchill had no love for him, either: 'I can't stand his booming voice and shifty little eyes. Keep that man away from me.'[5]

In London Churchill delivered a powerful speech to representatives of occupied Europe: 'We shall aid and stir the people of every conquered country to resistance and revolt ... he shall find no rest, no peace, no halting place, no parley.'

However, as the war progressed Hugh Dalton was told that the time was not ripe and a lot of unfortunate people would be shot. Dalton shrugged: 'These are the Prime Minister's orders, and must be carried out.' Between 1940 and 1943 SOE's operations were dogged by the brute fact of the Axis powers' military domination.[6, 7]

Of all Britain's wartime secret organisations, the Special Operations Executive, or the 'Ministry of Ungentlemanly Warfare' as it became known to its staff, remains the most controversial (it was Churchill who gave SOE its infamous epithet). The Nazis called its agents 'terrorists, gangsters or bandits', and of its leadership *The Times* commented that 'a few could only charitably be described as nutcases'. Professor Michael Foot noted that SOE 'was full of people with personalities like sledge-hammers'.

Author David Stafford refers to SOE as one 'of the most glamorous, brave and self-sacrificing "secret armies" of the war'.[8] It has also been described as an organisation specialising in 'assassination, sabotage, prisoner-of-war escape routes, female seduction, sophisticated blackmail, resistance armies' build-up, gun-running by parachute drops by land, by sea, forgery, currency deals and the making – and sometimes breaking – of foreign leaders and even governments'.[9]

Many of the SOE operatives were refugees from the Nazi-occupied countries who after completing their training were reinserted into their homelands on specific missions. The work was some of the most dangerous in the war.

In the early days the organisation was not highly regarded within Whitehall and was thought to cause more trouble than its achievements were worth. Existing intelligence and espionage services, particularly MI5 and MI6, local resistance groups and governments-in-exile all had cause to complain about its activities. From small beginnings, SOE was first started up in three 'gloomy rooms in St Ermin's Hotel' before moving to 64 Baker Street, a large five-floored modern office building in south-east Marylebone that had recently become vacant. Michael House was next door across the lane, headquarters of Marks and Spencer. Norgeby House was across the street, a brand new building taken over by the Treasury and built on commercial land once occupied by a hairdresser, a greengrocer, a milliner and a gownmaker. There was also Montague Mansions and eventually Bryanston Square, with offices in Norgeby House. The organisation was cleverly disguised by large name plates at the door marked 'Inter-Services Research Bureau'.

Although SOE's raison d'être was to support resistance movements in 1940, in most of Europe the occupied population had been stunned or intimidated into passivity, and resistance movements barely existed at the beginning of the war. In England once the immediate danger of invasion was over SOE set about recruiting potential employees in earnest. The whole idea of sending personnel into enemy-occupied countries who were in essence amateurs – although patriotic and trained to the best of SOE's ability – was an ambitious objective. In those early days of the war in 1940 there was little the fledgling organisation could do to set fire to anything as Churchill and his government had enough on their hands in trying to prevent an invasion by the Germans.

Towards the end of the year, when this danger looked to be over, SOE set about recruitment and developed a series of techniques for transporting its members and equipment to supply the European resistance. At this early stage, and owing to the secret nature of the organisation, its first recruits were often from the 'old boys' network or friends of friends and from the Army, Navy and Royal Air Force. At that time the only requirements were the ability to speak a foreign language and a willingness to jump out of an aeroplane.

Applicants joined for a variety of reasons. Robert Boiteux-Burdett, half-French and born in London, code named *Nicholas*, was stranded in London when war broke out:

> One day I was walking down Piccadilly and I met an old friend, and we started talking about the war and he said, 'What are you doing these days?' and I said, 'Nothing,' and he said, 'They're looking for silly buggers like you to parachute into France. They've asked me and I'm not mad, but you might be interested.' So I went straight to the War Office and volunteered.

Roger Landes, born in Paris of a French mother and an English father, came to live and work in London just before the war:

> When I arrived in London after my training I saw a British captain, the brother of the actor John Gielgud, who asked me questions in French and he said: 'Well, you've been trained as a wireless operator. We want to know if you will go back to France. You'll be dropped by parachute or fishing boat … you've got a good chance to be arrested, tortured and maybe shot. I'll give you five minutes to say yes or no.' Right away I said I will do it.

Of all the Axis-occupied countries in which SOE sought to foster subversion and sabotage, France appeared to offer the best opportunities. The region's countryside of rolling hills and woodlands offered good dropping zones for parachutists and airdrops of weapons and explosives. Night landings for the delivery and extraction of agents by Lysander and Hudson aircraft were not too difficult for expert pilots to achieve so long as the resistance reception parties had marked out the landing strips and shown the requisite identification signals. Once on the ground, agents who had adopted credible cover stories could merge into the local population of the industrial cities and ports. When conscription for forced labour in Germany was introduced in France in late 1942, young men were prompted to take to the hills, where they joined the pro-Gaullist *Forces francaises de l'interieur* (FFI) or the Communist *Francs tireurs et partisans* (FTP).

Two organisations primarily dealt with the training and operations of secret agents in France: the British-controlled French (F) Section, headed by Maurice Buckmaster, and the Gaullist Secret Service, the BCRA (*the Bureau Central de Renseignements et d'Action* (also known as the 'Free French') and headed by Colonel Passy. The BCRA was located in Duke Street behind Selfridge's department store. A liaison section staffed by both French and British personnel was known as RF Section and was headed by a British officer, Captain Eric Piquet-Wicks.

When the Eton-educated forty-one-year-old Buckmaster had been approached by SOE in 1941 to run their French Section, he was told that there had never been a situation quite like this before:

> We've recently formed a new organisation to deal with something that sounds very much up your street – subversive warfare in France. It's something quite fresh. You sound the man for the job. How about it? But we're in the early stages still. And that means it is going to take a long time to persuade people to see just what's needed.[10]

Over six feet tall with thinning, fair hair and very blue, slightly protruding eyes, Buckmaster had a natural talent for languages, particularly French and later German. Before the war he had spent some years in France where he became proficient in the language, and later worked for the Ford Motor Company in Paris as a senior executive. At Eton he had come to the notice of his teachers by teaching French to boys younger than himself who were trying to pass the Common Entrance Examination. When the Second World War began he was commissioned into the Intelligence Corps and was one of the last officers to be evacuated from the French coast near Dunkirk. From December 1941 he became head of 'F' Section. His strengths were a gift for leadership, immense energy and enthusiasm, and a love of people. He proved to be one of the greatest thorns in the side of the Nazis. It was said that Hitler so reviled Buckmaster that he had put him as the third person on a target list if the German invasion of Britain had gone ahead. Buckmaster was supported by a large staff of around forty men and women in Baker Street. It was his job to organise the activities of British agents sent into German-occupied France. He was described as having a 'gentle, slightly self-deprecatory manner and seemed unlikely to rise any further in the organisation', according to SOE's Controller for Western Europe, Robin Brook. 'He knows his job within the Section intimately, but never quite gets outside it,' and SOE head Major (later General) Colin Gubbins agreed, summarising him as a 'Staff Officer rather than a Commander'.[11]

Buckmaster had a staff of around fifteen in the earlier stages, rising to around thirty by the time the war finished, and ran what was described as 'a happy office' with staff meetings held regularly each Wednesday.

There is no doubt that Buckmaster was an approachable person with a ready smile – a caring, compassionate man deeply involved with his agents, a father figure to them all and far from careless and uncaring about their fate.[12] Leo Marks, SOE's cryptographer, was used to

> ... being thoroughly towelled down in the [boxing] ring between rounds but not by blue eyes of such extraordinary penetration. I didn't begin to understand the politics he was obliged to play to compete with de Gaulle and had no desire to. But I'd noticed that no matter how late I phoned to tell him that an indecipherable was broken, he was always waiting in his office, and his first concern was for the safety of the agent.[13]

SOE historian Professor Michael Foot felt that Buckmaster's problem lay in the deep-rooted attachment he felt for most of his agents, an attachment that many felt was soft and could cloud his judgement.[14]

In the end Buckmaster would be responsible for sending around 400 men and women into France, each with false identities, code names and operations.

Deputy head of 'F' Section was Nicholas Bodington, who had worked for Reuters in Paris. It is said that the relationship between Buckmaster and Bodington was not good: 'Bodington's swift and cutting intellect was bound to clash with that of the generously spirited father figure. There was no doubting his extraordinary courage and remarkably dexterous mind, but there wasn't one officer in F section who would have followed Bodington anywhere.'[15]

Some of SOE's employees were unaware exactly who they were working for. For one thing, SOE was not the official name – it meant different things to different people. The War Office referred to it as MOI (SP). It was known by others as the ISRB, the Joint Technical Board, or The Headquarters Special Training Schools, while the Admiralty referred to it as NID (Q) and the Air Ministry AI-10. Nobody outside SOE and few inside the organisation knew precisely with whom they were dealing.

Professor Foot says that SOE loved to cloak itself in code names, ciphers, symbols, aliases and numbers: 'I got on to somebody in F Section who would answer to three different names over the telephone with the same voice and was inclined to say: "I'm sorry, old boy, we can't help you at all." That was their general line.'[16]

Buckmaster's assistant was Vera Atkins, formerly Rosenberg, a thirty-three-year-old Romanian Jew, a fact she kept close to her chest and which technically made her a foreigner – suspicious during a time of war. This was hidden from everybody except Buckmaster. An extremely intelligent woman who spoke five languages fluently to many people she *was* SOE. Nobody in SOE was sure exactly what Vera's role was. She has been described variously as 'Buckmaster's second-in-command, an intelligence officer, his assistant or aide, or his secretary.' Noreen Riols recalled that 'Maurice was certainly pleasant to work with ... he always appeared to be in a hurry and thinking of his next appointment rather than the one in hand.'

Atkins looked after every aspect of the agents' welfare, arranging their accommodation, helping them to prepare for 'going into the field', reading and checking incoming wireless messages, and writing Buckmaster's daily resumés, which were known as 'comic cuts'. Stella King in her biography of Jacqueline Rudellat described Vera as saying she actually ran the French Section. Even Buckmaster was vague about her status. Nor was she his second-in-command. This title was given to Nicholas Bodington, his deputy, but apparently this was purely nominal: 'There was no second-in-command, Maurice ran the whole thing.'

Agent Yvonne Baseden described Vera as 'F' Section's éminence grise'.[17] 'She seemed to be ubiquitous. I first met her in Baker Street, cool, detached, single-mindedly preoccupied with the interests of those who had or had not come back from the field.'[18] Extremely tidy in her work, she had formidable organisational skills, tireless attention to detail, and a brilliant memory, all of which made her the perfect administrator. However, she 'was a secretive, cagey woman who could never admit she might ever have been guilty of having made a single mistake in her life'.[19]

Vera's designation was actually 'F. Int. – F Section Intelligence Officer', although she herself sometimes translated it as 'F. Interference'.

She terrified an eighteen-year-old Noreen Riols, who as a French-speaking secretary worked for Buckmaster. She described Vera as 'icy, so poised, so sophisticated. She smoked Balkan Sobranie cigarettes attached to a long cigarette holder, her bright blue eyes piercing whoever she was interviewing through a haze of smoke. Some of the agents nicknamed her "Madonna" or Marlene Dietrich. I think a rod of steel describes her better.'

The fledgling SOE started off slowly. Resources were limited and the thought of cloak-and-dagger operations concerned primarily with sabotage met with resistance from military establishments such as MI5 and MI6. When SOE was formed as a separate entity from SIS, inevitably rivalry existed between them. Though their functions were different, there were unavoidable instances of trespass: 'You cannot carry out clandestine operations without intelligence to guide you, and you cannot help acquiring intelligence in the course of your proceedings.'[20]

As David Stafford explains, 'SOE appeared to the Foreign Office and Chiefs of Staff as an unruly sixth-form schoolboy unable to keep his grubby fingers off the tablecloth while constantly demanding second helpings when there were none.'[21] MI6 worried about subversive operations interfering with intelligence gathering. Bomber Command objected at first to diverting aircraft for special operations, and no one trusted the amateurs at Baker Street.

Those with the best prospect of survival on SOE operations were the most ruthless and untrusting. But however strongly their instructors discouraged it, there was also a romantic, buccaneering streak about the organisation that brought into its ranks many men and women who would never have become professional spies for SIS.

Brigadier Colin McVeigh Gubbins was enlisted to run this 'dirty tricks' department. A forty-four-year-old, gimlet-eyed Scot, he was a born leader. Gubbins was an expert on subversion who had fought with an anti-Bolshevik force in northern Russia and against Michael Collin's guerillas in Ireland. He had also written an important pamphlet in the 1930s, and in 1940 had won a DSO for commanding the Independent Companies in Norway. He was a tough, professional soldier and more than a match for Dalton. He was described by one agent as 'a real Highland toughie, bloody brilliant'. He was known as a swashbuckler in his private life, partying all night – sometimes wearing a kilt – with members of the FANY, which provided cover for female agents sent into the field. According to instructor Kim Philby, who helped to create the SOE training course, it was rumoured that 'Gubbins could only find time for his girlfriends at breakfast. But he was man enough to keep them.' An SOE secretary recalled that there were a lot of 'bedtime stories' at Baker Street and that 'Gubbins was a lech'. But Gubbins was soon to be busy with other tasks such as sabotage and subversion. At the time of his inception into SOE he proved to be an energetic and enthusiastic organiser of British resistance. However, he was not, in Lord Selbourne's words, 'universally popular', though he did have the gift of inspiring confidence and spent as much time as he could with the younger agents in Cairo, by whom he was accepted not only as their commanding officer but 'as a battle-scarred member of their own tribe'. In Cairo he was to write that the city was 'a sinkhole of iniquity'.[22]

'When everything was at its blackest in July 1940 and the government was of course searching for any possible way of getting at the Germans to help our main forces while they reformed,' remembered Gubbins after the war, 'our task was our Charter and was simply to carry out all forms of irregular warfare against the Germans that we could possibly devise or think of –mostly, of course, behind their own lines from a straight-forward act of sabotage of factories or communications right up to open guerrilla warfare.' (*Gubbins and SOE.*)

By the time Diana joined SOE in 1943 Gubbins had become a Major-General and succeeded Charles Hambro, the banker, as head of the organisation. According to historian Max Hastings, 'From an early stage Gubbins was the most effective personality in SOE. He had a background in military intelligence who had served at the war office.' SOE's recruiting officer, Selwyn Jepson, was later to describe him as 'having the outward affectations of a regular Highland officer, but underneath it all, there was great sensitivity'.

SOE would end up recruiting, training and equipping more than 9,000 agents who would end up being infiltrated into many European countries, including Germany, as well as into the conflict in the Far East.

At the beginning, before SOE got off the ground, the organisation considered recruiting only men, but in the face of a good deal of opposition Selwyn Jepson came up with the argument that this was an antiquated rule:

I was faced with a good deal of opposition from the powers that be who said that women, under the Geneva Convention were not allowed to take combatant duties which they regarded resistance work in France as being. It took me some time to find a proper answer to that and then I found it. I discovered that the anti-aircraft units always had ATS officers on their strength, and that when it came to firing an anti-aircraft gun the person who pulled the lanyard that released the trigger was a woman, an ATS officer. The long and the short of it is that when Churchill growled at me: 'What are you doing?' I told him and then he said: 'You're using women in this?

'Yes, sir. Don't you think this is a very sensible thing to do?'

He said: 'Yes. Good luck to you.'

In my view women were very much better than men for the work. Women, as you must know, have a far greater capacity for cool and lonely courage than men.

For some time the French Section, and Selwyn Jepson in particular, were concerned as to how to put their women agents, some of whom had been drawn from civilian life, into uniform during the period of their training in England. They could not, obviously, train in plain clothes, since this would be bound to excite curiosity. They had to have a uniform that would provide them with a 'cover story' they could tell to their friends and relatives, and at the same time provide them with a sense of being in the Services. The ATS could not provide a cover on account of a clause in their constitution forbidding members to take part in active military operations. Jepson made contact with the Commandant of the Women's Transport Service (First Aid Nursing Yeomanry), a civil organisation which had in its constitution no such limiting clause. The Commandant readily gave permission for women members of the French Section to be enrolled in the FANY corps, to wear the uniform during their training and to remain members while in the field. It was still considered desirable to obtain for these women the rank of officer in one of the Armed Services before they were sent out into the field, since in the event of their capture the Germans might hesitate to sentence them to death; they could say they were officers of His Majesty's Forces and, if nothing else, such status might procure them better conditions of detention. In the end, the WAAF agreed to give honorary commissions to women agents.

In an interview with the BBC, Vera Atkins talked about this very subject:

> I've always found personally that being a woman has great advantages if you know how to play the thing right, and I believe that all the girls, the women who went out, had the same feeling. They were not as suspect as men, they had very subtle minds when it came to talking their way out of situations, they had many more cover stories to deliver than most men and they performed extremely well. Also, they were very conscientious – I'm not saying men are not. They were wonderful wireless operators and very cool and courageous. I think we assessed the chances of coming through at no more than fifty per cent.

In the summer of 1941 twenty-six-year-old Diana arrived back to a country at war and a joyful reunion with her mother. Mrs Rowden had bought a small mews flat in London, No 1 Cromwell Mews West, SW7, near the Natural History Museum. The flat would be home to Diana for the next two years. At first she found it difficult to settle, after living in the powder keg she had left behind; it was strange trying to reconcile the England of 1941 with the occupied, war-stricken and politically divided country she had left behind. From June 1941 active resistance in France was a very dangerous occupation, but in England there were no obvious outward signs of a country at war except for small details like the signposts being removed and sandbagged buildings in London. The people, stoic and seemingly unconcerned, went about their business much as usual. Downed Royal Air Force pilot William Simpson remarked about this stiff upper lip attitude:

> Did anyone realise that just across the English Channel crouched an army of gangsters, armed to the teeth and waiting only for the fall of Russia before springing on us? Yet, as the months passed I began to realise that this apparent apathy was to a large extent an illusion, and that in reality there was a wide consciousness of the gravity of the situation alive in English hearts.[23]

Only late in 1941 and early in 1942 did a small number of French people begin to stir from their lethargy and the shock of their defeat. Clandestine opposition newspapers were set up and, slowly but cautiously, meetings of like-minded people opposed to Vichy took place throughout the country. However, many of these people were arrested and shot, but more and more people joined the pockets of resistance that by now were springing up all over France. Links were forged with interested parties in London, the French Section of SOE, MI6, MI9, de Gaulle's BCRA and later the American OSS.

Diana longed to do something positive for the war effort and discussed her options with her mother. Many young women had volunteered for the services – the ATS (Auxiliary Territorial Service), the Wrens and the WAAFS, which was seen to possess a certain glamour by its association with aircrew. But not everyone believed that servicewomen were doing a good job. One woman told a Mass-Observation Survey: 'Those ATS girls are a disgrace. They come in this pub at night and line up against that wall. Soldiers give them drinks and when they're blind drunk they carry them out into the street.'[24]

When nothing was forthcoming Diana applied to the Air Ministry in Whitehall for a job. While there her ability with French came to the notice of Harry Sporberg, deputy head of SOE. Formerly a city solicitor and Hugh Dalton's private secretary, he was now deputy to Colin Gubbins. Sporberg had much to do with the day-to-day affairs of agents and was looking for a French-speaking secretary who could also do shorthand. He was immediately interested in Diana, and his letter dated 4 September 1941 reads:

> In connection with the attached letter on the subject of a certain Miss Diana Rowden ... What I am looking for is a French-speaking secretary who can also do French shorthand, but the letter rather reads as though this lady has no secretarial qualifications. If I am wrong and she has such qualifications and has not already been given a job, we should very much like to see her.[25]

Diana applied to the Women's Auxiliary Air Force (WAAF). This did not present a problem as already she was at the Air Ministry. Normally requirements were such that girls applying would have a basic health inspection as well as certain scholastic requirements for officers over the age of nineteen, having passed the School Certificate; language skills or wireless knowledge were particular advantages.

On 8 December 1941 Diana was given the service number '4193' and commissioned into the WAAF as an Assistant Section Officer. She remained in London until July 1942, when she was posted to RAF Moreton-in-Marsh, Gloucestershire, an airfield used by the Vickers Wellingtons of 21 Operational Training Unit (OTU), which saw aircraft regularly committed to either Bomber Command's big night-bombing raids on Germany. The station was enlivened by visits from the Luftwaffe, who managed to destroy a number of training aircraft on the ground. In the meantime, while Diana was working in the WAAF (by this time she was Acting Section Officer Rowden) she became ill and had to have an operation, apparently for appendicitis. She was sent to recover at the RAF Convalescent Home, the Grand Hotel at Torquay, and it was while she was there that she met Squadron Leader William Simpson. Simpson had received the DFC, the *Croix de Guerre* and the OBE. On a wartime flying mission in 1940 with Fighter Command's No. 12 Squadron he had been shot down in flames over Belgium and suffered disfiguring burns to his face and crippling injuries to his hands. He was to become one of the most famous of the 'Guinea Pigs' treated by New Zealand plastic surgeon Sir Archibald McIndoe.

Diana and Simpson had much in common. Both of them had been in France and had recently escaped, not out of a desire to return to

England, but more from the viewpoint of returning to carry on the war – Simpson in the hope he would return to flying even though he had been turned down for continued active service back in France, for obvious reasons, and Diana to fight back against the tyranny of the Nazis. They shared a mutual love of France and both were frustrated and plagued by the feelings that they had deserted her, that they should never have returned to England and its relative comfort until the war was over. Coincidentally, Simpson had also escaped from France and returned to England through Spain and Portugal. In 1955, when journalist Elizabeth Nicholas, Diana's school friend of Manor House days, was researching the fate of the four women SOE agents killed at Natzweiler concentration camp, she was surprised to hear that her friend William Simpson had also been a friend of Diana's. Nicholas invited Simpson to dinner and he told her of his meeting with Diana in Torquay. Very quickly they became friends, Diana telling him of her devotion to France and her urgent desire to return in order to prepare the way for liberation.

In his book *I Burned My Fingers* Simpson described the convalescent home as unique. It was in a beautiful setting with a view over the golf course and the sea. The atmosphere was one of freedom from unnecessary and tiresome restrictions. It was the perfect atmosphere in which to relax, one of tranquility and restfulness. The stay was intended to help him recover from his many surgeries, recover his health and put on weight. Simpson and Diana became very close. He was attracted to the calm, poised young woman, who did not in any way show repugnance toward the scarred young man.

Simpson was obsessed by thoughts of France:

I loved her as a man loves a beautiful and intelligent mistress who has given him solace and understanding. She had become like a mistress whom I loved dearly, yet could not reach. My heart ached at the memory of the suffering I had seen there. I saw again the queues of small, shivering children waiting for their paltry rations of blue skimmed milk. I felt the hunger and hopelessness which French men and women were feeling. These were serious feelings and they persisted for a very long time.

Many times Simpson and Diana chatted, often in French as Simpson was also fluent. She told him she had tried to think of every possibility that could enable her to return to France. Simpson, who was by now attached to SOE and working in the Operations Room, was impressed with her strength of character, her admirable education, her ability with languages. They discussed the misery the occupation had brought to France and their fear for the safety of their friends whom they had left behind: were they still with the Resistance or had they been shot or imprisoned? It is understandable therefore why Simpson thought he and Diana had so much in common. When Simpson left Torquay and was back in London again he immediately got in touch with his friends in SOE, describing Diana as 'a free spirit' with outstanding language skills, and reporting that 'she was healthy as a flea' and recommending her for training. In the meantime he had met up with Mrs Rowden in the mews flat in Kensington she shared with Diana. He was to tell Elizabeth Nicholas that he was very fond of Diana, a girl of striking character, though not in any way other than friendship: 'I wonder if I did right in recommending her?' Elizabeth Nicholas mentioned to Mrs Rowden about Simpson's worries and doubts, and Mrs Rowden replied, 'Tell your friend not to reproach himself. If it had not been him, it would have been someone else.' (*Death be not Proud.*)

It was inevitable. He need not wonder if he did right. Diana was determined to get back to France, and would have found a way somehow.

On Simpson's recommendation Diana was called for an interview on 6 October 1942 at Room 238 of the Hotel Victoria, in London's Northumberland Avenue. The note on her file reads: 'Has interesting linguistic qualifications which might make her of value for operational purposes'. It was signed Selwyn Jepson, Capt. However, at the bottom of the page is a further note: 'DNTU' (Did not turn up). It is unclear what went wrong – there could be several reasons. Certainly Diana, who wanted to return to fight in France more than anything, would have had a valid reason for not turning up. Maybe the time wasn't quite right. Having spoken to her mother about what she wanted to do, inevitably she would have met with opposition. It may have been illness on the part of her mother, or even Diana herself, or, as it was nearing Christmas, she may have wanted to delay her induction into SOE until the New Year. This last factor would be the most likely reason as the two women were very close and Diana may well have promised her mother she would wait until after the festive season.

She would not have wanted to let people down and it is most unlikely that she would not have made the necessary arrangements to cancel the interview. Diana remained on the Intelligence staff of the Chief of Air Staff.

By the beginning of 1943 all operations were planned, intelligence collated and filed, and new reports from agents in the field were starting to be received at Baker Street. Briefing sessions were held at a flat in Orchard Court. This was where operatives who were about to be dropped into France were given the very latest details about conditions there, in particular their own districts. If there were any possible doubts, such as in the case of a suspect agent working for the Germans in the *réseau,* the outgoing agent would be warned and would be told to take appropriate action to silence the man. The flat in Orchard Court became famous for its bathroom, which contained a black-tiled bath with marble surroundings and pink mirrors engraved with flowers. The bathroom had subdued lighting and thick carpet on the floor: 'From time to time agent Peter Churchill might be found, fully clothed in the dry tub, his feet resting on the taps, doing *The Times* crossword.'[26]

The Orchard Court flat was presided over by Arthur Park, SOE's major-domo or butler. He was middle-aged, had a prodigious memory and was beloved by the agents. He had lived most of his life in France, especially Paris where he had been a bank messenger in the Paris branch of the Westminster Bank. He knew every agent by his training pseudonym and made each one personally welcome when they arrived at the flat for briefing. His cheerful countenance was beloved by all the members of the French section and his tact was responsible for avoiding many awkward meetings between men who were not supposed to know each other's appearance. For security reasons, he had the difficult task of keeping agents of different nationalities apart, and would shut them in separate rooms after promising to personally give them a tour of the infamous black-tiled bathroom – if they behaved.

'Arthur had lived most of his life in France,' said Buckmaster, 'but after Dunkirk and the fall of France, had had to leave his French wife and hurriedly made his way to England to serve King and Country, only to discover on arrival he was too old for active service.' As Noreen Riols recalls, 'He was perfect for his job at Orchard Court, very firm, but very gentle. I asked him why he had been chosen. "The

General [Gubbins, head of SOE] told me it was because I knew how to keep my mouth shut," he replied smiling. Arthur was one of the last people they saw before leaving, and one of the first they saw upon their return.'

SOE was a new and unorthodox secret service wedded to a doctrine of subversion whose job was to cause mayhem and disorder, and this made the more orthodox SIS very hostile to the new organisation. SIS's activities were more discreet, and the two were soon in direct conflict. SOE had not become an effectively recognised unit in early 1941 when it made its first parachute drop behind enemy lines into Poland. Even then, it had to wage continued warfare with the service chiefs and the Foreign Office for a share in resources such as aircraft and weaponry, as well as proper recognition of its role. Because of Churchill's support, SOE survived. His support and his faith in European resistance provided a beacon of hope for the oppressed nations and all those who lived under Hitler's rule. But one of SOE's greatest handicaps was the continued hostility of SIS. General de Gaulle couldn't stand either of the two departments, saying both were thorns in his side.

In January 1943, just before Diana started her training, Stewart Menzies, 'C' of MI5, exhibited one of his frequent explosions of wrath about SOE to Sir Robert Bruce Lockhart, diplomat, journalist, author – rather like a present-day James Bond – who recorded the conversation: '"Could nothing be done about this show, which was bogus through and through?" Menzies demanded. They never achieved anything, they compromised all his agents, and they were amateurs in political matters. Menzies reckoned that if they could be suppressed Intelligence would benefit enormously.'[27]

Diana was commissioned in the Intelligence Corps in December 1942. A Personnel Form on her personal file, dated 4 March 1943, says, 'Applicant for employment as Agent in the field after training.' A further Personnel Form, dated 4 March 1943, mentions not only Diana's linguisitic qualifications but also geographical qualifications 'which might prove valuable operationally after training'. She was told to have her kit handy but not to bring it with her when she reported in.

On 15 March Section Officer Diana Rowden, No. 4193, was again invited to the Hotel Victoria in Northumberland Avenue. Room 238 had again been selected for the interview. Built in the 1880s, the hotel, a large brownstone building with an ornate sculpture decorating the façade, had 400 rooms and is said to have been a favourite haunt of King Edward VII and Lily Langtry. It was requisitioned for military use by the War Office in May 1940. Diana passed through the revolving glass-and-mahogany doors of the main entrance into the vast and ornate foyer panelled with rust-and-grey marble. After filling in a form where she stated her name and who her appointment was with, she was led by an attendant along a corridor into an old antiquated lift that led up to the second floor to Room 238. The room looked over a quiet inner courtyard. It contained an empty fire grate and a trestle table covered with a grey army blanket, which served as a desk. There were two chairs and a metal filing cabinet. Seated behind the desk and dressed in military uniform was Selwyn Jepson, a sharp-eyed forty-three-year-old Army Captain. Jepson worked under the pseudonym of 'Potter' and was recruiting officer for SOE. In civilian life he had been a writer of detective thrillers; his outstanding quality was as a shrewd judge of character. A report from SOE to Military Intelligence on his file in March, 1942 described him as being 'far ahead of anyone as a talent spotter'.

In post-war editions of *Who's Who* Jepson described himself briefly as 'author and occasional soldier'. In fact he had an impressive army record, having served in the Great War, been commissioned in the Royal Tank Corps and posted to Northern Ireland security in 1939. From Ireland he was transferred to Oxford to select suitable army officers for intelligence work, which led to his appointment with SOE. Jepson had a network of useful contacts that produced a steady flow of possible agents. Other sources were the three services, particularly the RAF, from where Diana was recruited. However, he had to overcome a steep hurdle in the shape of the Geneva Convention, which forbade women to take active roles in war and in which the women's branches of the Services were adamant in obeying, even though their commandant was sympathetic to Jepson's needs.

After the war Jepson described that time:

I would decide after the initial appointment ... whether I would want to go on with them. I simply went with the cover that having languages and a knowledge of France might be valuable in the war effort. Then they would go away. I would then have to refer their names and addresses to MI5 for vetting.[28] MI5 generally would say: 'Nothing known against'. Not a very positive vetting, but enough for me. Anyhow, by the time I'd interviewed them I'd had a pretty good idea of where their loyalties lay. For the most part they just hated Germany, hated the Germans and wanted to get into the war. I interviewed prospects entirely in civilian clothes, and that would automatically put us on a different personal level except when I was interviewing anyone in the services.

In the early days of SOE Jepson had a desk with nothing on it, but he soon decided it was too formal and threw out the desk and got an ordinary army-issue folding wooden table, which made it much easier: 'Then there was no sense of officialdom about it.'[29]

Diana walked into the almost bare room and saluted the man in civvies before her. Captain Jepson returned the salute and asked her to sit down. Then he looked down at some notes in front of him. She quickly stole a look around the room. It was furnished very simply with just two foldaway chairs.

'Miss Rowden, tell me about yourself. I see you are a Section Officer in the Women's Auxiliary Air Force. How long have you been with them?'

'Since 1941, sir.'

'I see you have lived in France. Tell me about your time there.'

'Well, I first went to France as a child ... with my mother and my brothers. We lived there for some years ... and then we came back to England.'

Then the questions came at her in fast, fluent French.

'*Vous parlez Francaise, Mademoiselle?*'

'*Oui, M'sieur.*'

'*Ou étiez-vous instruits?*' 'Where were you educated?'

'*En France et en Angleterre.* And when we returned to England, at the Manor House School in Limpsfield, then the Sorbonne where I studied languages.'

'*Vous avez vécu en France avant la guerre.* Tell me about that time.'

The 1920s. A long time ago and yet it seemed like it was yesterday. She didn't even stop to think, the words poured out as if she had been storing them up for a long time. The sea, the sun, the freedom ... it was all there clear in her mind, just waiting to be released. As she spoke her face changed, it became flushed and her eyes shone and she became very French, using her hands to illustrate a point or two. She built up a picture of a life of perfect happiness with her two brothers – no restrictions, no rules of any kind.

Jepson smiled. 'Miss Rowden, would you tell me which areas of France you are most familiar with?'

'Both northern and southern France, sir.' And then she told him of her time with the American Red Cross and her work with the escape lines.

'We need people like you. We're very short of good agents, especially ones with your ability: people who know France well, who know and love the country and its people. Would you be prepared to go back, and work behind the lines so to speak?'

Would she?

'I would want that more than anything, sir. You see, I want to do my bit, I want to help in whatever way I can. Just tell me when I can go.'

Jepson laughed. 'You would have to have at least a six-week period of training. We don't send agents in just like that. The job is very dangerous. There are serious risks involved; you would be risking your life. Some of our people have failed to return. You'll be in danger every moment of every day you are in France. And if you're caught we won't be able to help you. You will be completely on your own. You don't have to make up your mind just yet. Go home and think about everything I've said very carefully.'

Diana took a deep breath.

'I have thought about it … and I will do it. I have been hoping for just such an opportunity. I want to go back more than anything.'

'I can see you could be of great value to us. You have obvious qualifications, not just your strength with languages, but also because you have been over there in the thick of it, amongst the occupied forces. I recognise your singleness of purpose, your strengths. But… I still want you to think all this over very carefully. You see, I'm not sure if you have weighed up the risks. You haven't had time to consider. Be sure it's what you want to do. What I am trying to tell you is that the chances of surviving are approximately 50-50.'

Fifty-fifty.

'I am not trying to put you off,' said Jepson. 'On the contrary, we need people such as yourself – at this stage in the war, particularly. But I want you to be very sure.' He stood up and held out his hand. 'Please don't discuss this with anybody, but I'm sure you know that.'

'Sir ... if I join and you are happy with me, when would you want me to go?'

'Not for a while. After you're trained there would still be a period of perhaps a few weeks. I've arranged for you to have a week's leave. Go home and think about it and let me know what you decide. One thing, I'm sure I don't have to tell you is to be discreet, and I make this very clear, do not mention it to anyone, not even your family.'

He stood up and handed her a slip of paper with a telephone number written on it in very small print. 'That's all for the moment. We'll be in touch and thank you for coming to see me. If there are any questions, please get in touch with me.'

She held on to it very tightly.

'*Au revoir, monsieur.*'

He smiled at her again and shook her hand. '*Au revoir.*'[30]

Diana would have impressed Jepson. They were lucky to get her. Bilingual with the added advantages of Italian and Spanish, she would have the ability to blend seamlessly into the background. Her thoughts, her reasons for joining SOE, her obvious experience of having already lived in France, and the fact she had already made her own way back to England from occupied France were distinct plus points. But there was no disguising her distinctly English looks. That was a worry.

Jepson had spoken to Diana of the need for new recruits to help with the war effort as by now the tide was beginning to turn and the Allies were about to go on the offensive. On 10 November 1942 Churchill, buoyed after the desert victory in El Alamein, the Allied landings in North Africa, and prospects of success in Russia, had lifted the spirits of the British people with yet more encouraging words: 'This is not the end. It is not even the beginning of the end. But it is, perhaps, the end of the beginning.' By the spring of 1943 SOE was fully functioning in every theatre of war with agents inside Europe and throughout the Middle East, North Africa, and even some in Germany itself, with the emphasis on building up secret armies to support resistance in occupied countries to support a forthcoming Allied invasion.

However just after the time of Diana's interview, German troops marched into the unoccupied French zone, allegedly to save Vichy from invasion. Code-named Operation Anton, the move was ordered by Hitler after Pierre Laval, leader of the Vichy government, resisted pressure from Berlin to let German forces occupy Tunisia. A letter from Hitler to Marshal Petain justified the occupation by saying that he wanted to protect the south of France from an Allied invasion. Field Marshal von Rundstedt, the German commander, said that 'the attitude of the population is indifferent, except in Marseilles'.

George Millar, who had been born in Scotland but who had already been living in France, was desperate to go back. He spoke fluent French with a Scottish-English accent and joined SOE in the run-up to D-Day:

> If all else failed I had determined to get Beaverbrook to take me to see Churchill. After all, SOE was Churchill's baby, and I was his kind of person … This interview took place in a small hotel off Wigmore Street:
>
> 'We only accept volunteers, the SOE major [Buck] said. 'The best go into the field. If they're washouts in training we pitch 'em out.'
>
> 'No ashtray,' he said, as the charred fragments fell on his desk.
>
> I instantly formed a favourable opinion of the nodule that ran F section. For one thing the place was simply run, without pomposity or rank worship and the people running it were few. From their appearance of fatigue, worry, strain, I judged them to be hard working.

Buckmaster interviewed accepted candidates in Orchard Court in Portman Square. He also met them at this expensively furnished 1930s flat when they returned from France. There was no doubt over his devotion to the job, and especially to his agents. Marks also witnessed the same qualities but considered them to be strengths rather than weaknesses. As noted earlier: 'his first concern was for the safety of the agent.'

Leo Marks, head of SOE's coding department, was probably the greatest crytologist of the war. Short and stocky with a bulbous nose and captivating smile, he was a great personality. 'His door was always wide open and there always seemed to be a party going on inside,' said Noreen Riols. 'Apart from the fact that he was very popular, there was the added attraction that his mum always sent him to work laden with cakes and sandwiches, which he shared around – commodities that were not to be found on every table during the war.'

Another agent was Marcel Ruby. 'A Major in French army uniform greeted me. He introduced himself as Major Carpentier, recruiting officer for the BCRA. He tried to persuade me to join Colonel Buckmaster's outfit. I told him I would much rather join de Gaulle's mob.'

"Listen," he said, "it isn't all that easy to join SOE. You'll undergo a pretty unpleasant week at the training school, or madhouse as they call it. By way of compensation you'll find yourself living in a beautiful mansion set in lovely grounds." One of my main aims was to kick the Nazis out of France, destroy the Vichy regime, and put a new Republic in its place.

'The sort of person who volunteered was in the main someone prepared to operate on their own with a considerable amount of courage and prepared to take the very considerable risks of which they were made fully aware. I think we assessed the chances of coming through at one more than fifty per cent.'[31]

Diana did not have long to wait to hear from SOE. A letter arrived in the post at Moreton-in-Marsh asking that she attend a meeting of F-Section's Selection Board at Orchard Court on 18 March. This board consisted largely of psychologists, who made a thorough scientific assessment of each potential agent lasting several days. The careful method coincided with the general development of the Allied war effort: the slow assembly of a mass of meticulously designed war material designed to crush the Axis forces. By this new approach SOE certainly secured competent and even formidable agents – but some of the panache, some of the splendid derring-do of the early volunteers was missing.[32]

Before she had left home that morning she had made certain that her WAAF uniform was neatly pressed, her shoes polished and her hair freshly washed. Quickly adjusting her hat, she glanced into a small hand mirror and knocked on the interview door. Somebody said 'Come in', and she stepped into the room and saluted a sea of faces, her left hand in a tight fist at her side. She tried to quell her nerves, calm her thumping heart. Six men and one woman were seated at a table, looking at her inquisitively. They were Lewis Gielgud, chief recruiting officer and brother of John the actor, Selwyn Jepson, Major Maurice Buckmaster, Nicholas Bodington,

Vera Atkins, Major Jacques de Guelis, briefing officer, and Major Robert Bourne-Paterson, formerly a Scottish chartered accountant. They would already have read her history sheet detailing her languages, hobbies – stated as journalism, translations, yachting, gliding, swimming – and her intimately known areas: the French and Italian Rivieras, Normandy and Brittany.

'Ah … Miss Rowden,' said Major Bourne-Paterson, waving to a seat in front of them. 'Please take a seat.' He smiled at her. 'Please don't be nervous. I see you're currently stationed at Moreton-in-Marsh. We just want to establish one or two points with you. How long have you been there?'

'Ten months, sir.'

As before, the questions switched to fast, fluent French.

'*Je vois que vois connaissez les domaines de Normandie et de Bretagne et les Rivieras francaise et Italienne?* Tell us about that, if you please.' And so she told them, and in the telling she forgot her nerves, her memory of those happy times flooding back once again. Once or twice she could see them making notes and glancing at each other. When she finished they murmured quietly to each other as if going over what she had said. The woman named Vera Atkins glanced down at a pad in front of her: 'I see you are also fluent in Italian and Spanish.' And here she quickly changed to Italian. She had a deep voice with a pronounced way of articulating each syllable. As she spoke, Diana had the impression there was just the faintest trace of an accent which she could not place. Miss Atkins leaned forward and placed both tips of her fingers under her chin, a characteristic Diana would get to know well. 'I want you to tell me, if you can, something of the conditions in France, and how easy it was for you to get out of there and return to England. These things are important to us as we must know the current situation over there.' And Diana told them everything she knew at the time of her escape – what the rationing was like, whether or not the trains left on time, signs of resistance, etc.

Major Buckmaster looked at her keenly out of very blue eyes. She instinctively liked him and started to relax. 'Tell me, Diana, I see you have, or had, two brothers serving in the army, one in the K.R.R. Your youngest brother, Cyril, appears to have been discharged. Do you know the reason for that?'

Diana gulped. *So they knew that as well.* They had certainly dug deep.

She sat up very straight. 'He had been wounded at El Alamein, sir, and he is at the moment convalescing from his wounds.'

They looked at the clear-eyed girl in WAAF uniform, hands at her side, reddish-fair hair, the blue eyes, the freckled skin, the way she carried herself. Impeccable background, aristocratic, old Army family. In all, a poised and charming young woman. Her RAF report described her as 'willing and cheerful'. They were lucky to get her. Her initial interview had demonstrated her strength of character. She had a certain unobtrusiveness in manner. She wouldn't draw attention to herself. She would acquit herself perfectly, although the issue again raised itself that she would probably stand out like a sore thumb. She was ideal in every way – apart from not looking like a Frenchwoman.

Buckmaster glanced at the others. 'Well, I think that's about it, Diana. Frankly, we're impressed. You have had a considerable amount of administrative experience in different organisations in France, with the French Red Cross and the Anglo-American Ambulance Corps and the B. E. F., and you managed to escape from France by your own devices. For that, together with an excellent report from Air Ministry, and with your obvious command of the French language, we recommend your employment by 'F' Section. But please remember, this is not a final decision. We are merely accepting you into our training programme. If you are not happy about the work you have a perfect right to withdraw. The same applies to us: if we are not happy about you, we have the right to release you from this organisation or to post you to a different job. You will be notified shortly when you will commence your training.'

Diana stood up as the other members of the board did the same. She saluted. '*Je comprend et merci.* 'Thank you, sir. I'm very grateful I have been given this chance and I don't intend to let you down.'

The blue eyes twinkled at her as he got up and held out his hand. 'I'm sure you won't.'

Diana made a point of not letting herself show how excited she was or appearing too keen, which would have been hard to do because her one thought was to return to her beloved France. Walking on air, she let herself out, trying to close the door as quietly as posssible. *She was in! Merci, mon Dieu!* The waiting was over, and she would pass every test and do the best job she possibly could. She ran down the stairs of the hotel wanting to shout out: 'I'm going back!' It was a beautiful early spring morning and the sun almost stung her eyes. No doubt she was experiencing very deep emotions at this time. The board would have been impressed with her, and the fact that she looked quintessentially English must have been passed over. Maybe SOE at that stage of the war were prepared to take a punt on their English French-speaking agents? But without a doubt, they were lucky to get her. There were few fluent French-speaking would-be agents who were able to bring up-to-date information about conditions in the country and who were prepared to go back.

On that beautiful morning in London, nothing could stop Diana's happiness. She saluted the sentries outside, who smiled and saluted her back. She just stopped herself from jumping over the sandbags piled high on each side of the pavement, past a man wrapped in an old fur coat playing on a mouth organ a popular song at the time 'What'll I do?' Now all she had to do was to convince Mama.[33]

In November 1942 SOE's task was to train saboteurs and send them into Europe to organise and strengthen resistance. Burglary, safe-breaking, hand-to-hand combat and silent killing were the skills needed. Savile Row was busy making suits in the continental style and the Science Museum had gone into the forgery business, producing identity cards and papers for the organization.

5

A Wizard Time

I knew I had the makings of an agent in me, and I was not going to take no for an answer.

- George Millar

We were to be gangsters with the knowledge of gangsters, but with the behaviour if possible, of gentlemen.

- Second Lieutenant Robert Sheppard

I was told that I should be working outside the international law concerning soldiers and the only thing I could expect if I was caught would be a bullet in the back of the neck.

- Robert Boiteux

In 1943 the tide of the war was beginning to turn. Plans were underway for a second front and, even though SOE was still struggling for resources, there were some spectacular successes with Allied sabotage operations, such as the attack on the Hydro Norsk heavy water plant in occupied Norway. In the spring many SOE teams consisting of liaison officers and wireless operators were infiltrated into eastern European countries such as Greece, Albania, the Balkans and Yugoslavia. Plans for the invasion of Sicily by British and American forces were also being prepared. However in France, where SOE were inserting more people, building more circuits, preparing for the invasion and carrying out sabotage, casualties were high. Perhaps worst of all, many agents who had been dropped into Holland had fallen straight into enemy hands as a result of the capture of British radios.

Up to June 1943, at the time when Diana would be sent into France, trainee agents intended for insertion into the country began by being put through a stiff preliminary course of basic military and physical training. This was provided at various training schools in southern England and was conducted under commando cover.

On 18 March 1943, the same day as her interview with the Selection Board and having been formally accepted into SOE, Diana was posted to Al 10, a branch of Air Intelligence, as a means of enabling her transfer to French Section SOE. She also received promotion to Section Officer. A few days later, a letter from 'F' Section, signed by 'Capt.' (no name attached) arrived on the desk of the Officer-in-Charge at the Women's Transport Service in Whitehall, the WTS or FANY. This letter reiterated that he

> ... had known Miss D. H. Rowden socially for a considerable period and he had no hesitation at all in saying that she is, in my opinion, fully qualified to be a member of the FANY. She has never belonged to or had any connection with an organisation of a subversive character and is morally of good name. This lady will do excellent work in connection with the special employment in which it is proposed that she should serve.[1]

Diana duly signed the Official Secrets Act and was given a date to report for training. She would be attached to STS Training School No. 5 at Wanborough Manor in Surrey. After her interview with the Board, Diana had spoken with her mother for a long time. It was not an easy conversation. She could tell her mother very little, apart from the fact that she was to undergo a period of training, and when questioned said she was not allowed to say much more than that. Mrs Rowden had guessed correctly the reason for the training but did not know anything about the organisation Diana had joined or was about to join. But she sensed the danger involved; the motivation for this, of course, was fear for her daughter's safety. Mrs Rowden felt she had done enough already; there were others who could take up the fight. Let them go. The two women were very close and Diana struggled with the idea of leaving. She knew her mother was also worrying about Kit, who had returned home but was most unwell, and Maurice, who was still overseas in the Western Desert.

She let her mother finish before she said quietly:

Mama, I have not gone into this without a great deal of thought. I realise you're worried about me, and I would too if I was in your position, but I've seen first-hand what the Germans are capable of, and I know what the French are going through ... they're suffering terribly. But you see, I'm not afraid. If I stayed, and it would be easy to do this, I'd feel that somehow I was shirking my duty. Try not to worry too much ... I know how to look after myself. And if I don't go I'll be letting the side down. They're sending in agents and wireless operators who don't know France that well, some don't even speak the language properly. So you see, I have to go and try and help in some way. But first, I have to do my training and that's going to take some weeks. Don't worry yet, dear Mama.

And she gave a small laugh. 'They may not even take me in the end.'

Mrs Rowden sighed. 'Oh, they will, they will.'[2]

They said their goodbyes at Waterloo, Mrs Rowden insisting on accompanying Diana to the station for her journey to Surrey. It was a difficult goodbye. A cold wind had blown in from the north as they stood about waiting for the train to arrive. Diana looked very smart. It had taken her some time that morning to get ready – pressing her blue WAAF's uniform, polishing her black shoes, and checking there were no snags in her grey lisle stockings.

The parting from her mother in London had not gone well. It did not make any difference that the platform was crowded with people, most of whom were in service uniform. They tried to make small talk, but Diana could see how distressed her mother was, even though Mrs Rowden tried to be cheerful. At this moment this same scene was being played out at railway stations all over the country: partings between loved ones, last farewells, the traveller hopping from one leg to the other, vacillating between excitement and pent-up fear, waiting ... waiting for the train that never seemed to come, and when it finally did, it seemed to take forever to leave.

At the basic military and physical training facility at Wanborough Manor in Surrey, inquisitive locals were told that commando training was in progress. Potential agents sometimes believed the same themselves. The course provided a convenient chance to get rid of unpromising candidates. Groups of trainees arrived at Guildford railway station, approximately thirty miles from London. Since the beginning of the war all road and rail signs throughout the country had been removed to prevent assisting the enemy, whether in the form of an invasion force or a lone spy. A covered army truck waited for them in the station forecourt. Diana climbed into the truck with the others, somewhat pensive. No doubt she wondered what lay ahead of her; how would she acquit herself? So much depended on the next few weeks.

The manor was just a few miles away, a trip which normally took less than ten minutes by car but took about an hour, the truck ambling around the beautiful English countryside, up and down lanes, hills and byways. This was not only an exercise in patience – the reason behind it was so that no agent, if caught and interrogated, would ever be able to divulge the exact whereabouts of the training establishment. French was to be spoken at all times with theoretical classes conducted also in French.

Wanborough, the school for would-be agents, was the first port of call for the agents. It had been built in 1527 and was nestled on the northern slopes of a chalk ridge, the Hog's Back, the long, low hill that stretches between Guildford and Farnham and leading to Stonehenge. The gabled sixteenth-century manor house itself, built during Elizabethan times with its brown- and red-brick chimneys, was remote and well out of sight of any passers-by, hidden behind a huge fourteenth-century timbered tithe barn sheltered at one side by a little Saxon church. Extensive grounds were dotted with shrubs, grasses and mature trees. There were comfortable dormitories, plenty of hot water for baths and some of the best food the agents had seen in ages.

The school was run by Major Roger de Wesselow of the Coldstream Guards, a kind and charming man and a personal friend and fellow officer of Sir Charles Hambro, the banker who became the director of SOE.

'He believed in leading from the front and even though he was over sixty, never failed to take part in the early morning cross-country run over the Hog's Back,' remembered Francis Cammearts. 'In the evenings when work stopped we climbed over the Hog's Back again to a pub in the village.' (*Pacifist at War*, Ray Jenkins.)

The idea behind the course was to sort out which people would make good agents. The first day of the course they were introduced to Major de Wesselow, a tall, thin man with a black moustache:

Ladies ... [looking at Diana and Eliane Plewman] and Gentlemen ... you will be given three weeks' intensive instruction in this school of subversive activity. You will receive instruction in map-reading, demolition, weapons-training, Morse code, fieldcraft and hand-to-hand combat. You will be worked very hard and there will be no slacking. Most importantly you'll need physical endurance, and patience. Nobody outside this school knows what goes on here and nobody must know. All letters are censored and the telephone must not be used. If you can't take it you'll be returned to your units forthwith.

The major made it clear to the students that during PT he would not tolerate any reference to their parentage, insisting that if some of the pupils did not appear to be born athletes, they had other qualities, and that any comparison between their movements and those of a crippled washerwoman would be strictly frowned upon.

Head of French Section, Maurice Buckmaster recalled spending much time at Wanborough:

A marvellous colonel, de Wesselow ran it. We used to sit up half the night talking about various people. We also used to test them out on how they reacted under a little bit too much drink. We'd give them an extra drink or two and see how they behaved. Then we'd wake them up in the middle of the night with a sudden bright light and see what language they exclaimed in, whether they said 'God Almighty! Or whether they said, '*Mon Dieu!*'

French Section recruits, male and female, gathered, about twelve in each group and accompanied by conducting officers trained in self-defence, in the use of arms, the use of cover – moving around at night and so on – and all sorts of things which seemed to be a little remote from wartime activities. They had to learn what the rules were in France: when you could get a cup of coffee or couldn't, that sort of thing, what a ration card entitled you to.[3]

There were plenty of early morning runs and exercises that built up as training went on. In the grounds of the manor the would-be agents learned to set charges to destroy railway tracks. 'Never run away from a charge, you might trip up after a step or two and knock yourself out. Then you'll go up with the target,' the explosives expert told his trainees. Buckmaster continued:

In the bar, which was open all day, prospective agents who had drunk too deeply were coaxed by FANY participants in the 'game' into revealing details of their previous history. Not unnaturally, this sometimes bred relationships of undue intimacy, and it was not uncommon for a candidate to be whisked off overnight to some camp in Scotland for subsequent reassignment to his unit or some other branch of the Service. This form of psychological test was eventually abandoned because it resulted in too much wastage, not only among would-be agents but also among female volunteers, whose feelings of compassion dissuaded them from playing the game any longer.[4]

... The courses at Wanborough were theoretical: how to become a poised, competent agent capable of weighing up a course of action before embarking on it; how to react under severe and prolonged interrogation; how to acquire the sixth sense that would alert one to the presence of a tail; how to avoid traps.'[5]

'I remember a sergeant giving us our first lesson in unarmed combat,' said Brian Stonehouse. 'We were all second lieutenants there, officers and gentleman, and he started by saying: "The first thing you have to learn in unarmed combat is to grab your opponent by the balls." Then he stopped and said, "Oh, sorry gentlemen, and ladies. I forgot officers have testicles."'[1]

A trainee wireless operator, Henri Diacono, described Wanborough as such:

There were between 15 and 18 in each course, including a couple of young women. They used some tricks on us, to teach us, for instance, not to be caught by booby traps. One day we were going down the demolition pit along a small path and I saw a branch of a tree had fallen across the middle of the path. The first thing I did was to give it a big kick and there was a terrible explosion just near me. That taught me to be more careful.

They also taught us how we could hide, how it was more easy to hide at night when the moon was shining than when it was completely dark. When the moon was bright you could hide in the shadows and when it was completely dark there wasn't any shade at all and you were much more conspicuous.

Sometimes they took us for a walk in a forest with revolvers in our hands and targets came up suddenly and we had to shoot very fast. There was a conducting officer who was a captain and his job was to get very friendly with us, and he used to take us out in town and have us drink a little but more than we should have drunk and after that judge our comportment, if we talked too much. Although it was important it was like a game for us, you know.[6]

That first day all new recruits smiled politely at each other. Trainees would never learn their real names, only their code names, mainly to instill a sense of security in them from the start.

Diana was in Training Group 27Y. She would stay in this group right throughout her training. Her fellow trainees included Eliane Plewman, Pierre Reynaud, Robert Maloubier, Jacques Ledoux, Eric Cauchi, George Hiller, and Paul Tessier.[7] Diana and twenty-five-year-old Eliane, who had been described as having a 'vivid personality', were to become friends throughout their training. She was Anglo-Spanish, recently married, dark haired with fair skin.

A fact not widely known is that some of Wanborough's trainees had been former German prisoners-of-war who had been turned and were willing to work as double agents. They were commonly known as 'Bonzos'. Wanborough was guarded by Military Police and serviced by FANYs, the usually well-bred women from good families who worked as secretaries, typists, accounting clerks, radio operators, etc.

As George Millar recounts:

They sent me off to a country house which was called a school. It was better than any other school I had known. There were Frenchmen and a few of us Britons and Americans. We were lectured to in French or in English, or more often in a mixture of the two languages. We were called students. In the main rooms the outhouses, the fields and coppices we were taught to use firearms and clean them, to destroy things with explosives and to carry out raids on interesting objectives like Gestapo jails. We were taught to use the forward-crouching stand and the quick, snap-shooting method. Some of us got so accurate with the pistols that we were like King George V knocking down driven grouse. As the targets popped up from one screened side of the range to the other, our arms leaped to the horizontal and the automatic, a blue, shining continuation of our arms spoke 'crack-crack' and again 'crack-crack'.[8]

One of the instructors was Leslie Fernandez:

During training we attempted to prepare them physically, building up their stamina by hikes through rough countryside. All were taught close combat which gave them confidence even if most were not very good at it. Some of the girls didn't have the physique though some had tremendous mental stamina. You would not expect well brought up girls to go up behind someone and slit their throats, though if they were grappled, there were several particularly nasty little tricks that were handed on to us by the Shanghai police.

Two instructors, Donald Fairbairn and William Sykes, formerly Shanghai policemen, taught unarmed combat and quick shooting reactions, such as how to kill four people in a room whilst falling down on the ground near the door lintel to make oneself a difficult target. Sykes' methods of unarmed combat and silent killing were such that many were able in the years to come to save themselves personally owing to his instructions. In 1942 the Germans published a pamphlet which portrayed his methods, and used it in neutral countries to enlist sympathy against the diabolical British.

Sykes showed students a new style of handling a pistol using a two-handed grip, knees bent and firing from waist level. This 'quick on the draw' method was invented by SOE. Bill Sykes, a quiet and mild man who spoke like a bishop and who always wore a dark polo neck sweater and black corduroy pants, had been the fastest draw in the Far East, holding the record for drawing from a shoulder hoster, cocking the gun in the withdrawal and hitting the target. In his lectures he would say the most gruesome things in his soft bishop's voice: 'During unarmed combat, if you get the chance insert a finger into a corner of your opponent's mouth and tear it. You will find the mouth tears very easily.' After describing particularly vicious ways of crippling and disarming an enemy, he would often end with the remark, 'and then kick him in the testicles'.[9] 'The first thing you do when you handle any weapon is to prove to yourself that it is not loaded,' said Sykes.

> Get out of your mind that the pistol is a weapon of self-defence. It is not. It's a weapon of attack, in just the same way as the rifle, the machine gun or any other combat weapon.
>
> The difference between the pistol and these others is that the pistol has a short barrel; it fires blunt-nosed pistol ammo and is therefore a short range weapon. The normal combat range is not more than 12–15 yards. When you're attacking the enemy so close you have to be able to move with extreme speed; you must be able to kill from any position and in any sort of light – even in complete darkness. You will be keyed up and excited, nervously alert, you will crouch, your body balanced on the balls of your feet in a position from which you can move swiftly in any direction. You make your entry into the house stealthily and start searching for the enemy moving along passages, up or down stairs, listening and feeling for any signs of danger. Suddenly, on turning a corner, you come face to face with the enemy. Without a second's hesitation you must fire and kill him before he has a chance to kill you.
>
> To summarise: You will always fire from the crouch position – you will never be in the upright position. (*SOE Syllabus: Lessons in Ungentlemanly Warfare*)

On the firing range Diana wore battle dress – slacks and a blue serge blouse of the same type that she had worn in the WAAF. Cardboard cut-out replicas of Germans stood against sandbags.

'Have you ever fired a handgun before, Miss?' asked Sykes.

'No, sir.'

'Right. Listen up, everybody. Listen good and listen hard. This is a Smith and Wesson – commonly used. I'm going to show you a few things to familiarise you with some basic weapons you're likely to come across. Here we have two submachine guns. This one is a Mark 11S, silenced version – the type the French Resistance groups are using. There are thirty-two rounds in this magazine.

'Now this little bit of machinery is known as the Sten … calibre, 9mm. Rate of fire, 500 rounds per minute. It's in standard use with our own forces. It's natural that you'll compare the Sten with the Tommy Gun.

'Why would you be wrong?'

Silence in the room. All faces trying to look intelligent.

'It fires 9 mm Luger ammo. It is approx three pounds lighter than the Thompson. It has a very simple mechanism. Now, the Sten is ideally suited for all types of close-combat fighting. The lightness and design of the gun enables it to be used with extreme speed from the shoulder at all ranges – max effective range approx 175 yards.

'You can fire single rounds or put him on automatic – like so – and let go the whole mag like a fart in a gale. That's what the wild boys across the channel do, so I'm told. Discourage this where you can.'[10]

'Now ... who would like to have a go?'

Diana stepped forward. 'I'll have a go, sir,' and she held out her hand. The gun was surprisingly light. She took aim carefully, trying to line up the target and gripping the pistol tightly. The instructor came forward. 'Not so tight, miss. Now, that's better. Right ... off you go.'

She fired, getting down on one knee, her eye never leaving the target. The first shot tore the sandbag apart. The next was better. This time she felt a little more relaxed and the next shot ripped into the mannequin into the chest area.

'Very good, Miss. Much better. Just remember not to grip the trigger too tightly. Now, anyone else?' He looked across at Bob Maloubier. 'I want you to have a go at this one, sir. It's a German Schmeisser – an MP 40. The Resistance uses these too. They're good at close quarters when you're up against several people at once.'

Maloubier gripped the Schmeisser and obliterated the head of the mannequin in one fast burst of the gun. He looked amazed as if he couldn't quite believe what he had done. He wasn't so good at the Bren, succeeding in tearing some of the legs off the mannequin. And when he used the Smith and Wesson he succeeded only in nicking the shoulder of the target. 'I'm afraid you're dead, sir. Now, who else wants to have a go?'

'Right. Take this for example. A semi-automatic Walther PPK. Seven-round magazine goes in the butt, like so. Right? Now ... pull the slider back and you're in business. See? Handy little bugger, isn't it? Just small enough to pop into your handbag, ladies. Even though it's small, it will do the business nicely. Remember ladies and gents – and hear me well – this whole business rests entirely on being on the alert, the surprise of the moment. Practise taking it out of your bag and getting in the firing position – try not to think about it – practise, practise, and you'll soon be able to aim and fire all in one smooth go.

'Now, we're going to move closer to our targets – about 10 or 12 yards away from the target. If he's close enough for you to hold the gun against him when you pull the trigger, do it that way, but you should never be further away than you are now. Simply throw up your arm and point the gun at him. Keep both eyes open and fire very fast.'

Diana took aim, closing her eyes and picturing the placement of the target in her head and fired very quickly. Bang! Bang! Bang! Three shots in quick succession. She opened her eyes and blushed with excitement. She had fired accurately, hitting the target in the area of the chest and stomach. She was breathing fast. She had done well. Some of the party clapped their hands.

'Well done, Miss,' said the instructor. 'But could you do it for real?'

'If it was a matter of life and death, sir, I think I could. And if I was angry enough.' She thought of what she had seen in France, the devastation on the roads leading out of Paris, the Stukas dive-bombing the innocents, the families, women and children and animals slaughtered on the roads, the flies buzzing around the dead bodies in the stifling June sun. Yes, she could do it. It was payback time now.

'I'm going to show you one more thing today and then you lot can go,' said Sykes. He pointed to another Walther with a round cylinder of polished black steel screwed on to the end of the barrel. 'This is what's called a Carswell silencer. Specially developed for use by SOE agents. Now watch carefully you lot.' His arm swung up. He didn't appear to take aim; he fired twice, shooting out the central mass of the target. The only sound was the dull *thud thud* of the bullets hitting the target.

Diana was a natural shot. It may be that she had inherited some of her Scottish ancestors' abilities to shoot and stalk wild life and game. She listened very carefully to her instructors and was not afraid when handling firearms. She recognized immediately just how good Major Sykes was as a teacher, and she determined to do well. She knew a lot hinged on her getting a good report.

'Forget all you've been taught about pistols,' Sykes told the class. 'I'll teach you how to get two rounds away quick as light. Remember this very important fact: until you can shoot straight by instinct out of your pocket or if need be backwards under your arm or lying in bed, you're not a shot. Regard your pistol as your pointing finger.

'Faster, faster! Don't pause or you're dead. Two rounds in each man, another two just in case. Quick – now change mags. Too slow, you over there. You have precisely one to two seconds before it's all over. Very good, Rowden. But some of you ...' He clicked his tongue. '*Merde!* You slackers over there. Sit up and take notice. Do you want a woman to beat you? *Maintenant ... tout le monde!* Do it again ... and again.

'And finally ... '*Restez!* Listen, and listen good, you're getting better but I want you to practise – all the time, even in your sleep.'

Diana enjoyed this part of the course very much and had a natural aptitude for it. Donald Fairbairn taught the art of silent killing, an extreme version of unarmed combat. It was a combination of jiu-jitsu, karate and Shanghai waterfront practice. Pearl Witherington felt she could never have been able to use a weapon against someone in cold blood:

I think that's a feminine issue. I think women are made to give life, not to take it. When they said, 'If you're attacked you've got to do such and such a thing,' I thought: right, if I'm attacked, I'll try. In other words, I took in everything they said without questioning it; not once did I think it was daft or pointless.

One thing that made me wretched was wondering what would happen to Mummy if I didn't come back. I asked to see Vera Atkins to find out what would happen in that event. She said I had to ask the colonel. So I did, but to no avail. He said: 'What would your mother do if a bomb fell on you in London?' His reply didn't satisfy me so I went to the RAF to see my former boss from the British embassy, Douglas Colyer. He promised he would do whatever was necessary.[11]

This very legitimate worry also concerned Diana but she tried to put it out of her mind. She knew that for the moment she couldn't do anything about it, so instead she concentrated hard on passing the course.

Tony Brooks was more pragmatic. 'I really did not think I would come back. I accepted it was probably the end of the road.'

Diana enjoyed her time at Wanborough and soon became very fit. Together with Eliane Plewman they would go for runs through the woods surrounding the extensive grounds. Then they would run back to the manor house out of breath, collapse on the lawn and laugh. Eliane was a much more open personality then Diana, but the two girls got on very well. Diana was also very friendly with Bob Maloubier. They were not emotionally involved but spent much time together socially. He remembers Diana as

... a sweet girl, red haired and a bit spotty but with lovely blue eyes. She was a strong person, very English in appearance and manner, and would generally wear a ribbon in her hair. She was one of the best students in our training group, better even than some of the men. She was very clear-headed, calm, not an excitable person. She excelled in everything she did in her training, everything that is except Morse.

Many nights during breaks in their training they would go up to London, where they would often stay at Diana's mews flat. Evenings were spent sharing drinks and playing cards before they were assigned their missions. There would be parties at the flat in Cornwall Mews West, where Diana, a very good cook, would do most of the cooking. She was good at making meals with whatever rations were available. They were gay evenings, the agents enjoying letting off steam and taking advantage of the early summer weather. They were now nearly at the end of their training.

As training progressed instructors were able to assess and observe whether agents were 'made of stern stuff'. Their conduct was watched carefully, as were their relations with others. And at the end of the course unpromising candidates or people who were obviously not going to make it through to the end were sent back.

The instructors made regular reports on their trainees and the school's commandant passed them on with his comments to Baker Street. At the end of the course the school made its final reports, recommending some trainees, making negative reports on others.

As George Millar remembered in *Maquis*:

There was at Wanborough a tall engineer. When it was time to say goodbye to Wanborough and move on to a different type of training, he stood at the door to shake everybody's hands and to say goodbye to each person. 'Don't forget what I taught you. If you're involved in a sabotage operation do as we have taught you. Always try and reconnoitre the target yourself. Make good use of what you have been taught.'

Diana's first training report bears out her prowess with firearms. Somewhere in her past she had become a highly proficient shot including grenades, and so impressed the training staff at Wanborough that it was noted that ... 'Miss Rowden is very fit, very good in fieldcraft and excellent with guns.'

A further report noted that Diana

... was a strange mixture, very intelligent in many ways but very slow in learning any new subject. Well educated, reliable and has courage. She should do well provided her job did not entail technical details or involved memory work.

Her signaling has been a grief to herself and others. It is not worthwhile persevering with it as it only discourages her. She hates being beaten by any subject so must have got through a lot of hate down here. I think she has really enjoyed the course and could be useful.

At the end of the course another report noted that she 'was very conscientious and has tried really hard. Her rather slow progress in some subjects has depressed her, but on other subjects she has been quite up to standard. She has been a pleasant student to instruct.'[12]

From Wanborough some of the agents went on to Arisaig, a beautiful remote part on the west coast of the Scottish Highlands in Inverness-shire, near Mallaig. Although Diana is mentioned in one or two sources as having gone to Scotland, nothing of this nature appears in her personal file. Agents such as Noor Inayat-Khan, Yolande Beekman, Cicely Lefort, Vera Leigh and Eliane Plewman all show no evidence of paramilitary training in Scotland. (All would lose their lives.) Leigh's file is quite specific that she went straight from Wanborough to Beaulieu. Also, agents such as Pearl Witherington undertook paramilitary instruction for three weeks at the beginning of her training. Any agent who did not do the full paramilitary training in Scotland would probably view their initial training at Wanborough as paramilitary, given that it included weapons training, use of explosives, basic unarmed combat, etc. Scotland went on to give more advanced training than that at Wanborough, and it is sometimes forgotten that women were largely seen as couriers or radio operators, so for some time they were not deemed to need advanced paramilitary instruction. By the summer of 1943, around the time that Diana left for France, experience gained and ability shown by some women already in the field, such as Andrée Borrel, showed that women could do more.

At that stage in the war, mid-1943, many agents were inserted into France quickly, a fact that some historians feel was too soon, some of them not having had a suitable enough time for training. This fact is not borne out by those who returned safely, who felt that they had been adequately trained. Professor Foot was inclined to think that the training system was too short. 'The objection often urged against SOE that amateurs were sent into the field to combat the "professionals" of the German counter-intelligence services who were bound to outwit them, is based on a faulty appreciation. In wartime an amateur could frequently do as well as a professional.'[13]

Had Diana gone to Arisaig, undoubtedly she would have enjoyed it. She was half-Scottish and would have loved the beautiful, rugged part of Scotland where the now almost fully fledged agents fished for salmon, went on deer stalks, and generally got very fit.

Diana's training report is then silent for a month. Some members of her course, including her friend Eliane Plewman, attended the usual parachute course in late April at STS. 51 at Ringway airport, near Manchester, but there is no record that Diana went to Ringway. One reason perhaps could be her operation in 1941, which had been deemed a serious one and which would have precluded her from jumping.

The agents were 'finished' at the Beaulieu estate in the New Forest, in Hampshire. There they were allocated to various schools, which had the collective name of 'The Houses in the Woods', for obvious reasons. The actual 'House in the Wood' had over thirty rooms and had been taken over as an officers' mess for members of the staff, and was indeed buried in a wood. It could only be approached by driving up a long track through woodland, which beyond the house ultimately led to an area known as Hartford Heath and a large gravel roundabout surrounding a small island of tall trees; other tracks led from the roundabout through the woods to 'The Rings', Hartford House, 'The Vineyard' and Boarmans. Diana went to Boarmans.

STS Training School 36, Boarmans, is close to The Vineyards. The agents and staff referred to Beaulieu as 'the gangster school'. It was to become famous as the preferred house for F Section trainees. Many women agents were trained there. It was ideal in its location as it was in a remote area of land not visible from the road and could only be approached by crossing a cattle grid and driving down a long private track. On the day I was taken to the Beaulieu estate and Boarmans by Elspeth Forbes-Robertson it had been raining for some time, and the track was difficult and muddy to negotiate. Elspeth had already spoken to the present owner of the house, who had said we were welcome to look around. She gave us the impression that she knew very little about the history of the house but was eager to help us.

As we drove up the long, gravelled, immaculately landscaped driveway, the tall, red-stoned house came into view. Boarmans had been built around the year 1935 by Commander E. C. Wrey, who had been called up at the outbreak of the war. It was at Boarmans that the first batch of 'F' Section women agents arrived. They were Yvonne Rudellat, a Canadian, Andrée Borrel, who was to die in Natzweiler, Marie-Therese le Chene and Blanche Charlet, courier for Brian Stonehouse.

Although the house has been modernised since the war, it has retained much of its character. Mrs Chamberlain the owner explained it is much as it was during the time the agents were there. As one enters the front door into the hall there is a wide wooden stairway leading up to the bedrooms above. I imagine the agents running up and down the stairs, relaxing in their rooms, and going on 'reconnaisance' in the several acres of grounds. Off the dining room there is a snug and smaller room that Mrs Chamberlain tells us was used during the war as a study. The view from the now modern kitchen and dining area is magnificent and I wander around taking photographs. The wide expanse of lawn leading down to a copse far below seems to stretch for miles. We are shown a map of the original red-brick house, which is easily recognisable; very little has changed.

'At the end of 1940, the British government established on the Beaulieu estate in the New Forest a very peculiar school indeed,' writes Cyril Cunningham:

Its curriculum included burglary, forgery, sabotage, slander, blackmail and murder. By the end of the war over three thousand men and women had graduated in some or all of these highly undesirable skills and became agents or officials of the SOE. Most of those trained as agents were then infiltrated into the mainland of Europe to inspire and assist the resistance movements in German-occupied territories. About forty per cent of them were caught by the Nazis and many of those met terrible ends.[14]

Some returning agents like Phillipe de Vomecourt felt there were deficiencies in the teaching at Beaulieu:

While in England I enjoyed myself at the so-called 'finishing school' for saboteurs, bringing myself up-to-date on weapon training and the use of explosives. I felt [there were] deficiencies in the org[anisation] as seen from the other end. I felt that the headquarters' administration and executive staff were far too static, that insufficient use was made of agents most recently returned from France. Only they could provide reliable information about the constantly changing papers which ordinary French were expected to carry. Only they could pass on to agents about to be dropped the all-important details of existence, a knowledge of which might mean the difference between life and death. What food was available to ordinary people, what procedure to expect on the trains, even the latest jokes about the Germans, all this could be invaluable help to an agent going to France. Yet it seemed to me that SOE were too often content to reply upon reports given to them a year or two years earlier.

By now France was a furnace. Everyone knew that D-Day was imminent; the Germans were killing indiscriminately in their attempts to wipe out the Resistance ... the whole country was burning with fear, hatred and revenge. I reckoned the odds at ten to one against my coming out alive.[15]

Diana and the rest of Party 27Y were addressed on the first day by Lieutenant-Colonel Stanley Woolwych, the commandant at Beaulieu; previously he had been its chief instructor. He had been an intelligence officer in the 1914–18 war and was perfect for his role at Beaulieu. A committed Christian, he was also a linguist, photographer and accomplished pianist – as many of the students found to their pleasure when he played the grand piano every day for an hour before breakfast. He installed in them the belief that subversion, properly applied, was one of the most potent weapons one could use:

> Damage the enemy's communication and production, and undermine the morale of the enemy. If you follow conscientitiously in the field all that we teach you here, although we cannot guarantee your safety we think your chance of being picked up is very small. Never relax your precautions when you're in the field, and never fool yourself that the enemy is asleep. They may be watching you all the time, so watch your step. Remember the best agents are never caught.

Remember the best agents are never caught. Diana took those words with her, not only throughout her training, but all through her time in France.

Noreen Riols was very much in awe of Colonel Woolwych, but everybody called him 'Woollybags'. 'He organised everything in this rather large house called The Rings. We used to go over to the office every day and do things like typing, answering telephones, and running around doing what anybody wanted.'

Lord Montague of Beaulieu writes:

> The permanent instructing staff, some of whom were there throughout the war, and the officers were in the habit of dining with us regularly, playing tennis and attending parties, and the younger ones paying court to my sisters. Consequently, we got to know the instructors very well, but it was not until VE Day that we found out what and whom they were instructing. We also learned that the Germans, as a result of their interrogation of captured SOE agents, knew a great deal about what went on at Beaulieu, and apparently there was a report in Nazi files fully describing my family, including the name of my dog.
>
> All at Beaulieu are proud of how this small Hampshire village played such a vital part in defeating the enemy and giving support and succour to those valiant men and women behind the enemy lines.
>
> All the instructors were in uniform, but I wondered once or twice whether their peacetime professions were entirely legal![16]

Chief instructor during 1943–44 was Major Paul Dehn, expert on propaganda. He taught codes, ciphers and secret inks. Dehn bubbled with fun and wit in the mess hall, and in the classroom he was first-rate, being especially well-informed on propaganda techniques. After the war he became a scriptwriter of movies including James Bond.

Another instructor was Kim Philby. Agents thought him handsome, charming, efficient – everybody liked him. With his brilliant mind he had organised the training programme for Beaulieu. Early on in the war he had rapidly climbed the ladder of 'the firm', as the Intelligence Service was called, to become head of the highly sensitive Russian Section at the Foreign Office.

Professor Foot, in *SOE in France,* made special mention that during the training courses agents had it drummed into them that their task was not only aggressive but that they must make aggression part of their characters, to eat and sleep and live with it, and absorb it into themselves entirely; and also that they must be wholly self-reliant, always inured to disappointment, patient in waiting for an opening, always ready to pounce on any chance, however fleeting, of harming the enemy.

'All the women were satisfactory in training,' says Noreen Riols:

> They trained in classes with the men and it was noticeable that they were much better than the men in many of the skills that the work required. Funnily enough they took up pistol shooting with great ability. I don't know what the psychological drive was out there but there wasn't one of them who wasn't keen on it, even when the pistol was a .45 automatic with a recoil so shattering they would sometimes fall over. They would just get up and fire again. It was that sort of determination that was so impressive.

Francis Cammaerts remembered his time at Beaulieu very well:

> Beaulieu was the last port of call and was the first point at which you got a very shrewd idea of the kind of thing you might be asked to do. It was where, in a sense it was most difficult for the teachers to instruct you. They had certain basics you had to learn, like what the German uniforms were like, what the ranks were. You also had to get some wisdom on following people in the street, or being aware of being followed, but they also set

up imaginary situations which might be something you'd face abroad. I remember being taught about opening locks and the use of keys and the nature of different kinds of keys and how to get by when you had to break the curfew. For instance if you needed to move in the streets when there was a curfew you had to have a story like you were a doctor who had to visit a patient who was dying. But most importantly, you had to avoid being caught.'

Tony Brooks considered Beaulieu to be the most important part of his training:

About 2 o'clock in the morning we were woken up by batmen and mess waiters we recognised but dressed as German troops with tin hats on and rifles with bayonets. We were thrown out of bed ... this was a very valuable experience. Other people, in fact two on my course, said, 'Oh, for fuck's sake, let's get back to bed.' And I regret to say neither of those chaps survived. They were both caught and both died. I took it very seriously. That's why I'm here. (BBC documentary *Secret Memories SOE*)

They came for her at two in the morning. Two big men dressed in black SS uniforms. She knew they were SS because she had been taught to identify all the enemy uniforms. It began with a bucket of iced water thrown in her face so quickly as to induce an involuntary inhalation, which made her sinuses feel as if they were on fire. While she was still choking, one of the thugs grabbed her hair, pulling back on her head, and the other slapped her viciously about the face. Then some more iced water was thrown in her face. She tried to catch her breath and almost choked. Then the chair was pulled out from under her and she was thrown in a corner. She started to shake and couldn't stop. She had never been so cold in her life. She was only wearing a light nightgown and tried desperately to cover herself, but it was hopeless. They shouted at her, calling her an English bitch, a whore, a dirty spy, an *Englischer swein*. Then she was hauled back to bed. Half an hour later, they were back, rougher than ever. They threw her against the chair, one pressing a gun into her temple. The lights were harsh and hurt her eyes, already sore from lack of sleep. *'Qui est Raymond? Qui sont vos amis ici?'*

Then she was dragged downstairs into a room she had never seen before. The walls were very thick and damp. She could see moisture running down them and the shaking started again. She was roughly tied into a chair, then her face was slapped again. 'We know who you are, you dirty English spy. Don't bother screaming, no one can hear you. You think you're so clever, don't you. Well, you're never getting out of here.'

The questions went on and on. '*Nom? Addresse? Qui est Raymond?* Where did you get that money we found on you?'

Diana gritted her teeth and murmured over and over again: '*Je n'ai rien à dire.* I have nothing to say. *Vous pouvez faire ce que vous voulez.* You can do what you want. I will tell you nothing. *Rien.*'

The two instructors looked at each other. One of them said quietly, 'She has courage this one. I don't think we'll get anything much out of her.' Then he held out his hand to her. 'Very good! You can go back to bed now!'

The teaching at Beaulieu was continually updated throughout the war years and any natural skills or acquired accomplishments of the staff were added to the syllabus, such as those of Kim Philby, although he passed on only a particle of his talent; Nobby Clark, the king's gamekeeper and a commando-trained major; and Paul Dehn, not only a capable and amusing instructor but the instigator of many of the practical schemes and ingenious exercises. Hardy Amies, dressmaker to Queen Elizabeth II, and who had lived in Germany during the 1930s and spoke the language fluently, was a liaison officer between SOE headquarters and the Beaulieu training school. He appeared at intervals, wearing a beautifully cut uniform that he had designed himself, which was the envy of his SOE colleagues. One of his jobs was to talk about the structure of the German army. It was rather important that agents should, for instance, be able to distinguish between the green uniforms of the *Schutzpolitzei*, the German semi-military town police who kept law and order, and the SS.

After Diana and Eliane Plewman finished their security training at Beaulieu they were assigned to a training mission in Nottingham, undertaken between 30 May and 4 June, with the Ninety Six Hours Scheme. This was a training exercise set up for couriers wherein the students were required to reconnoitre the area and make arrangements for communications between Nottingham and Derby. This involved setting up 'live' and 'dead' letterdrops, sending 'veiled' language messages and recruiting possible informants. The report on this exercise was mixed, with Diana being criticised for incomplete reports of her activities. However, the general comment was:

> Miss S submitted a very full report on most aspects of her scheme, omitting however any mention of her contact or the Police Interrogation, as well as more details about her choice of RV, Boites-aux-lettres, etc. It seemed that she worked most industriously and the good impression gained of her abilities whilst on the Course, was confirmed.[17]

When Diana returned to the mews in London after her training was completed, she told her mother that the manor house, with its charming red and brown brick façade and its tall chimneys, reminded her of the school in Limpsfield – 'without any of the teenage miseries and anxieties'.

On 30 May 1943 Diana had her final report. It was signed by Major Allan Wilkinson, Staff Instructor for Commandant, B Group. Diana's training report is in direct contradiction to Bob Maloubier's comments about her being the best of the all the trainees:

> She does not seem to be of more than average intelligence and is not very quick. She tried extremely hard and was very anxious to learn. Her practical work, although often rather unimaginative, was nevertheless carried out with care. Her personality, though pleasant, is rather uninspiring. However, she has no particular powers of leadership and is not really capable of occupying an executive position but should be a reliable subordinate in carrying out a straight-forward task.
>
> Codes. Innocent letter based on Playfair with conventions. Double transposition with conventions. She found codes unusually difficult and needs much further practice.[18]

SOE agent George Langelaan, who had been a correspondent for the *New York Times*, was very positive about his SOE training:

> At the end of my training I knew that I could fight more intelligently and efficiently than the majority of men and that,

single-handed, I was capable of blowing up a bridge, of sinking a ship, of putting a railway engine out of action in a matter of seconds with a mere spanner, or of derailing an express train with my overcoat. I had been taught to drive a locomotive, how to kill an enraged dog with my bare hands, jump from a fast-moving train, throw a horse, decode a message, make invisible ink, and receive and transmit Morse.

George Millar was rushed through the schools,

> ... so that the picture of each one became blurred into a moving film and I learned for certain what I had always suspected, that Britain is strong because of her cranks. The most apparent factor of her strength is the steadiness of the stodgy, dull, ugly, ordinary people and their readiness to face all problems cheerfully, packed together in a cohesive mass. But in time of war, and especially in odd organisations like the one in which I found myself, the British crank makes himself felt, you see the importance of the great body of Britishers who occupy themselves seriously with crazy things.[19]

It is important to note that while there was deliberate separation of SOE's French sections – RF at Dorset Square and Buckmaster's 'F' at Orchard Court – agents were inclined to socialise with each other at their respective training schools. This allowed the suspicion to arise that some operations must have been compromised before they had a chance to get going.

How good was security in Baker Street? According to Dutchman Guido Zembsch-Schreve, who was known as the only agent who could not speak 'proper' English, and joined SOE in 1942:

> I thought security in Baker Street wasn't all that hot, especially in the early days. They asked me to wait before launching into a discussion of subjects that should not, in the normal course of events, have been aired in my presence. Then, suddenly remembering that I was still in the room, they told me to come back the next day. Sensitised by my prior training, I was astonished at their amateurism and neglect of elementary security measures, so astonished that I wondered if they were deliberately testing my discretion.[20]

At the end of their training, Diana and Eliane wished each other luck and returned to their respective homes before orders came for their departure to France. Neither knew if they would ever return to England. On the night of 14/15 August Eliane was parachuted into the Jura to act as courier for Charles Skepper and Arthur Steele (Laurent), who would act as wireless operator. All three agents would not survive.

Diana returned to Baker Street to finalise preparations for France. Agents leaving for enemy-occupied territory were photographed before they left and were told to make a will. A copy on file shows that she left her property to be divided between her mother and her two brothers, Christopher and Maurice. A small sum of money would be given to Colonel M. V. B. Hill.

For the last time Mrs Rowden tried to press home her worry over her daughter going – especially leaving at this stage in the war, when fighting was particularly fierce. They discussed her options, such as waiting for a while; when it was certain that the war had been won, maybe *then* she could go to France to help with the cleaning-up. In the few days while waiting to be recalled, Diana had very carefully thought over her task ahead. Mrs Rowden had been carrying a heavy weight, the weight of fear, for a long time ever since Diana had joined SOE: 'Have you really considered the danger, that you may be captured, or shot as a spy?'

'Yes, there will be danger. I've been told what to expect, I'll do my best to stay alive.'[21]

Diana did not tell her mother any details of her operation, where she was going or what she would be doing, other than the fact she was returning to France. Inevitably sometimes she would have been torn between remaining in England for her mother's sake and returning to the country where she knew she could help, if only in a small way. She knew there was no option. It was a mixture of living on the edge of danger, knowing she could fall and yet not letting go. It was like hanging on to a tight rope with all the strength she could muster, looking down into the abyss, knowing there was a good chance she would fall, but not wanting to slide to safety. She was ready to go: 'Mama, I can't wait it out until the end of the war. What would I do? I can't let them down after all these weeks of training. I promise I'll take care. It's a very poor show out there and I can't let the Nazis destroy all that I love.'

Christian Rowden looked at her daughter with a mixture of fear and pride.

She would be perfect for the job, this horrendous task which could take her away from her forever.

Diana had no idea just how dangerous the situation was in France, especially for British agents. Nobody, not the agents nor SOE, knew that some agents' radios had been captured by the Germans. It had started in Holland in 1942 when a German colonel, Hermann Giskes of the *Abwehr*, had masterminded the radio game, or *Funkspiel*. It all began when a Dutch informer, a *V-Manner*, had infiltrated an SOE circuit in Holland and pretended to be a resister. One of those he betrayed to the Germans was an SOE wireless operator, Hubert Lauwers, who had been captured with his wireless set. Eventually Lauwers reluctantly agreed to the Germans' demand that he continue to transmit under their instructions; unknown to the Germans, he would leave out his security code. He assumed that Baker Street would spot this and be on the alert. To his amazement, London ignored the absence of his code and replied that another agent would be sent in by parachute. Incredibly, for over a year the Dutch Section 'N' (for Netherlands) continued to send more agents, most of whom were met on the ground by a German reception committee. Even when as time went on and Louwers became more desperate he inserted the word CAUGHT in his messages, 'N' Section *still* went on sending information about the arrival of agents and parachute drops of arms and ammunition. When another captured radio officer refused to transmit any messages for the Germans and insisted that he had never been given a security check, the Germans had one of their men transmit a message to London on the agent's set. INSTRUCT NEW OPERATOR IN USE OF SECURITY CHECK, came back the signal. The agent was then forced to reveal it.

By this time the Germans were transmitting to London on seventeen different wireless sets and at the end of the wireless games had received fifty-eight agents and repeated drops of munitions, including a new secret plastic explosive and valuable currency in gold. This was referred to as 'the worst Allied defeat in the espionage war'.[22]

The *Abwehr*-code named *Nordpol,* or *Das Englandspiel* (the England Game) as it was known to the SD, was the story of how Herman Giskes of the *Abwehr* broke into SOE's Intelligence in

Holland. This travesty, one could say bordering on the criminal, caused the capture of fifty-eight Dutch agents, of whom fifty-seven died in Mauthausen Concentration Camp, the deaths or capture of numerous Special Duty air crews, plus a great loss of supplies. All landed straight into the hands of the Germans. Leo Marks, SOE's code encryptor extraordinaire, had felt something was wrong: he was sure that the radio traffic had been infiltrated, so he gathered evidence and presented it to General Gubbins. Gubbins told him to shut his mouth and report directly to him in future if he had any worries and not to tell a soul. Marks did as he was told, but this was not the end of the story. Incredibly, agents were still sent into Holland. Marks never did find out the reason why Gubbins took not one step to put an end to the wireless games.

And nobody knew back in London that one of the biggest circuits in France, *Prosper*, had already been blown, which would eventually bring about the arrests and deaths of hundreds of people. It was into this quagmire that Diana and three other SOE agents were about to be dropped.

6

Fair Stood the Wind For France

I know that I shall meet my fate
Somewhere among the clouds above

- W. B. Yeats

'*Ici Londres. Les Français parlent aux Français.*' This is London. The French speaking to the French. This BBC message was sent out from Broadcasting House in London to let the Resistance know that the four agents were on their way. Messages from the BBC in its broadcasts to Europe were always preceded by Beethoven's Fifth Symphony, three dots and a dash, the code for V for Victory.

These programmes in French were produced by a brilliant team of journalists, writers, university professors and politicians. Every evening the news of the day was commented on by Pierre Bourdan, a trusted, well-known French journalist. He did not hesitate to say, 'I will not hide the truth from you. Tonight the news is very bad.'

At the end of her course at Beaulieu, Diana had been fitted out with new French clothing and a .32 automatic. These outfits were specially designed for them by a Jewish refugee tailor from Vienna who had a workshop in Whitechapel. The cut of a jacket or the way a shirt collar was set or its buttons and zip fasteners differed from country to country. After changing their uniform, their personal effects were packed into a suitcase and placed in a locker to await their return – or, should they not return, they would be sent on to their next-of-kin. In 1943, when things began to heat up for SOE and more and more agents were being trained and sent into the field, the facilities at

Orchard Court became rather strained and the overflow of agents was taken to another flat at 32 Wimpole Street.

The point of departure was often a time for excitement and fear. On the eve of leaving for France Brian Stonehouse, a British wireless operator code named *Celeste*, could not settle. He played *J'Attendrai* and other French love songs over and over again:

> My father must have guessed. At Tempsford all the FANYS were there and there was this big goodbye. Maurice I think was there and gave me a silver cigarette case and a nice watch and then we got into the plane. It was a hot night, I had a bit of a nap and I woke up and said, 'What are all those headlights?' In fact they were searchlights over the northern coast of France, and then there was some firing, which was a bit scary.

Denise Bloch on her first mission into France had been tasked with escorting Brian Stonehouse to help him with his French. He could speak it perfectly well but with an English accent. He had been the childhood friend of agent Jacqueline Nearne in Boulogne-sur-Mer.

On 16 June 1943, a warm balmy early summer's day, two open-top Cabriolets took four agents to RAF Tangmere airfield in West Sussex. They were Diana Rowden, Cicely Lefort, Noor Inayat Khan and Charles Skepper. Noor, code named *Madeleine,* was the direct descendant of Tipu Sultan, an Indian Sufi mystic. She was a small, exotic-looking girl with long dark hair. She was very beautiful. She had been born in the Kremlin on New Year's Day 1914 and has been described as having a smooth dark skin, huge dark eyes and a graceful mouth. She had been trained as a wireless operator and would be joining Emile Garry of the *Cinéma réseau*, a sub-circuit of *Prosper,* one of the biggest circuits in France. Professor Foot has described Noor as 'a fascinating Indian princess ... Her appearance, noticeably un-French, was as striking as her character, which was strong and flexible as a rapier-blade; she radiated grace.'[1] She had spent much of her life in France and was bilingual in French and English, although she spoke each with a trace of foreign accent. Noor had escaped to England with her mother and brother from France in 1940 and had been working as a wireless operator in the WAAF before being transferred to SOE in February 1943. This was her second attempt to go to France. In May she had flown from Tangmere to Compiègne, but because there had been no reception upon arrival they had no option but to abandon the operation and return to base. On this day she wore a green oilskin coat over her skirt and blouse.

The other woman agent was Cecily Margot Lefort or Cecile as she is sometimes known, code named *Alice*. She was middle-aged, of Irish descent, and had spent her childhood in both Ireland and England. Born in London in 1900, she was married to a French doctor and was living a comfortable lifestyle in Paris when war broke out. A keen yachtswoman, she was fond of all sport. At the age of forty-three she was considerably older than the other women agents. In 1941 she had joined the WAAF, and then in 1943 SOE had recruited her to work as a courier with Francis Cammaerts's *Jockey* circuit in the Basses Alpes. Although she had lived in Paris for some years, she spoke French with an English accent.

The only male in the party, Major Charles Milne Skepper, code named *Bernard*, described by Professor Foot as 'older and staider than the others', was to travel south with Cecily Lefort to take charge of the *Monk* circuit. He would be joined later by Arthur Steele (*Laurent*) as his wireless operator. Skepper had fought against the Japanese in the Far East in 1941, been wounded and taken prisoner. Suffering from beri-beri, he was certified as 100 per cent disabled by the International Red Cross for Japanese prisoners and taken to Gibraltar. He never regained his full health but pleaded with the War Office to allow him to join SOE as an intelligence agent.

Diana wore a smart jacket and skirt tailored in the French style and beautiful black shoes that looked as though they had just come out of a Coco Chanel showroom. Her clothes and shoes were in keeping with her *Juliette Rondeau* cover story.

This was to be a double Lysander operation. Their destination: Angers in Western France on the banks of the River Marne, which feeds the Loire in the Marne-et-Loire Department, 300 kilometres from Paris by train. Diana and Charles would be flown into France by James McCairns of 161 Squadron and Noor and Cecily by Bunny Rymills.

Departing agents were driven to Orchard Court in the afternoon prior to leaving to change into their French clothes. As previously mentioned, these outfits were specially tailored to match the custom in their target zones. Had they been infiltrated into France wearing British-tailored clothes, even with the original labels removed, and

Galeries Lafayette or *Printemps* sewn in their place, this could have betrayed them. When they arrived at the flat in Orchard Court, their new outfits would be waiting for them. This was the last place they were taken to before departing for the field. Arthur Park's firm handshake, his warm smile of encouragement and his friendly pat on the back as they left Orchard Court were precious memories for many agents long after the war was over.

Agent Guido Zembsch-Shreve spoke of being driven in an

> ... enormous great American gas-guzzling station wagon, painted in sand and spinach but with civilian number plates and civilian licence disc, driven by an extremely glamorous girl in a very smart FANY uniform. Then they were given their new identity papers, ration cards, work permits and a sum of false French (made in England) money. A small suitcase was crammed with temporary rations, tins of food, cigarettes and chocolate, which could also be used for bargaining since such luxuries were almost unobtainable in France.

Women agents rarely carried guns, although it is noted that Diana carried a .32 revolver. Like the men, they were given a sharp double-edged knife for silent killing in case their grip on an enemy throat was not strong enough. Most male agents carried pistols, although it was always risky if found by the enemy. They all carried large sums of the local currency, usually in the region of a million francs.

When SOE decided the fully trained agents were to be deployed with the Resistance movements in enemy-occupied European countries, mainly France, they called on the RAF for assistance. To meet aircraft requirements initially Bomber Command formed a flight of obsolete Whitley aircraft at RAF Stradishall, under the command of Squadron Leader Charles Pickard DFC, who had recently completed a tour of bomber operations with 99 Squadron at RAF Newmarket. Most of the flying personnel were Czech escapees.

As the Resistance movements grew in numbers, there was a greater need for weaponry and other supplies, and it became necessary for Pickard's flight to be supplemented. This was achieved by turning RAF Tempsford in Bedfordshire into a base for the additional requirements. 138 Squadron was posted in and equipped with Halifax aircraft, and was later joined by 161 Squadron commanded by Wing Commander 'Mouse' Fielden, who was Captain of the King's Flight. Fielden was destined to become the Group Captain commanding RAF Tempsford.

The Halifaxes were gradually fazed out when the Stirlings arrived, though for a time both were in operation together. In addition to the customary sorties where agents, supplies and weaponry were delivered to the Resistance receptions, 161 Squadron was engaged in taking agents in and picking them up by actually landing in designated fields. The aircraft used for this work were Hudsons and, more frequently, Lysanders.

The Westland Lysander was a high-wing, single-engine monoplane powered by a Bristol Mercury engine. It had been designed originally for Army Co-operation reconnaissance. The aircraft had a remarkably short landing and take-off run, which made it ideal for the Resistance work when agents required transportation. In addition to the pilot the Lysander could carry two or three (at the most) passengers. This was a disadvantage because the pilot had to fly without a navigator.

For use in 161 Squadron the Lysander had been modified by stripping it of all guns and armour and making the rear cockpit suitable for the agents. The canopy was replaced by a sliding perspex unit that allowed rapid entry and exit; a ladder was also attached to the port side of the fuselage to assist ease of access for passengers. A rearward-facing two-seater bench for the passengers with a locker beneath was installed, and a shelf was built at the rear of the cockpit that could also be used as a seat.

The limited range of the Lysander was increased by the addition of a reserve fuel tank fitted to the fuselage between the wheels. To increase the range even further, the Lysander flight was moved to RAF Tangmere, on the south coast near Chichester, a week either side of the full moon period. Aircrew and agents were accommodated in a cottage situated in the grounds of the airfield.

One of the Lysander's great advantages was its fixed and sturdy undercarriage, suitable for landing on rough ground. Its range was around 600 miles, extended to 900 with the addition of reserve tanks mounted outside the fuselage. Cruising speed was 165 mph.

The young, brave, highly skilled Special Duty pilots, expected to navigate to Europe, their only friends the stars and a map on their knees, were always aware that the aircraft was liable to attack from both flak and night fighters. They took their lives in their hands every time they flew into enemy-occupied territory. The target was like looking for a needle in a haystack in a blacked-out countryside, the pilot desperately trying to find a small field, a tiny glimmer of light, a pre-arranged signal, maybe three small flickering lights made from torches with batteries very likely about to run out – to say nothing of the people awaiting down below. Were they friend or foe? Germans or collaborators?

Squadron Leader (later Group Captain) Hugh Verity DSO & Bar, DFC described the Lysander as

> ... a beautiful little plane to fly and very manoeuvrable, ideal for getting in and out of small landing grounds. Every moon period ... one week before and one week after full moon, all the Lysanders and their ground crews were detached from the main squadron to be based at Tangmere on the south coast, because that was well on the way to our target areas in France.[2]

It was late in the afternoon when the four agents in the care of Vera Atkins left suburban London, driving past buildings with sandbags piled in front, past rows of red-brick, semi-detached Victorian houses, each with a small lawn in front and a latched gate. The green-topped Cabriolet drove at a steady pace and soon they were on the outskirts of Surrey, driving along leafy tree-lined roads. Vera spoke very little on the journey and Noor seemed quiet, almost dreamy. Each of the agents would have been absorbed in their own thoughts; almost certainly uppermost among them would have been whether they would succeed in their mission and if they would ever see England, 'that green and pleasant land', again.

Then they were in Sussex, with its low open hills and the sweet scent of the countryside. Jean Overton-Fuller's biography *Madeleine* painted a descriptive scene of that English summer day in the country:

> A lovely June day, the air was fresh, the sun shining, and the English country at its sweetest. They drove through the Surrey lanes with hedges filled with dog roses and honeysuckle, and when they passed into the more open country of East Sussex marguerites bobbed their heads in the fields of green corn, and here and there a lark sang.

It was nearly evening when they arrived at the cottage in Tangmere from where they would fly to France. The red-bricked seventeenth-century cottage halfway along a narrow country lane was set back from the road. This was Tangmere Cottage on the Channel coast near Chichester, which housed both pilots and agents while they awaited embarkation to France or other European countries. Its location was perfect. Just across the road from the entrance to Tangmere Airfield, it was hidden from view, sheltered by tall boxwood trees and high hedges. It was English in every respect, with its ivy-covered walls, small, green-shuttered windows and flower and vegetable gardens. The interior was chintzy, the curtains and sofas shabby and comfortable, the walls thick and the ceilings low. And the bar was always open. Surely a home away from home! Every effort had been made to provide comfort for the agents' last taste of English civilisation before they left for foreign soils. That day it was crowded with departing agents, their escorting officers and various other staff who had travelled down from London. Figures, some in uniform, scurried here and there in the dim light.

Upon entry the scent of many men and women was suffocating; a mixture of fright and excitement permeated the air that warm early summer evening. Diana felt numb from the mental strain of repeating over and over again her cover story and password: *'Je m'appelle Juliette Rondeau ... Je viens de la part de Diane – la fille de Christiane.'* I come from Diana ... Christiane's daughter. And the reply: *'Vous voulez dire la fille de Guillaume?'* You mean the daughter of Guillaume?

Robin Hooper, one of the pilots, having discovered pencilled Roman numeral numbers around the walls of the dining room thought the cottage may have been a Roman Catholic chapel at one time. There were six bedrooms on the first floor, each room with six beds with small, thin mattresses. Here the agents could rest or read and try and calm their nerves. The ground floor comprised a kitchen which also served as an informal guardroom and two living rooms. On the left was the dining room, with two long trestle tables with places already laid. From the kitchen the sounds of a meal being prepared could be heard. The cooking was usually done by the FANY (First Aid Nursing Yeomanry) who did little, if any, nursing. When the Americans heard about this shortened acronym they thought it was a hoot and were continually in fits of laughter.

On the right of the living rooms was the black-beamed Operations Room, with its comforable easy chairs and a large table in the middle with maps and a green scrambler telephone. In the early days the telephone was black, but when the green scrambler was installed the old Post Office engineer sat on the floor smoking and muttering, 'Mr Churchill's got one of these. Mr Anthony's (Eden) got one. I don't know why you young buggers want one of these.'[3]

Some people played table tennis or cards; others sat around talking. For those who had been waiting around all day to leave or waiting for a change in the weather, the pilots and the agents would play music, singing along to well-known songs as *'Sur le pont d'Avignon'*. Somebody put on 'Everytime We Say Goodbye', causing someone to yell across the room, 'Turn that bloody thing off!' which produced nervous laughs.

On that early summer's evening, with the smell of roses and lavender heavy on the air, somebody must have liked the lovely wartime song *'J'Attendrai'* because it was played over and over again on the radiogram – a song especially poignant for those who were leaving their loved ones or were thinking about someone special who they had left behind. And always there was the thought: would they meet up again?

By now the reception committee in France would have been alerted to the imminent arrival of the plane by a BBC message inserted in the *messages personnels*. It could have been something innocuous like *'Grand-mere Nadine est en visite chez sa petite-fille ce soir'*.

A thin, good-humoured man went up to Diana and Noor. 'Welcome to Tangmere,' he said, a smile on his long face. This was Flight Lieutenant James McCairns, always known as 'Mac'.

'I'll be running you in tonight. And supper's on its way. There may even be a decent claret.' The son of an English engineer, McCairns had been born in 1919 at Niagara Falls but after living in England from the age of twelve spoke and even looked like an Englishman. In 1940 he had been a sergeant-pilot in 616 Squadron under Douglas Bader, whom he worshipped. The following year he was shot down, wounded and captured, but escaped and eventually on his return to Britain became a Lysander pilot with 161 Squadron. Mac was small, and had a good deal of nervous energy and a bright twinkle in his eye. His hair, which was rather long for those days, was brushed straight back from his forehead. Hugh Verity likened him to the young Prince Peter of Yugoslavia, 'frightfully polite, with an odd pseudo-Scots, half-American accent'.[4]

In the dining room places were laid along two trestle tables in front of bare, whitewashed stone walls. This was the final meal agents would have on English soil, referred to by many as 'The Last Supper' and eaten by very few. However, it was a gay dinner and all four passengers appeared relaxed, although there would have been the inevitable tightness in the stomach. When they had finished their dinner, Verity took the four agents to the operations room and pointed to a large map on the wall of France bearing red marks.

'Now chaps ... these marks indicate high risk areas for flak, and in order to give it a wide berth from Bayeaux we'll be flying a single heading all the way down here to Angers where we'll pick up the Loire River. That's the tricky part. After that it's quite simple really. We'll follow the Loire up to Tours, then pick up the Cher and run on into our field, east of the city on the north bank of the river. A good field which we've used many times.' (*We Landed by Moonlight*.)

He then showed them a picture taken by the RAF Photographic Reconnaisance Unit of the landing field, three kilometres north-north-west of Angers. The four agents sat around the table while Verity discussed the Met report and that evening's operation, *Teacher*: 'You should be able to see clearly the loop of the Loire. The weather report's not bad. For the first hundred miles inland Northern France there may be patches of low cloud and some rain storms but the rest of the trip should run smoothly. Mac is one of our best pilots. He'll be dropping you at our usual field, La Vieux Briollay, not far above the Loire's junction with the Sarthe. There will be a few passengers to pick up after landing so time on the ground must be kept to a minimum.'

Then came the last-minute checks – Diana's valise, her pockets, looking for anything potentially suspicious like bus or film tickets, English cigarettes, a box of Swan Vesta matches, even a cigarette end and 'Player's Please' written on travel timetables. SOE's dentist had already inspected her fillings and changed one or two to Continental fillings. Even the turn-ups on Skepper's trousers were unfolded and carefully brushed in case they had collected some British dust between Orchard Court and the airfield.

Some far-sighted Frenchman had smuggled a set of currency plates out of France in the middle of the chaos in 1940. Since then every secret organisation in England had been printing the currency it needed to finance its clandestine operations in France from those plates.

Their conducting officer, Maurice Astley, reached for a tiny cellophane packet containing a dozen round green pills: 'Here's your Benzedrine. If you simply have to keep going, never take more than one every 12 hours – otherwise you won't be able to sleep again … for a long time.'

Agents who went overseas were offered the 'L' pill. This was a lethal dose of cyanide, in case of capture. The usual practice was to have it sewn into the lining of an item of clothing where it was unlikely to be discovered in the event of a search; some had it hidden in a false lipstick container or in a cavity in one of their shoes. Death usually took place in seconds. Others refused, either because of religious convictions or other reasons such as being unable to live with the foreboding presence of the pill.

'They make them in this square shape so you won't mistake them for anything else, even in the dark,' said Maurice Astley. 'It's quick-disolving. Thirty seconds and it's all over. I'm told it's quite painless, you won't know a thing.'

There is no evidence that Diana carried the 'L' pill, and I would suspect from what I know of her that she would have refused. She did tell one of the others on her course, believed to be Eliane Plewman, that she wasn't afraid of torture, and in the event of capture 'she wouldn't tell them a thing'. Also, having been brought up with a strong religious background, it is unlikely she would have carried the pill.

The Archbishop of Westminster had issued a dispensation to all Roman Catholic agents who felt obliged to take it to avoid talking under torture. The Church would therefore not consider it suicide and no mortal sin was attached to it. Not all agents took the pill. A Dutch agent, Joss Gemmeke, refused, saying in a programme on the BBC after the war: 'I didn't want to take the "L" pill, it was against all my convictions.'[5]

Vera Atkins was not in favour of agents having the means of sudden death, but whether or not she conveyed these thoughts is not known. On the aforementioned BBC documentary programme, she said:

My personal conviction is that it is dangerous to live with the means of sudden death. It is too easy. It is your job to survive. It's too bloody easy to kill yourself. The daily business of living … the whole business of living a new life and realising you have to be so cautious of every little thing.[6]

The night was lit by a very full moon as the four agents were driven out to the airfield in a large Army-issue Ford station wagon. One feature distinguished this from the one that had delivered them to Tangmere: all its windows except the driver's windshield were painted black to block out all distinguishing features of the airfield, so that if agents were caught and interrogated they would be unable to inform their captors.

As an extra last-minute precaution, Vera looked meticulously through the agents' pockets to see if there was anything English on their person. She checked clothing labels, laundry tags, examining everything for tell-tale signs that they had come from England. She gave them packets of cigarettes and a recent French newspaper to complete their disguise.

It is known that Vera was worried about this trip. At the time her uneasiness was put down to Cicely Lefort's poor French accent and Diana's very English looks: she was English to her fingertips and it showed in her fair, wavy hair. On *Secret Agent,* a BBC television programme made in the 1980s, Vera spoke about Operation Teacher and that fatal trip to France, in particular what happened to the women at Natzweiler. She made a certain gesture when she spoke about the agents' tragic deaths: when she spoke about Noor and Diana, she would lean forward, placing both her hands under her chin, her face away from the camera.

The checks complete, Vera, by now wearing an Irvin flying jacket, gave each agent a chance to see her alone, should they wish. She took Noor up to the bathroom, and as they spoke for a moment, Vera was relieved to find that Noor seemed quite relaxed, almost elated. She spoke to Diana, who asked her if anything happened to her would she delay in letting her mother know until the last possible moment.

At dispersal the tall, thin figure of Buckmaster in a raincoat, the collar turned up in the cool night air, was waiting to see them off. The four agents climbed out of the car with their valises and walked towards him. He greeted them and kissed the girls on both cheeks. He took Diana's hand and pressed something into it. The blue eyes smiled at her: 'This is a token of our appreciation – for all you have done, for all you are about to do.' It was a solid gold compact. He gave the same to Cecily and Noor. Charles received a set of gold cufflinks: 'They're gold – in case you need to pawn them.'

In the event of dignitaries or agents returning to England Buckmaster was always on the tarmac, waiting to greet the new arrivals when they landed in the early hours of the morning. 'I don't know when he slept,' said Noreen Riols, who as a young eighteen-year-old worked in Baker Street:

> He worked eighteen hours a day, often leaving the office around seven in the evening to go home to Chelsea for dinner with his wife, returning a couple of hours later and working until three or four in the morning. And he was always back at his desk again next morning at the usual time.

Then it was time to leave. Vera kissed the girls then raised her hand. 'Well then … *Merde!*', traditional words used by agents and crew for 'Good luck' or 'Break a leg!' Harry Peulevé literally did go on to do that: parachuting out of a plane he landed awkwardly and one of his legs was broken so badly he had no option but to go to hospital, from where he would eventually escape.

Diana and Charles would be the first to depart. They walked out to the Lysander that stood on the tarmac. It looked like a giant black bird with webbed feet – waiting patiently to take them across the Channel to a country Diana loved, now overrun by a vicious and tyrannical enemy.

By now the moon was huge and white. Mac, a torch in his hand, did last minute checks of the aircraft. He came towards them and explained the take-off procedure and how to climb into the Lysander. A small ladder was fixed to the port side of the aircraft and he demonstrated how they would board and disembark. Then he showed them to their seats at the rear of the cockpit facing the tail: 'You'll be sitting aft. These are your microphones so you can speak to me. Let me know if you can see any night fighters, won't you. Now sit back, make yourselves comfortable and enjoy the ride! Forty minutes over water and we should make the French coast, a bit west of Bayeaux.'

He watched while they strapped themselves in, then wished them *bonne chance*. As the Lysander revved its engines and Mac was given a green Aldis lamp signal as clearance, RT silence was observed. The Mercury engines whirred and at 11.15 p.m. exactly Lysander E V9822 taxied along the tarmac, Mac pushing the throttle forward, and they were off – just like that. The black bird lifted into the moonlit summer sky, studded with stars, and turned south-east towards occupied France. Seconds later the other Lysander with Noor Inayat Khan and Cecily Lefort on board followed. Operation Teacher was on its way.

Back at the cottage, Hugh Verity remarked that tonight was an exceptionally good moon for Lysander ops; in fact this June had been a very good moon period altogether. The 'long hot summer' of 1943 provided wonderful moons for Lysanders, and an increasing number of flights was recorded into France from April through to the September harvest moon.

On the seventieth anniversary of VE Day at Tangmere, almost to the day when Diana left England in 1944, I stand on this same field and breathe in the sweetness of the English countryside. It is a place of memories, of sights and smells, so tangible, so powerful that I want to reach out and touch these figures walking out to the aircraft waiting on the tarmac. They brush past me, these people in RAF uniform or in plain clothes. I walk out to the tarmac almost expecting to hear the roar of an aircraft engine. I look up into the sky, shaded in blue and white. It is very quiet, hardly a sound is to be heard in the beautiful Sussex countryside, far away from the noise of the museum which is crowded with visitors this anniversary weekend. There are no planes taking off today, no echoes of the voices of pilots and agents, just their shadows. Only a few dusty hangars remain on this lonely airfield. I think of the agents, in particular Diana, a suitcase in her hand, walking determinedly out to the Lysander with her companions on that moonlit night in June. I imagined Diana's mother, with her mixture of fear and intense pride, looking grey and haggard, saying her last goodbye to her daughter earlier, holding her daughter's hand tightly: 'You know – it's not too late. No one will think ill of you if you change your mind.'

Diana would have tried to calm her mother's fears. 'It will be all right, mother – it will be all right.' But it was too late; she couldn't turn back now. She would have had to put aside her mother's worry for her safety and concentrate instead on her mission. There would also have been the joy at returning to the country she loved. And when the little aircraft landed, she would stand at last on the hot dry earth of the French countryside.

Scottish-born agent George Millar, who was returning to France, gives a particularly good description of the nerves experienced by many agents when they left England, some for the last time:

They told me that I should see the colonel before I left. This was a particularly sympathetic and admirable colonel. His talents, industry and kindliness had coloured the whole organization and had done much towards keeping me alive during the past two months. I was scared of the colonel, one always is.

So I took off my leather coat and trousers, rubbed them on the filthy floor and walked and stamped on them. They looked better. When I had mixed some water and dust in the wash basin and rubbed the mixture in wet they looked so much better that I did the same for my beret.

A vast American station wagon stood outside the front door. And three people, the colonel, the Intelligent Gentlewoman and the young captain were waiting on the pavement to say goodbye. The usual French words were exchanged that are supposed to bring good luck.

The colonel said something very kind to me in his soft voice. I suddenly felt that I wanted to make a go of it for him. While I was savouring this feeling he handed me an astonishing present, gold cuff-links, made from four great chunks of gold and two gold anchor cables.

'A small present from all of us. We like to give all of you some little personal thing before you leave. Something you can use and think that we are behind you, with you in a sense. We are not all strong enough or young enough to go into the field ourselves. You don't smoke, I know, so I bought these for you. They are gold and they have no English markings on them. So they might come in useful; you should be able to hock them if you run out of money.'

We all moved away. They all waved. A light rain was falling. It was five o'clock. The after-work rush for ordinary people was beginning. I suddenly liked all the ordinary people of London, a quite exceptional feeling for me.

Three figures were moving slowly back, off the wet pavement. It was goodbye.[7]

When the Lysander had taken off, Vera returned to the cottage. Upstairs in the agents' bedroom she found a few items they had left behind. Among Diana's papers were three address books, a small atlas, a passport and some personal papers. One wonders why she had left these behind. It could have been just an oversight, due to nerves, or she may have had acted intuitively, a feeling perhaps that she might not return. There was also a paperback that somebody had left, called *Remarkable Women*. After the war, when searching for the lost women agents, Vera remarked to Hugh Verity that 'the book will have to be re-written after these girls have done their stuff'.

Years later, in 1975, Vera recalled to Hugh Verity that the only trace of nerves that night was in a slightly trembling cigarette. They were on their way to Natzweiler-Struthof concentration camp for a ceremony which included the unveiling of the only plaque in the crematorium by the Prime Minister of France, Monsieur Chirac. Diana Rowden's name is on this plaque.

'What's our chance of running into night fighters?' asked Skepper.

'Unlikely. Jerry is too busy nowadays scrambling fighters in France to go and protect the Fatherland,' Mac replied.

Bunny Rymills, piloting the other Lysander, was unaware he had left his transmitter on, and 'broadcast to all and sundry. Black mark!' For most of the way McCairns in the other Lysander was aware of a conversation taking place in the other Lysander which could clearly be heard by all. And so it went on for some thirty minutes: step by step, Bunny pointing out all the landmarks to his passengers.'Now madame, we are approaching your beautiful country. Isn't it lovely in the moonlight.' Back came the answer in soft accented French: 'Yes, I think it is heavenly. What is the town over there?' Mac wondered what the German listening-service, which intercepted all the broadcasts, thought of this running commentary and how annoyed they must have been at their inability to stop the flights.

Hugh Verity found the flights to France in Lysanders fascinating,

Partly because of the skill required. It gave one a sense of achievement if you could pull it off successfully, but largely because of the contacts one had with the passengers who were amazingly interesting and stimulating people. They were equipped with microphones so that they could speak to the pilot and we asked them to let us know if they could see any night fighers. Sometimes they were too chatty. The pilot had to think what he was doing with his navigation and so on and had to switch off the intercom in order to have a little time to think. But most of the agents were no problem at all.[8]

He continued:

It was only natural, particularly just before take-off, going to France that some of them would be a little over-excited or they would be unnaturally quiet. But their demeanour when they were picked up in France and were brought back to Tangmere for a night-flying breakfast, maybe with champagne, was something else again, because they were so overjoyed to be free of the constant tension and fear of living in the clandestine world in France and bubbling over with stories about all their exciting activities.[9]

As they neared the French coast the Lysander banked westwards to avoid the anti-aircraft guns at Cherbourg, and headed for the less heavily defended coast of Brittany. Diana stared through the perspex windows of the aircraft and watched the French countryside moving swiftly below them, the shadow of the Lysander looking like a giant bird. This was the country she knew very well.

The voice of Mac cut into her thoughts: 'That's the Loire beneath us.' In the moonlight it looked like a thread of silver meandering through the valley beneath them. Mac continued, flying a thousand feet above the blacked-out countryside, all the time checking that the Loire was still beneath them. 'Not too far now. When we're near the field I'll let you know.'

They were on track and the flight had been uneventful; McCairns was an old hand.

He spoke over the intercom: 'Fifteen minutes, so be ready.'

Then he descended to 500 feet in the brilliant moonlight. He made radio contact with Flying Officer Rymills, and when he confimed that he was over the rendevous at 01.00 gave the word to proceed to the target. From a distance of four miles the signal 'SC' could be seen. McCairns received Rymill's answering signal, 'RA'.

Ahead Diana could make out three lights in the shape of a letter 'L'. It was the Lysander's clandestine landing pattern, a design first laid out on the tablecloth of a Soho restaurant, Spaghetti Palace, in 1942. The field was safe or as safe as the pilots could hope for. She could see figures dimly on the ground.

'I've landed here before,' said McCairns, 'so I know my stuff. In and out very fast. You know the drill.'

Losing height in preparation for landing, the Lysander lined up with the landing lights, then facing into the wind the plane landed and bounced on the surface of the field, its two great feet landing on the grass beneath them.

Some years later Diana's school friend Elizabeth Nicholas recalled rather poetically the night of 16/17 June as she lay in her warm bed listening to the planes as they passed overhead:

> At the time of course I did not know that Diana was somewhere in France. But when I heard what happened to her … I remembered another June … peaceful rivers and men fishing in the kindly dusk. Diana had seen England for the last time, and never again would she feel the springing English turf beneath her feet, nor hear English voices murmuring softly across an English field. On that night she had a year and twenty days left on earth; and of those months nearly eight were spent in prison. (*Death be not Proud*)

The agents hurried to disembark and climbed down the ladder. For a moment Diana stood still and breathed in the smell of the French countryside. It had a certain scent: the musk of high summer, a smell she remembered well. Members of the resistance were waiting for them, scarves tied around their necks, Sten guns in hand with magazines sticking out of their pockets. Some time was spent on the ground whilst all incoming luggage was unloaded and several more cases from the outgoing agents were loaded in turn. McCairns wrote in his report: 'The field was excellent, very good surface of crop combined with a long run. At 0.13 I took off, gave the o.k. to P/O Rymills and circled until he had completed his drop. We then both set course for base and landed at 0.3.00.' Nearing the English coast he would turn on his IFF device – the Secret Identification 'Friend or Foe device' that sent automatic 'friendly' signals to British radar stations.

After dropping Noor and Cecily, Bunny Rymills was to tell Hugh Verity upon his return to base that 'Cecily Lefort looked like a vicar's wife. Her French did not seem to me to be all that hot.'

These SOE flights, which have often been described by some pilots as 'taxi runs, of which they were just the drivers', were anything but. They were deadly aerial wartime operations. 'There was a sense of excitement in flying on Special Operations compared with the usual Bomber Command sortie, although the danger was always present from flak and German night fighters prowling the skies from heavily defended areas if one drifted off course,' says Squadron Leader Geoffrey Rothwell, who was attached to 138 Squadron based in Tempsford, and who undertook many Special Duty operations not only to France but to other enemy-occupied European countries. 'Flying an aircraft such as a Lysander was always difficult as it had no navigational aids other than a map resting on one's knees, and one had to try to search for a distant field and a small pinprick of light – three flashlights stuck into turf a couple of hundred yards apart.'[10]

Every night during the moon period these brave young pilots, most of them in their early twenties, flew the small lightweight aircraft with its funny webbed feet, searching for a river, a railway line or a road junction which might give them the bearing they needed. The task has been described as searching for a postage stamp hidden at night in a football field.

SOE's Air Operations man, Henri Dericourt, greeted the four agents as they descended from the plane. An extraordinary comment about these landings in France was made by agent Pierre Raynaud, who had been in the same training party, 27Y, with Diana: 'When the plane landed at our usual landing strip at Vieux Briolley, a group of German officers happened to be hunting boar in the nearby wood about a mile away. They took no interest in us ... I passed through Paris without difficulty.'[11]

Of the three women who arrived together on 16 June, Noor Khan was the only one whose mission lay in Paris. Diana was to set off for the Jura and Cecily Lefort was bound for the Drome as agent Francis Cammaert's courier. Remy Clement, Dericourt's second in command and friend and fellow pilot whom he had recruited for SOE, was at the landing ground to receive the two Lysanders that night.

Noor Khan and Cecily Lefort travelled into Paris by train with Remy Clement. Although Dericourt was a friend, Clement did not share Dericourt's personality. He had grave doubts about working outside the law. The SD had agreed to keep clear of Clement but allowed him to be at the landing ground to receive the Lysanders.

He had laid out the lights in the correct pattern and had guided the aircraft in; he saw the three women and the single man climb down the ladder on to the grass and the five passengers he had waiting with him hurrying across to take their place. The incoming passengers were greeted by the reception committee, and the aircraft took off along the line of torches.

So from the moment they stepped on to the field, all four agents were under the surveillance of the SD (the *Sicherheitsdienst*) and the Bony-Lafont 'shadows', the French gangster collaborators in the pay of the Gestapo who followed many of the newly arrived agents from the landing fields to the train stations. But for how long? According to some historians, these contemptible men are said to have followed the agents through to Paris and two on to their long journeys: Khan and Leigh staying in Paris, Skepper to Marseilles in the south and Diana to the Jura in the east. According to Jean Overton-Fuller in her book *Double Webs*, Dr Goetz of the *Sicherheitsdienst* boasted that they knew of the landing of the F-Section agents that night of 16 June. However, there is no conclusive documentary evidence to support this claim. One would also think that Diana and the others, who had been taught to pick up a tail in training, would have been ultra cautious.

So the four agents were left alone – for the moment. The incoming agents had no idea that their arrival had been watched by the SD, but somehow Diana and Skepper managed to give them the slip.

Diana's mission in France was to act as courier for the organiser known as 'Bob' (John Starr) of the *Acrobat* circuit in the Jura. The operation was known as Chaplain. Her instructions once she had landed in France were to proceed immediately to Paris, where she could stay for two or three days to acclimatise herself. She would then proceed to St Amour, where she would contact 'Bob' through a Mlle Bereziat at an *epicurie* on the Place des Quatre Vents. Her cover story and papers were in the name of Juliette Therese Rondeau and she was to be known as 'Paulette' in the field. Bob's circuit password was: '*La peche rend-elle par ici?*' Is the fishing good around here? The reply would be: '*Oui, j'ai pris dix poissons la derniere fois que j'y suis allé.*' Yes, I caught ten fish last time I went. The number of fish would be according to the period of the month – for e.g. *une dizaine* – from the first to the tenth when the passwords were used.

Diana was to let London know as soon as possible the address of a postbox through which she could be contacted in the event of her being separated from her circuit; she was to send them the address of a cachette in case she should find herself in difficulties. In this event she would go to her cachette and advise London of the circumstances by wireless telegraph or, failing that, by coded letter or card to a Senor Albuquerque Ramos, Apartment 511 in Lisbon.

Dericourt greeted the agents and indicated there were bicycles available for their use in a belt of trees close by. Dericourt, SOE's Air Movements officer for F Section, was a tall, stocky man in his thirties who had joined the French Air Force and been a pilot for Air France before the war. He would become the subject of bitter controversy as to his true allegiance, which raged in the latter months of the war and afterwards. A protracted investigation and his trial investigating whether he was a double agent or even a *triple jeu*, still discussed to this present day, took place in Paris in 1948. At the trial he stated he had been acquainted before the war with several Lufthansa pilots whom he had regularly met when flying the Le Bourget-Cologne route. In 1941 he had escaped to England by the 'Pat' escape route through Spain and Gibraltar. On reaching England his love of flying prompted him into contact with British Intelligence, and with his excellent knowledge of navigation and Continental air routes, he was readily accepted by the RAF. In 1942 he was posted to 138 Special Duties Squadron at Tempsford, serving under Squadron Leader Charles Pickard DFC, and dropped agents and supplies mainly in the Cher-Loire area. When sea 'pick-ups' of agents became too risky, the French Section decided to increase Lysander operations – much the easier option – and Dericourt was approached with the idea of organising such air missions. He agreed and in 1943 Dericourt, now '*Gilbert*', was put in sole charge of all Lysander operations.

Now in haste, he ushered the agents to the edge of the field while the two aircraft made their take-offs once more. He gave the agents directions to the local station at Angers. The girls had little time to make their hurried farewells in the dark, just a quick smile, whispered words of encouragement, and a quiet *bonne chance*. Clement guided his new charges, Noor and Cecily, along the dark roads to the country station and waited for the early trains.[12] Diana and Skepper made their way separately and bought tickets at the station for their short trip to Paris.

Remy Clement felt their tension and anxiety, and even many years later remembered the bewilderment of those first few hours for them:

It was safer for a man and women to travel together, and a woman carrying a set which looked like a suitcase was not so suspect. It was very difficult for them to come from England where they had been protected to a foreign country. To come under cover of night to a field in an occupied country, and to be met and taken away by a man whose face they had not seen before. There were so many things they didn't know about France – the ration cards, clothing, the ID papers that kept changing, and the curfew.[13]

Diana was more schooled than the others about the current situation in France. It was, after all, not so long ago that she had been there herself.

Francois Mitterand, future President of the French Republic, remarked after the war:

Dericourt's operation was smooth, quiet, unfussy and absolutely on time. The way he handled his passengers and the way he herded the cattle in the field where the plane was due to land I could only but admire. The operation took place without interference. The security was perfect, which was not surprising when you knew the facts.

Noor Inayat Khan was going to act as radio operator for Francis Suttill, the *Prosper* network's *chef de réseau*. However, unknown to her and F Section her network had been blown and was under German control. Baker Street, believing that *Prosper's* radio operator, Frank Pickersgill, had not been compromised, continued to exchange messages with the now German-controlled *Madeleine* (Noor Khan) post in Paris. Pickersgill had been caught more than four months earlier.

Leo Marks was in charge of SOE's coding at Baker Street. While grim power struggles were raging throughout every directorate in SOE, Marks was engaged in a still grimmer one with SOE's second-in-command, Nicolas Bodington, whom he referred to as Edgar Allan Poe: 'He went backwards and forwards to France as if he had a private ferry.' Marks spoke about the time Buckmaster came into his office and thanked him for breaking Bodington's indecipherable code:

... but he'd already done that on the telephone and Buckmaster never said anything twice. RF complained that he never said anything once. I suspected Buckmaster had come for some other reason.

'How reliable are our security checks?' he asked sharply.

He was the first country section head to ask that question.

'They're no more than a gesture to give the agents confidence.' I told him why in some detail.

'Can they ever be relied upon?'

I told him that if an agent was caught before he was sent any messages he could get away with giving them the wrong security check because they'd have no back traffic to compare it with. But not otherwise.

'What's being done about it?'

'We're working on a wholly new concept of agents' codes.'

'Can't anything be done in the meantime?'

I told him that as long as the poem-code was in use there were only two things the country sections could do: they should ask their agents personal questions – to which they alone would know the answers, and they should use prearranged phrases in their messages to which the agents must reply in a prearranged way. I warned him that these phrases must be used only once in case the agent's traffic was being read.

'We already do something of the sort. I'll make sure it's done on a regular basis.'

'Colonel Buckmaster' – he'd just been promoted – 'is there anyone in particular you're worried about?'

A microdot of hesitation. 'It was a general question. I'll consult you if I am.'

That night I went through the back traffic of all the F-section agents. It contained the usual mixture of Morse mutilation, wrong checks, right checks, no checks. If I were Buckmaster, I'd be worried about all of them and I was convinced he was.

Rumour began to spread that there was an outbreak of insanity in the Signals directorate. It was well founded. Agents were making so many mistakes in their coding that breaking their indecipherables single-handed against the clock was like being the only doctor in a hospital full of terminal patients. And the biggest indecipherable of all was SOE itself. Claude Dansey would still be in charge of agents' codes – but this could be changed at the flick of a mood-swing.[14]

Major Francis Suttill, referred to by Buckmaster as a 'marvellous Englishman, with a clear intellectual vision', and who had been a barrister in England, had run the circuit *Prosper* for over two years. The circuit was the largest in Paris, in the north of the country, with tentacles stretching all over the rest of France. Highly intelligent, fearless and a natural leader, Suttill was one of SOE's best agents. Buckmaster was to say of Suttill: 'In four months, *Prosper* had established excellent relations with the big Parisian Resistance groups, and was progressing well in the task of coordinating their activities.'

Buckmaster so admired Suttill that he was to say that 'of all the men we were to send to France I think I admired and respected him the most.'[15]

Suttill's courier and co-organiser was a twenty-two-year-old nurse, Andrée Borrel, code named *Denise*, a strong, tough Frenchwoman who was also a member of SOE; Borrel was the first SOE woman agent to be parachuted into France. After the betrayal of the 'Pat' escape line where she had been working, she had made her own way to London where she had been accepted immediately into 'F' Section. Andrée was known for her extreme courage and coolness. In March 1943 Suttill was to write of her: 'Everyone who has come into contact with her in her work agrees with me that she is the best of us all.'[16]

According to agent Harry Rée, quoted in *Shadows in the Fog*,

Suttill had the logical perspicacity which is so often found allied to Gallic features. Born to a French mother and British father he was dark haired with clear grey eyes, and with a classic profile this made him a striking man. He had left his family back in England, a wife who had studied medicine at Oxford before the war and two young sons, the elder also named Francis, and John. 'It was not until he spoke that one realised the full extent of his charm and balance,' remembered Rée. 'It was a joy to work with a man whose brain cut like a knife into the problems we put before him. He never made the mistake of minimizing the difficulties of his mission, and he took as much care over the study of his brief as if he had found it difficult to understand.'[17]

However, *Prosper* had become infiltrated with enemy agents, and in June the circuit was blown wide open. This was serious not only for the *Prosper* network but also for the adjoining Paris Resistance, for the circuit covered Beauvais and Tours, Chartres and Melun, and therefore considerable overlaps were unavoidable.

According to Buckmaster, *Prosper's* downfall had probably been the work of the notorious Heinrich Bleicher, a German businessman before the war who had become attached to the German *Abwehr* and who had made it his job to expose members of the Resistance and British agents. Owing to Bleicher's cunning, good fortune and a certain ability, Suttill as well as Andrée Borrel, Gilbert Norman, *Archambaud* and over 1,500 of the Resistance were seized, tortured, shot, or deported to concentration camps. Bleicher was heard to say triumphantly, 'We have wiped out the Buckmaster organization.'[18] (As Francis J. Suttill's book about the Prosper network, *Shadows in the Fog*, shows, Buckmaster's analysis of the disaster was however wrong.)

With the arrest of Francis Suttill other agents were rounded up, eventually giving rise in London to suspicions of treachery, poor security and mismanagement of the circuit. It is thought that poor allied security led to the virtual destruction of *Prosper*. However, Buckmaster makes the point that when at one stage he recalled Suttill to London, during his absence the vigilance which was so much a part of Suttill's had been relaxed in spite of the careful measures adopted by *Archambaud*, his wireless operator, and Andrée Borrel. Buckmaster also notes that Suttill, 'overworked and already under a grave strain', sent messages to London that suggested he was worried about some of the recruits made by various sub-sections.

Buckmaster has nothing but praise for Suttill:

He knew well enough never to go beyond his limitations of which there were few. He was a tireless organizer in the Paris area. Paris was, far and away, the most dangerous place in which to work; it was swarming with Germans and with security police of every description. Nevertheless, Francis fashioned, in the face of every hazard, a model organization. It attempted nothing beyond its abilities nor failed at anything within them. It may be argued that I should have brought him out of France; that view misunderstands the nature of war: Francis was a very capable, a very brilliant officer, and could not be – nor would want to be – withdrawn because the work was tough.[19]

SIS was quickly aware of the disaster, and it was later recalled how Claude Dansey, head of SIS, remarked, 'Have you heard the latest news? SOE's in the shit. They've bought it in France. The Germans are mopping them up all over the place.'

In the summer of 1943 Suttill, having been caught by the Gestapo, was tortured, imprisoned in Fresnes Prison, and taken to the concentration camps of Flossenburg and Sachsenhausen.[20]

Among the five outgoing passengers to England on 17 June 1943 lies a tragically unlucky story regarding two of their number, Flight Lieutenant Jack Agazarian, code named *Marcel*, a radio operator for *Prosper* and his wife Francine, a courier for Francis Suttill who had been in France since March 1943. Francis Suttill had decided at short notice that Agazarian should go to England for a rest after a chance encounter with two 'Dutch agents' in Paris, having no idea that these men were actually Germans involved in counter-espionage. Jack and Francine were very lucky to get out of France that night because the breakup of the *Prosper* circuit was literally just a few hours away.[21]

Having had to cut short his break in England, Agazarian was told to return to France. One of the agents due to fly to England had been arrested and Agazarian was to replace him. Agazarian did not know at this stage that *Prosper* had been blown but he and London were suspicious. In an extraordinary move Buckmaster's second-in-command Nicholas Bodington decided to toss a coin as to who should attend a meeting at one of the circuit's so-called 'safe' cafés. Agazarian lost and turned up at the café, where he was immediately arrested. He was tortured, imprisoned and afterwards thrown into a concentration camp where he was eventually executed.

Professor Foot writes that Francine had to leave France because she was not tough physically like Andrée Borrel, Suttill's main courier, and could not take the strain of courier work in the infiltrated *Prosper* area.

'There has since been some speculation as to why Jack was sent to France on that second mission,' says Noreen Riols. 'Both he and his wife had just started to take some leave when he was recalled to accompany Nicholas Bodington, Buckmaster's second-in-command, on a short mission into France to contact a high-up *SD* officer, believed to be Boemelberg, who was actually a friend of Henri Dericourt's, and who Bodington had known before the war.'[22] One would think any other available radio operator could have gone in his place, and when Agazarian protested that he was on leave, Bodington assured him it was only for a few days and then he could rejoin his wife. We only have Bodington's word for all this. Agazarian never returned. He was caught and murdered in Flossenburg Concentration Camp. Just before he was hanged he managed to smuggle out a letter to his wife: 'I am in the last cell so they will be coming for me very soon. I just want to thank you for everything and tell you that I love you.'

Francine Agazarian went each year to Flossenburg to commemorate the massacre there, but sadly died shortly before the unveiling of the plaque honouring her husband and his comrades.[23]

Dericourt often travelled on the same train with incoming agents. 'He would have informed the Gestapo in advance of the drop and told them at which mainline station the agents would arrive the following morning,' says Noreen Riols:

> The French police would be waiting at the barrier to do a spot check, which was not unusual. He would give a prearranged signal, often an almost imperceptible nod or inclination of his head as he passed or walked behind the agent approaching the barrier. Some were never seen alive again. Because of the treachery of Dericourt after the collapse of *Prosper*, F Section's resistance in France threatened to come to an end. One thousand five hundred people were arrested and hundreds of agents and locally recruited résistants belonging to the group were seized, tortured and deported to concentration camps and sent to their deaths.[24]

In the 1950s Maurice Buckmaster wrote two books about SOE, *Specially Employed* and *They Fought Alone*. He described his thoughts on recruiting women and sending them into France at a particularly dangerous stage in the war:

> Some agents went to their death with that serene defiance which typified the gallant women of SOE. Some people have suggested

that we should never have sent women on these missions at all. I cannot agree. Women are as brave and as responsible as men; often more so. They are entitled to a share in the defence of their beliefs no less than are men.[25]

PART TWO

Resistance in the Jura

Free men cannot start a war, but once it has started, they can fight on in defeat.

- John Steinbeck

On arrival at the *Gare d'Angers* Juliette Therese Rondeau joined a small line of people outside the ticket office. She gave no sign of recognition to Skepper, who was waiting in line behind her. In a very short time the queue grew, although it was early in the morning. Some of the people were itinerant workers, forced labour for the Germans. They were pale, thin and dressed in dowdy dark clothes. Involuntarily she stared down at her skirt and jacket.

'Un billet pour Lons-le-Saunier, s'il vous plait.'

'There's a stop at Marne-la-Vallée–Chessy, then Paris-Montparnesse, then Dijon, where you'll change again for your journey to Lons, Mam'selle,' replied the ticket seller. 'A long trip for you, *Oui?*'

'*Ah oui, M'sieur.*'

As he handed over her ticket, he looked at her closely, his eyes travelling over her hair, her face. '*Ayez soin dans la region de Paris.*' Take care in the region of Paris.

Was he warning her, and if so, why should he do so? But they had told her about Paris. 'You have to be careful at all times, especially around the stations. Trust nobody, the girl in the *tabac* where one gets one's tobacco ration, a surly neighbour, even the *conçierge*. *La Gare* is always watched. You will recognise these people by their leather jackets and hats, but there will be others who will be on the lookout all the time for people like you – agents who have recently arrived.

126

They'll be plainly dressed, informers, or the *Milice*, members of the French police in their black and white uniforms.' Referred to as 'the scum of the earth' by the Resistance, these men and women were not only equal to but even more vicious than the Germans, more violent than the Gestapo, and they were always armed.

Diana did not need to be reminded of the conditions in France. It was only two years since she had last been there, but she accepted what she had been told and knew this stage in the war, in 1943, was far more dangerous than in 1941 when she was last living there. She was now Juliette Rondeau. It had a nice ring to it. She had done well so far, managing to get to the railway station without being apprehended, and giving no indication that she knew Charles Skepper, the man waiting patiently in the queue behind her.

The train steamed into the station and she hauled the bike up the steps and put it into the rear of the compartment, then retrieved her suitcase and her valise. A man wearing a black beret offered to put her heavy suitcase up on the rack. She accepted but when he reached for her valise she refused very politely. '*Non, merci, c'est bon.*' In it were many French francs and her personal *carte d'identité* made out in the name of Juliette Therese Rondeau.

She smiled at him then moved to a window seat at the far end of the carriage. People brushed past her, desperate for a seat. She straightened her back, trying to settle, and leaned her head against the grimy window. The smell of many *gauloises* permeated the carriage. No English cigarettes here. A train journey like any other? Oh no. This was France at war. The train moved slowly out of the station, shaking from side to side and blowing out dirty grey smoke as it gathered speed on its way south-east. How tired she was. For a moment she closed her eyes, all the time willing herself not to go to sleep, mindful of her training and everything she had been taught. *Try not to sleep or if you do, don't sleep too deeply. It's dangerous.* At that time she did not know that an exhausted SOE agent on a train journey had gone into a deep sleep and started to talk in English.

The train sped up and her head dropped as she slipped into a fitful doze; then something woke her with a start.

'*Montparnasse! Montparnasse!*' The journey to Paris had gone very quickly. People were getting off, and she collected her luggage and her bike and joined the throng exiting the train. Her heart quickened.

There was a *barrage* ahead. The *Feldgendarmerie* in their grey-green uniforms were at the junction between the exit and the gates. They were routinely checking all tickets and randomly opening luggage. She joined a long queue.

'The dirty *Boche* are everywhere,' murmured a young woman alongside her as she stubbed out a cigarette butt hard on to the ground with the heel of her shoe. 'God help us if our IDs are out of date.'

Diana glanced at her quickly. 'Would you like to go through with me?'

The girl nodded and gripped her arm and they plodded forward slowly. Juliette Rondeau breathed deeply, the way she had been taught. *Look straight ahead, act indifferent as if this is something you have done many times.*

Now they were in front of a lieutenant. She recognized the badges of rank; she had been taught this at Beaulieu.

'One at a time, *s'il vous plait.*' Then he beckoned to Diana. '*Vous ... attendez ici.*' Wait. Then: '*Votre carte?*'

She handed over her *carte d'identité* then waited while the contents of her suitcase were gone through slowly and carefully. Then he looked at her.

'You seem to have a lot of luggage, *Mademoiselle. Votre destination?*'

'Lons-le-Saunier, M'sieur.

'Ah,' He pursed his lips. 'And the purpose of your trip?'

'*Je suis en vacance a Jura pour visiter ma tante.*' And she raised her eyes and managed to look bored.'She is very old, you understand.' And she gave the soldier a pleasant, half-flirtatious smile.

A moment – or two – then he stamped her card.

'*Vous pouvoir allez.*'

'*Pardon?*'

'*Allez. Allez!*'

She went, grabbing all her luggage and her bike, and walked through the gates to find her platform for the next leg of the trip. She looked back just once : the young girl who had accompanied her was being led away.

Diana had to be very careful. Montparnasse was a busy part of the Paris area and would be heavily garrisoned. And it was alive with informers. Travelling was very dangerous and there were numerous and strict controls on all the trains, and she had a distance of over six hundred kilometres by rail before she reached her destination.

Now she waited for the train for Dijon, the closest port of call to the Jura, and where she would have to change again for Lons-le-Saunier. While waiting she noticed people sitting outside cafés, the waiters wearing the same blue-and-white striped aprons wiping down the tables, one of the memories she had stored away when she was in England. Maybe not everything had changed in France since she had been away.

On the train headed for Dijon she settled down once again in a compartment near the back in case the Germans came on board to check tickets. It would give her a little time to prepare until the danger was over. The train drew slowly out of the Gare Montparnasse, past posters plastered on the walls, the crudely drawn black and white sketches which screamed out *Recherché!* Wanted!, past the gendarme activity on the platform. A blur of faces: soldiers in grey-green uniforms questioning people, long-haired youths being roughed up by the Germans. These must be the *zazous* she had heard about in London, the jazz-loving youngsters with their greasy hair and baggy trousers who didn't seem to care about being arrested, always seeming to be in trouble. They congregated mostly on the Boulevard Lafayette; the Germans had no interest in them.

She dozed off. When she opened her eyes, after what seemed only a few minutes, they were travelling through the countryside. This was her France – it was everything she remembered. Nothing had changed in the two years she had been away. As the train stopped at some small towns she could see children in grey smocks on their way to school, their satchels over their shoulders, and as it made its way again she glimpsed figures working in the fields, the village church, its spire sticking up in the air.

At one point the train stopped at a small station a little longer than it should. She looked out the window. What was happening? Heavy footsteps sounded along the passage, and then the compartment door opened. German soldiers gave just a cursory glance into her compartment then moved on.

The train rumbled through the pleasant countryside, sometimes coming to a sudden stop for repairs on the track. There were mixed reactions. One man shook his fist and, pointing upwards, raised his voice: 'Always there is trouble ... it's either the damned Resistance or the *Anglais*.'

'What about the bloody SNCF?' shouted another.

At each station more people got on. There were not enough seats and many passengers were forced into the corridors, holding on to the straps overhead, their valises at their feet, while others who had been lucky enough to get a seat sat jammed together, their faces pinched and grey, their clothes ill-fitting and shabby looking as if they hadn't had a decent meal for some time.

Melt into the scenery. Remember what you have been taught. Act like one of them – which wasn't hard to do because by now she felt she had come home.[1]

Diana was heading for the Franche-Comté region of the Jura, an area south-east of Dijon of wild mountains and deep pine forests. It was an area strongly patriotic and full of *résistants* with one idea on their minds: to rid their country of the damned *Boche*. Because of its geographical situation it was ideally suited to this aim. It was also the home of the *Maquis,* the young who had fled the towns and villages to avoid deportation to Germany for forced labour in the war factories of the *Reich*. In the densely wooded hills and mountains hundreds of these young Frenchmen were clamouring for military instruction and weapons that they needed to fight.

The people of this area of the Franche-Comté, meaning 'Free County', have an unusually powerful sense of liberty. E. H. Cookridge describes it 'as having the spirit of the mountains, perhaps the nearness of the Swiss cantons with their long tradition of freedom, justice and equality which goes back to the struggles of the Middle Ages'. More specifically, during the second half of the nineteenth century a philosophy of anarchism gained a strong foothold. The Franche-Comté might well be called the cradle of anarchy, for it was the home of Proudhon, the great philosopher-printer from Besançon. Indeed, anarchy penetrated so deeply into the spirit of this region as to assume the proportions of a popular movement from the 1860s to 1880s. The most ardent anarchists were found among the class of independent artisans, especially the watchmakers, and these same people were now active in the Resistance.

This ageless region goes back to the Paleolithic Age, and its history is long and varied. Once the territory of the County of Burgundy, from 888 it had become separated from the neighbouring Duchy of Burgundy upon the latter's incorporation into the Kingdom of France in 1477. The tough, proud, and courageous people have had to be so, as the area has been invaded and conquered many times and incorporated into other territories. They are a people whose natural instincts are moulded and enhanced by a spirit of freedom, equality and justice – and their opposites – which is particularly hard to quell. Consequently, Diana would be working in a strong resistance area where she would at least have a chance of survival.

The journey to the Jura seemed to take forever, moving over 600 kilometres from the dropping zone at Villeveque, with all the stops and starts involved, but finally the train steamed into the station at Lons-le-Saunier, the main town in the Jura. Diana was entering a *departement* of pastures and vineyards, stone villages, spruce forests and wild mountains close to the Swiss border. Lons-le-Saunier was garrisoned by the Germans. From Lons Diana boarded a *tacot*, a small train on wooden wheels, to the town of St Amour, her destination. It was a beautiful late spring afternoon with blossoms in full pink bloom, and she smelt for the first time the certain smell of the Jura countryside; it was the smell of the fields, flowers, pines and wild thyme. She trudged up the road from the railway station carrying her heavy case of clothes and belongings and wheeling her bicycle, finally arriving at the charming, haphazard little town with its small, winding cobbled streets, pretty houses and a strangely octagonal *place*. Tired and dusty from her long train journey, she finally found the Hotel du Commerce where she would stay until such time as she met up with John Starr. The Hotel du Commerce was a three-storeyed, well-proportioned building with wrought-iron balconies. The proprietor was one Madame Laurencin, a short, dark-haired woman who was an active member of the Resistance and had lodged many of its members. She looked at the patently English woman standing in front of her and immediately gave her a small, dark room at the back of the hotel close to the roof where, if necessary, she could make a quick escape. Diana's name was never entered in the hotel's register so there was nothing to show she had ever stayed there. 'They were not difficult to fool, if one kept one's wits,' said Madame Laurencin, speaking of the Germans. 'I put these people in rooms at the back; they could get on to a roof, and from there down the back of the hotel and so escape if things became hot. But it was never necessary. We had no trouble at all.'

It was in a quiet room at the Hotel du Commerce that Diana met Captain John Starr, the organiser of the *Acrobat* circuit. He told her what had been happening in the region, that originally he had decided to develop his circuit around Lons, and that his contact with Clermont-Ferrand, Brian Rafferty, had been arrested just before Starr had arrived. This region of France had fast become a dangerous point of congregation for F Section agents. He also told her about Harry Rée, *chef du réseaux* in the Jura.

Harry Rée, the English SOE agent, wrote a very clear definition of the situation in France at the time:

> From the summer of 1942 onwards it was very difficult to know just what the French were thinking. We were continually getting contradictory reports. Some said that nearly all were in favour of de Gaulle, others that they were in favour of Vichy. Most reports indicated that the British were highly unpopular. The general feeling, we learned, was that we had let the French down at Dunkirk, and had added injury to insult at Oran and Dakar. It was thought that, apart from the working classes, Parisians were particularly anti-British. The slowly dripping venom of Radio Paris and of the German-controlled Vichy press was apparently having its effect. It was evident that resistance to the occupying forces was merely sporadic and lacking in organisation. The idea of patriotism – those French men and women who could not tolerate the thought of a captive France were concerned only with escape to a free country. They were totally disorganised and because they had few, if any, means of communication with the outside world were prone to despair.[2]

In contradiction to this, agent Claude de Baissac had reported to London that 'many arrests are made every day in France as nearly everyone is now engaged in some subversive operation or other'.[3]

Originally from Manchester, Captain Harry Rée started off the war as a conscientious objector, but just before the fall of France he realised that he

> … didn't think political objection stood up logically in the current scheme of things. The war was much more than a capitalist war. I think the concentration camp business and the anti-Jewish business convinced me that I, with the rest of the country, should do everything possible to defeat the whole Nazi thing because of its racial policies.[4]

Buckmaster had selected Rée for a special task – to assist Maurice Southgate, who was in charge of the SOE network at Clermont-Ferrand, to destroy the Michelin works that manufactured tyres for the German war effort. He was dropped into France on 15 April 1943 in the company of Amedee Mainguard, from Mauritius. When eventually Rée reached Clermont-Ferrand, the plans for the sabotage against the Michelin works had been changed and he was ordered to go to the Jura region instead. Brian Rafferty, code name *Michel*, an Irishman whom Rée had met earlier in Clermont-Ferrand, arrived with instructions from London. The last time Rafferty visited, he met Raymond Lazzeri at Lons. This visit was to end in disaster. Both of these brave, patriotic men were arrested and taken to the Gestapo prison at Dijon. Rée attempted to rescue them but the prison was heavily guarded.

Ree had contacts in Lons-le-Saunier and took charge of a new network there. Despite his accent being not altogether convincing, he was able to explain this away by saying he came from Alsace:

They'd got some contacts up in the Jura where there were some *Maquis* starting up in the hills. Would I go up there and contact these groups and try to organise them, get some *parachutages* and start arming them? It was about the time that the Germans had started calling up young French people to go and work in Germany. Those who didn't want to do so and were against the Germans would get themselves false ID cards and go up into the hills and join the *Maquis*.

When he had first arrived in the Jura, Rée set about organising camps for the *Maquis,* establishing local resistance groups, organising weapon drops, and finding suitable drop spots for the reception of arms and sabotage material. He visited remote mountain *Maquis* camps recruiting *maquisards* who had dodged conscription, impatient to get into battle. Not all were teenagers but all were young men eager to rid their country of the oppressors. They longed for the day when the English would supply guns and explosives. During the day they would earn their keep by working for local farmers or as tradesmen; they were a mixture of cobblers, watch repairers, electricians. At night they trained as soldiers. Rée was careful not to promise them supplies, though the Resistance leaders and especially the youngsters in the camps were impatient for action. He was hampered by the fact that he had no radio communication with Clermont-Ferrand and no orders from Baker Street.

In the course of his work Rée had picked up contacts in Dijon, in the Jura, and in Doubs, and it was to the development of these that he was to devote himself. After installing both John Starr and radio operator John Young as coordinators in local resistance activities, together with the help of a *résistant* by the name of Pierre Martin, they managed to get together several sabotage groups and Starr organised one or two sabotage operations. But Rée had not taken to Starr, disliking his assertive manner, and worried about the security of the circuit. Michael Foot was later to describe Starr as 'self-opinionated and over-confident who put it around the neighbourhood that he was a powerful figure in the intelligence service and would need the best of everything'.

Around this time a round-up of suspects in the area of Lons-le-Saunier prompted Baker Street to move Rée south to Belfort to start a new *réseau*. This was to be known as *Stockbroker*, a network which would work in conjunction with *Acrobat*, and he was glad to be sent off on his own to establish a line for communication to London through Switzerland. Many arrests had been made and the area became too hot for Rée, who moved his headquarters to Vallentigny, a village near Montbeliard close to the Swiss border. He hid out spasmodically at the house of Eugene Barbier, who worked as an accountant at the nearby Sochaux works of the Peugeot car company. Rée made a practice of never staying at M. Barbier's house for more than a day or two, and was constantly on the move travelling between his various resistance groups and visiting the Maquis camps up in the hills.

On meeting Diana in the Commerce, Starr was concerned that she did not look sufficiently French, but despite this, on talking to her soon discovered she would be an invaluable asset to the *réseaux*. Starr was a dapper little man with a pale face and a silky moustache, who was on his second mission in France; he had parachuted into France near Blye in May 1943 to organise a network in the Dijon area. On his previous mission, in August 1942, he had joined the *Carte* organisation under André Girard, a painter who had been working for SOE. Starr's job was organising food supplies for the group. 'Building a network is like making a ladder,' said John's brother, George, always known as *Le Patron* and organiser of the *Wheelwright* circuit. 'You fix one rung.

You stand on it. You jump on it. If it holds, you build the next one. It takes time. The people who wanted to do it in five minutes got caught. I was bloody lucky.'

Both John and George Starr had spent their youth in France but were British subjects. John was on his second mission and had been living in Lons-le-Saunier since May 1943. He had been a commercial artist and advertising agent in Paris before the war and had married a French girl. His French seemed perfect to Harry Rée. Starr had taken with him an excellent wireless operator, Lieutenant John Cuthbert Young, code-named *Gabriel,* and they were anxiously awaiting their courier. Young was a Scotsman, a pleasant Catholic who had met his French wife while travelling for an insurance company. He was the son of an army officer, and in Rée's words was 'a youngster with a pleasant manner and a rugged physique'. However, Young's Geordie accent was so atrocious that he had to be kept hidden as much as possible. One of the French Resistance men on meeting him for the first time had commented: '*Eh bien, mon vieux, il n'y a pas se tromper. Il voudrait mieux, que tu parles le moins possible.*' Well, my friend, there is no mistake. It would be best if you speak as little as possible.

Starr always thought it was very brave of Young to come to France with such a disadvantage. He could not even go into a café on his own and had to be very careful never at any time to speak too loudly. However, finding suitable places from which Young could transmit was to be an ongoing problem. One of the Jura's toughest *Maquisards,* Gut Grancher, had collected Starr and Young from Clermont-Ferrand, and with the help of Henri Clerc, the wine merchant from St Amour and head of the local resistance, had eventually found a safe place for them to stay at the medieval Château d'Andelot, a vacated castle high in the hills above St Amour, owned by a rich American who had returned to the States at the beginning of the war. The castle was richly furnished and well stocked with vintage wines and champagne, which the old caretaker somehow had succeeded in keeping from the Germans.

Young found the old castle 'most impressive but a very weird place to be living in alone, especially at night'. It reminded him of stories of his boyhood, and he wondered if the people down in the village would say the place was haunted if his candlelight was seen as he went from one room to another.

The meals were supplied by the caretaker and his wife, who cooked in their little house outside the castle. Although there was nobody living in the château, at midday the caretaker would go into the chapel and ring the bells as a signal to Starr that dinner was ready. His meal was brought in by the two of them and then they would leave, always locking the gates behind them. It was a lonely existence for Young except for the times when he would meet up with Harry Rée or another *résistant* such as Henri Clerc. As an extra precaution Young transmitted on batteries so that if the Germans in an attempt to locate his position cut off the current section by section, the transmission would still carry on. Initially he transmitted once or twice from high in the hills above St Amour, then left and went to stay on a farm. When Young returned from the farm Starr moved into the château with him and they worked together on messages for London.

On one occasion, after Young had sent out a message under extremely difficult conditions, one came back from London saying that his transmission was poor and that he should be more careful when sending and make some effort. Young was conscientious, a staunch and kindly man, and this message was hurtful. John Starr, who was with him in the castle when this message came through, felt that it was only right that he, as Young's chief, should send a return message to London. Accordingly, he asked Young to send the following message: 'Reception committee awaiting armchair critics. *Ici et la ça fait deux.*' In other words, one sees things differently.

This did not go down well in London and the reply finished with the words, 'END OF MESSAGE NOT APPRECIATED'.

Starr took Diana to meet Henri Clerc, the local resistance leader. Clerc was a seller of wine, particularly the famous Beaujolais of the region. The Germans had looted much of the stock, though Clerc had managed to hide a few precious bottles. A big, burly man, he towered over his lovely wife Yvonne. 'Clerc was one of the most cheerful, kindly and helpful people I met in France,' said Rée. Clerc regularly covered a large region, calling at restaurants, cafés and bistros where he sold his goods. His attitude to the defeat of 1940 was simple: either one accepted it or one did not. If those he spoke with seemed to accept it, he let it go; if they did not, he at once started discussions as to what could be done to turn defeat into victory. From the beginning he had undertaken resistance in a small way. He thought that, whilst salvation must in the end be brought from outside France, the happy day when the Germans would be chased away could be brought much nearer if men and women inside France worked actively to secure their own release. He never doubted that victory would in the end be achieved.

Acrobat at first grew very quickly, and for the last weeks of June and the first weeeks of July Diana worked hard with Starr, carrying messages between the thriving local Resistance groups and helping to receive the arms drops that *Gabriel* arranged over his radio. Starr by now had divided himself between St Amour and the château there and Henri Clerc, organising arms drops and putting people in touch with one another.

It was the Clercs who introduced Diana to John Young, who had returned from a break on a farm and was back at the château. They met in a café in the local *place*. Diana quickly realised that while they were together she would have to do all the talking.

Diana got on extremely well with the Clercs. They had a small daughter who went to the local school and Diana quickly befriended the little girl, who loved her new 'cousin'. They lived in a typical very old two-storey house built over the *caves*. It had dark polished floors and was very well furnished, with books everywhere. The kitchen boasted great, massive beams. There was a wine cellar on the lower floor with wide stone vaults, with many bottles of the dark red Beaujaolais. Diana was invited many times to dinner. A wooden staircase led to a delightful veranda, where sometimes they were joined by Harry Rée and other *résistants*. They would sip their Beaujolais and watch the sky slowly deepen to a deep navy blue. It was times like these that Diana knew without a doubt that she had made the right decision to return to France. She was very happy here in this beautiful part of the country.[5] It was still very spring-like, and the smell of the pink blossoms hung heavy on the air. Tall poplar trees lined the villages and the men sat around smoking their pipes. Jean Simon was a close friend of the Clercs, Diana and Harry Rée. On evenings like the one above, he would quote from *Le Croix de Bois: Tu sais, quand tout cela sera fini, nous dirons – c'etait le bon temps, quand même.* 'When all this over we will say it was a good time even so.'

Very quickly Diana became familiar with the local Resistance, its activities and its members. One such man was Jean Simon, a tough and energetic bank clerk, known as 'Claude' to everybody because he had come from the village of St Claude, a cathedral town nearby; it was he who had introduced Harry Rée to Henry Clerc. Simon had an extraordinary attitude to life, always positive and physically energetic; but he would not survive the war.

Diana met the other resistance men of the area and very quickly she went to work. At this time, June 1943, it was getting more dangerous to move around. The Germans had introduced the *Service du Travail Obligatoire,* the STO, forced labour for nearly all able-bodied men. The outcome of this measure was that people like John Starr and Henri Clerc had either to be in essential occupations, like Clerc in the wine trade, or else they were transported as free labour to Germany – hence the upsurge of young men who had joined the Maquis in the Jura. Cities like Paris were conspicuous in their lack of males, and were full of women, old people and young children.

When Starr failed to keep a rendevous with Rée on 14 July, it was no surprise to Rée to learn a few days later that he had been arrested. He had been betrayed by Pierre Martin, a double agent. Harry Rée had been introduced to Martin by a draper at Chaussin, Paupal. Martin was a big man, strong and willful with a certain element of charm, who was held in awe by some members of the local resistance. On their first meeting Martin had told Rée he had previously been an officer with the *Deuxième Bureau* of the French Military Intelligence. But right from the beginning Rée had reservations and suspicions about Martin. One reason was that he was overly talkative about his so-called 'daring achievements' in the Resistance. He always claimed he was a true *résistant* and had a car and a Gestapo *permis de conduire,* in explanation he told Rée that he was driving Gestapo officers who had no idea of his Resistance activities. Rée did not trust him. There was also the additional matter of London, who wanted to recall Rée; but he did not want to leave the area until Martin had been dealt with. By this time Martin was under the protection of the German field police, the *Feldpolitzei,* because he sensed his cover had been blown. Jean Simon wanted to kill him, but he wanted to do this in such a way that he could kill him immediately, that is to try and get him into the open and, if possible, alone without protection.

There is some disagreement as to who exactly killed Pierre Martin, who was living near Besançon where he felt safe. E. H. Cookridge says it was Jean Simon (Claude) who did this, while others say it was Eric Cauchi, code named *Pedro,* who had trained with Diana in Party 27Y and who had been parachuted into the area on 23 July to assist John Young. Cauchi was to become one of the best sub-agents in the area. Whoever the killer was had found Martin sitting in a restaurant in the Café de Belfort, Besançon, reading a newspaper, and had shot him through the open pages of the paper. The actual story of what happened was reported in a newspaper under the heading 'Assassination in a restaurant': 'At about 19.50 two young men who were eating at one of the tables, had fired several shots at another diner sitting alone, a Monsieur P.M. ... Hit by several bullets in the chest, abdomen, and head, the victim died within twenty minutes.'

The report mentioned there were two assassins, so it could have been both Simon and Cauchi.

A hue and cry for the assassins ensued, but they all escaped. Simon sent a full report to Rée three days later in which the shooting of Martin was mentioned among other things: 'We managed to regain our respective homes. That skunk P. [Pierre Martin] kept me freezing for eight days and I nearly caught my death.'

After Martin's death the Germans, enraged by the successful 'terrorist coup', made savage reprisals. It was through the traitor Martin that they had knowledge of many of the Resistance leaders. The Germans had let them remain at large, hoping to gain an even greater knowledge of the activities of Rée's network, but now the Gestapo decided the time had come to strike.

Cauchi himself was later to lose his life. He and Simon were shot by the Gestapo in Sochaux on 5 February 1944.

The friends Diana made, such as the Clercs and Madame Laurencin, were true and trustworthy – strong, salt-of-the-earth people, all hard working and willing to help the *petite Anglaise* who had come all the way from England with her slight accent to help them in their fight for their country. They were all pleased to be able to do something.

Diana found it was easy to get identity cards. When she had first met Harry Rée he told her that his own identity card, which had been issued in England, did not pass muster when he came to the Jura and he had had to change it immediately. His friend had said to him, 'Oh, that's no good, we'll get you another from the Mairie tomorrow.'[6] Such was life in the Jura in 1943. After the war, Rée described Diana as 'a very pleasant and serious young woman'.

An interesting side to Rée is shown by the remarks made by his students, here remembered and compared to his fellow teacher, Francis

Cammaerts, who although a conscientitious objector like Rée, joined SOE as an agent in France:

> Both Cammaerts and Rée's teaching was exciting and informal. Rée told us that his Southend Road landlady had been Miss United Kingdom – and then after a long pause '… in about 1900.' They were very different. Cammaerts was a quiet, no-nonsense man who was respected by his students. Rée was ebullient and his frequent shout of 'Shut up, blast you!' was surprisingly effective because we knew a good teacher when we saw one.[7]

Diana stayed with the Clercs for a long time, spending many nights under their roof. They all got along very well. Elizabeth Nicholas describes Yvonne Clerc's face as 'lovely, with a quality of pale transparency and an expression of great sweetness'. In the quiet summer evenings if there were no resistance acitivies, they would talk long into the night. Yvonne and Diana had similar characters; they were quiet, reflective and gentle. Diana would help with the household chores and other duties. Yvonne would later describe this time together 'as a time of splendour and tragedy'.

Diana soon met many interesting *résistants* who had quickly become experts in the little villages of the Jura. They ranged from peasants to the local petit-bourgeoisie, small factory owners, hotel and shopkeepers, clerks, butchers, and grocers. Although many of the young men had been called up to work in Germany, some managed to avoid this and assumed different identities. Many got away with it. There was Robert Doriot, a former airman, Bothey, the baker at Dampierre, Paupal, and the little draper at Chaussin who single-handedly blew up a heavily laden troop train.

Among these also was Gut Grancher, a former journalist and Air Force pilot who had picked up John Starr and John Young after they had parachuted in; Rée had entrusted Gut to receive many of their incoming containers, and after the war referred to him as 'one of the best types of *résistants* in the Jura'. George Millar referred to him as 'Max'. He had been taken in a barber's shop at Clairvaux, near Mouchard. In an effort to extract information from him the Gestapo had beaten him almost senseless, and then they had carried him off in their *traction-avant*, the front-wheel-drive Citroën, the French car the Germans in France preferred to all the others.

Early photo of Diana. (Courtesy of Yvonne Clerc)

Left: Aldred Clement Rowden (1888–1935). (From *Royal Academy Illustrated* 1914)

Below: Tilford Church. (Author's collection)

Right: Photo of Diana and her brothers on the beach at Cannes. (Courtesy of Victoria Boyle)

Below: The extended Rowden family. (Author's collection)

Above: Manor House school, Limpsfield. (Author's collection)

Left: The young Rowden family (from left to right: Maurice, aged nineteen, Diana, aged twenty, Cecil, aged fourteen). Possibly taken at the docks on a visit to England from France at the time their father died; they are wearing winter clothes (Aldred died in December 1935). (Author's collection)

Above: Twelfth-century cloisters of Beaulieu. (Author's collection)

Right: 64 Baker Street, headquarters of the Special Operations Executive from 1940 onwards. *Inset*: plaque commemorating the organisation, 'which supported resistance in all enemy-occupied countries'. (Author's collection)

Above: No. 1 Cornwall Mews building (white buiding on right). This is the flat in Knightsbridge owned by Mrs Rowden during the war, and where Diana and friends of SOE Party 27Y gathered. (Author's collection)

Left: James McCairns, who piloted Diana into France. (Courtesy of Tangmere Museum)

Above: Harry Rée
at back in uniform
with Jura *résistants*.
(Courtesy of Paul
McCue)

Right: An SOE airdrop.
(Courtesy of Tangmere
Museum)

Diana in uniform.
(Courtesy of Paul McCue)

Harry Rée, from his personal file.
(Courtesy of Steven Kippax)

John Starr.
(Courtesy of David Harrison)

Vera Atkins.
(Courtesy of Paul McCue)

Raoul Janier-Dubry.
(Courtesy of Janier-Dubry family)

André Maugenet aka the 'true' *Benoit*.
(Courtesy of Paul McCue)

Brian Stonehouse, from his personal file.

Left: M. Henri Clerc. (Courtesy of Yvonne Clerc)

Below: Rosemary Chetwynd-Stapylton (second from left) and Mark Chetwynd-Stapylton (third from left), Victoria Boyle's parents. (Courtesy of Victoria Boyle)

Above: Robert 'Bob' Maloubier (third from left). (Author's collection)

Right: The cyanide-containing 'L' Pill. Agents had the choice of whether or not to take this with them into the field. (Courtesy of David Harrison)

Diana's ring and cigarette holder. (Author's collection)

Barn in Jura where Henri Clerc and Diana stored arms. (Courtesy of Paul McCue)

The sawmill at Clairvaux-le-lacs. (Courtesy of Janier-Dubry family)

Telegraph House, where Mrs Rowden lived in the South Downs. (Author's collection)

Val-d'Épy, where Diana stayed with Madame Rhaithouze. (Courtesy of Paul McCue)

Château d'Andelot, St Amour in the Jura. (Author's collection)

Gestapo Headquarters in Lons-le-Saunier. (Author's collection)

Karlsruhe prisonl. (Author's collection)

Natzweiler entrance. (Author's collection)

Natzweiler layout. (Author's collection)

Yvonne Clerc, who sheltered Diana Rowden in St Amour, Jura. Taken in May 2015. (Author's collection)

Right: Valençay Memorial. (Author's collection)

Below: Arriving at Natzweiler for a memorial service, Victoria Boyle (second from left), Anne Chetwynd-Stapylton (right). (Courtesy of Victoria Boyle)

Diana on-site memorial.
(Courtesy of Victoria Boyle)

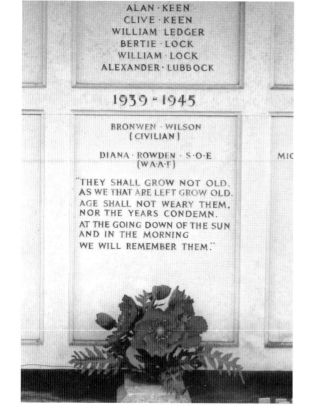

ALAN · KEEN
CLIVE · KEEN
WILLIAM · LEDGER
BERTIE · LOCK
WILLIAM · LOCK
ALEXANDER · LUBBOCK

1939 - 1945

BRONWEN · WILSON
(CIVILIAN)

DIANA · ROWDEN · S·O·E
(W·A·A·F)

"THEY SHALL GROW NOT OLD,
AS WE THAT ARE LEFT GROW OLD,
AGE SHALL NOT WEARY THEM,
NOR THE YEARS CONDEMN.
AT THE GOING DOWN OF THE SUN
AND IN THE MORNING
WE WILL REMEMBER THEM."

Diana commemorated in
stone at the Runnymede
Royal Air Force Memorial,
Surrey. (Author's collection)

His huge body was one mass of bruises and cuts, for they had beaten him with blows about the head and shoulders and kicked him savagely with their hobnailed boots. But Gut was known as a calm and brave man and did not talk. He had worked for a long time in the Resistance and knew everybody in the area, and when the Germans knew they would get nothing out of him they simply dumped him in the woods. It was here that some fellow members of the Maquis found him two days later. He recovered and carried on his Resistance activities.

Andre Jeanney was another *résistant,* a brave young officer who had fought in Charles de Gaulle's 5th Tank Division. All of these men were of great help to Harry Rée.

On the other side of the coin were the people who were frightened of the severe retaliation by the Boche if they were caught helping the Resistance, people too frightened to do anything illegal outside of their normal routine, like Robert, who was a Vichy man. Rée found him a sad character, a mixture of indecision and worry – perhaps just an ordinary, not very bright Petainist, as he was once described to Rée the first time he met him. At a meal together, Rée was told that as a loyal Petain supporter Robert kept strictly to the rations out of a sense of duty because the *Marechal* had told him so. 'I don't know if I've made the right decision,' he told Rée. Indeed, this man epitomised the type of Petainist who had followed the *Marechal,* for the best of reasons within his or her limitations, as did a great many Frenchmen and women, especially in 1943. Between the years 1940 to 1944 this prevailing attitude was to 'just fall in with the *Boche,* think of your family, don't rock the boat'.

A person like Robert was such a contrast to the Comte de Brouville, always known as Albert, a close friend of Rée's and who became close to Diana, a man who had a colourful way with words, referring to the *Milice* as 'the scum of the jails, brutalised of the most brutal, cream of the offal, they worked for German money and food for their carnal appetites'.

One man who worked in the car factory at Peugeot was known as '*Bigame*' as he had two girlfriends, both of whom he kept on a string, one in Switzerland and the other in France. There was twenty-year-old Raymond Lazzeri, who had escaped from a prisoner-of-war camp and who could always be seen cycling like mad everywhere. These men were all active, strong and resilient, who took great risks and made great demands of themselves and others. Referring to St Amour where

Diana was based, the word went around: 'This Maquis is by far the best armed in the whole area.'[8]

Making good use of the bike she had been given, Diana journeyed around the area, retrieving agents' messages so that John Young could transmit them back to London. She was the sole link between all of the agents in the Jura region and its only wireless operator, John Young. It was physically exhausting work, made even more difficult by the constant threat of German roadblocks. When in the cities or large towns especially, she had to constantly think and remember small things, such as never to ask for a *café au lait*. It could be fatal if the wrong person overheard. In wartime France there was no such thing.

'Most agents lived in a state of perpetual terror,' said Michael Foot:

They had to be extremely fit, tireless, constantly on guard knowing all the time that somebody might betray them for money or favours. They knew they were all under sentence of death. It was not only the Germans and the Gestapo who posed this threat, there were many French civilians who hated SOE agents and the resistance groups because their activities brought savage reprisals upon innocent people in towns and villages.[9]

Diana loved the Jura. The weather had warmed up and in the villages flowers bloomed in gardens and in baskets outside houses and shops. Roses and clematis climbed over trellises and walls. She became very fit, cycling long distances, or going by train, delivering and receiving messages. However, the roads in the Jura were dangerous, as the *Boche* had put restriction after restriction on the traffic, and many times she was stopped at road blocks and her papers inspected. Once she was arrested at a checkpoint but cleverly managed to slip away while the soldiers' attention was diverted elsewhere. Somehow she always managed to stay one step ahead of the enemy.

After the setbacks during the summer of 1943, in which the *Prosper* network had been destroyed and a number of officers captured, London had to rely on Young's radio post for maintaining contact with several other SOE agents and networks. Diana not only assisted *Gabriel* in operating his radio post but also maintained a regular courier service for Rée's network between his various groups at

Montbeliard, Besançon, Lons-le-Sounier, Belfort and other towns. On many occasions she helped Rée's men to arrange the reception of containers.

On 16 July Harry Rée heard through a contact that Field Marshal Rommel's train was passing through their area, so the Resistance set out to derail it. The train did not arrive and the attempt ended in failure. Rée, who had organised another derailment at Dijon, began to suspect a traitor among his informants. SOE agents had to disappear and quickly.

He sent word to Young and Diana and, after safeguarding as many in the two circuits as possible, escaped over the mountains into Switzerland in August. He returned with a second set of forged papers, the originals having been discarded as a poor forgery, and became Henri Rehmann from Alsace, a cultivateur, domiciled at Lons-le-Saunier. His mission was to make contact with Andre van der Straeten, a lieutenant in the French Army with a group at Valentigny and foreman in the Peugeot works.

On her trips into the mountains, the views far below on to pine-studded woods and streams were such that sometimes Diana would get off her bike and stand in awe. On her journeys back and forth to the Château d'Andelot the wind blowing across the valley from the mountains rippled the streams far below into waves of soft silk. The Alps were always breathtaking, looming above her like giant cones coated in icing sugar. At other times, when they were covered by a light mist, they were soft as gossamer. Their invincibility reminded her of the occupants of this part of France; like the people, they were unyielding, unbreakable, eternal. A surge of pride would flow through her that she had been sent here. She knew more than ever now she had done the right thing to leave England. If she could help these brave, indomitable people of the mountains – if she could help them win this great struggle – then she would have accomplished something

She delighted in spending time in the beautiful country of the Jura, and from the people I have spoken to and the accounts I have read of her work, she seemed to be very happy at this time in her life, despite the fact she was continually on the alert. She had made many friends, one of whom, Yvonne Clerc, told me: 'Diana said, "When this is all over, I shall come back and maybe live here where I have been so happy."'

Diana often accompanied Henri Clerc to parachute grounds when arms were to be dropped. Five parachute drops, cross-marked on the Michelin map #70, were made by M. Clerc. One was just by the Château d'Andelot; another was found to the south-west of St Amour, hard by a hamlet named Chamandre; the third was to the south-east, beneath le Point Lancette les Granges; the fourth located to the north, near Orgelet; and the fifth lay southeast of Lons-le-Saunier, near Blye.

These missions would take place after curfew but were very dangerous as there would have been German patrols always on the lookout. On a moonlit night, after they had received the message on the BBC to let them know the drop was on, they would usually leave for the dropping grounds around 10.30 p.m. on their bikes. This would be a field, always surrounded by trees, where the equipment could be well hidden. The plane would usually pass overhead about 12.30 p.m. During her training Diana had been shown how to put down the torches to lead the aircraft into the wind. She would set lights and flares and wait patiently in the dark for the sound of an aircraft carrying with it a load of arms and explosives, which, if all went well, would float down to where she stood. Henri Clerc was enthusiastic about the dropping of arms: 'They had in the end received plenty of ammunition and made good use of it.'

Diana had waited patiently with Clerc. They had cycled together, taking extreme care not to be discovered by the dreaded *Boche*. Clerc had one desire: to turn defeat into victory. He never deviated from this reasoning, nor doubted that victory would, in the end, be achieved.

She would also frequently accompany members of the *Maquis* to parachute grounds at the dead of night where, having carefully concealed their bicycles, they would await the dark silhouette and roar of an RAF aircraft as it disgorged its arms and ammunition over their carefully placed lamps and flares. The local *Maquis* knew the country like the back of their hands, most of them having been born there. They knew how to live off the land without help from the local people, who nevertheless often took the risk of offering help. Many were related, some of them being the sons, cousins and brothers of local citizens.

It was part of Diana's job to request supplies from London. Not only did she help to find and pinpoint suitable landing grounds for these local *Maquis*, she was also responsible for many successful drops of arms and ammunition, including Bren guns, which were the ideal weapon for the *Maquis*. The Bren was strong and portable, but could be known to jam.

As early as May 1943, before the insertion of Diana into the Jura, Rée had come to Montbeliard just in time for the first RAF raid on the Peugeot works at Sochaux in the arrondissement of Montbeliard. This first raid on the factory was a tragic affair. The factory was untouched and the bombs fell wide, causing very heavy casualties in the neighbouring village. By early July Rée had made his first contact with the Peugeot management, who proved very helpful indeed. Rée found to his great satisfaction that the Peugeot people themselves were toying with the idea of sabotaging their own factory in order to stop production, thereby preventing a repetition of the disastrous bombardment by the RAF. Nothing could have been more convenient from Rée's point of view. Through Roger Fouillette, an Alsatian Artillery Captain, he made the acquaintance of Pierre Lucas, chief electrician of Peugeot, who became very enthusiastic when Rée was able to point out to him the practicability of putting the factory out of action by sabotage. Delighted with the possibility of avoiding further loss of life through RAF action, he showed Henri all over the factory and its machinery.

In the meantime Rée had advised London of what was happening. SOE had obtained a grudging and conditional agreement from the RAF to postpone further efforts against what was rapidly becoming their favourite target. Reasonably enough, the condition was that properly effective action should be taken from the ground.

On the night of 3 November 1943 a party of six workmen under the leadership of Andre Jeanney entered the works to make their first attack. Coached by Rée, they carefully placed their charges on transformers and compressors, made their way out, and sat back in anticipation to await the expected results. However, nothing happened. Subsequent examination revealed that, despite the careful coaching, the detonators had been put in the wrong way round.

On 5 November – Guy Fawkes no doubt providing the inspiration – the attack was repeated, this time with success. Thereafter many successful attacks were made on the Peugeot factory and similar works in the district. These were carefully analysed in London and, although it was often touch and go, the RAF was successfully dissuaded from making another air attack.

Newspapers reported the sabotage on the Peugeot factory on 5 November: 'Industrial sabotage is being used with greater success than Allied bombing at the Peugeot plant, which is producing war equipment on the Germans' orders. Following the RAF raid on 14 July, the manufacturing of turrets for tanks has been interrupted indefinitely.'

The successful demolition of the Peugeot plant resulted in three months' interruption in the making of tanks for the German army – a wonderful morale booster for the Resistance.

Eventually, in 1944, when the 159th Infantry Regiment had liberated the region, it was largely the arms which Diana had helped to collect that both equipped and helped to rebuild its shattered morale. Diana had played her part in making this operation possible. 'That too was a result of *Paulette's* work,' said Clerc. 'She helped to get us arms when we were in hiding; she helped build our morale; the 159th Regiment owed much to her.' In August, Rée was forced into hiding, and he stayed in hiding until the region was liberated. After the war, he told Noreen Riols, who worked for F Section, that the bombing of the Peugeot factory 'had been a good job for a conchie'.

Diana was a good friend and comrade to all the local Maquis; she was always a tireless worker and without fear. One day she had to deliver some messages a long way away, and took advantage of the offer of a ride with three *résistants*, Jean Simon, Albert and Gut Grancher, all very active in the local effort. These men were in the habit of blaming everything on the war – it was always *c'est la guerre, c'est la vie!* The three of them were tightly squeezed into the cab of the old van. Each man held a gun, except Gut who had hidden his somewhere close in the car; Diana was unarmed on this trip. To avoid driving on the roads they took the small tracks that cut through the forest. Suddenly on rounding a bend they saw a gleaming black Citroën blocking the road in front of them. It had 'Gestapo' written all over it. With a squeal of brakes Gut reversed, backing frantically, and tore into the forest. With Diana and Albert crouching down on the floor, Gut put his foot down on the accelerator as trees shot past them in a blur. By this time there was no sign of the Citroën. They stopped just once, to pick up Paul Guyot, another *résistant*, at Clairvaux, an area judged dangerous as there were always Germans around. As soon as they thought they were safe, Gut told them to get out and climb into the back, but still keep their heads down.

It had been a narrow escape.

As railway stations were particularly dangerous with the *Milice* or Germans on the prowl, it was more sensible to get off at a little railway station and cycle into the main town rather than go into the main railway station. As Francis Cammaerts remarks, 'There was also a tendency that if things were going right to get careless and sometimes one was tempted to do things one shouldn't, such as meet others or go to nightclubs.'[10] At every railway station Diana had to continually remember what she had been taught, the basic rule of an agent: *Be observant and inconspicuous.*

One day, returning to the Jura on a train from courier work as far away as Paris, she had the feeling she was being followed. There was no outward sign, just an uncanny feeling. She looked at the other passengers: most were asleep or appeared to be dozing. She got up and went into the crowded corridor and looked out of the window at the passing scenery. It was a very light afternoon and she could see the reflection of the passengers behind her, some reclining against the passageway door, others propped up against luggage racks or sitting on suitcases. Her Beaulieu training had taught her to spot a 'tail', and very quickly she noticed the two men. They weren't too hard to spot as both of them were wearing felt hats and overcoats and were smoking cigarettes. Typical Gestapo. She quietly walked back to her seat and opened a book. As she looked up whilst reading, she noticed one of the men had come into the carriage and was looking at her. She decided very quickly how she would give them the slip.

Diana, even without the schooling she had received from SOE, was a very clear thinking young woman. She knew she must somehow get off the crowded train without being spotted, and she knew she must do it very quickly so the men would be in no position to follow her. Keeping her cool, giving no indication she had noticed the men and continuing to read her book, she waited for an opportunity to leave the train. Finally, it slowed as it approached the next station and people got up and made their way to the exit. Diana stayed where she was until the last possible moment before the doors closed, then she jumped up and rushed to the door just before they shut. She didn't look behind her – nor did she see the anger on the men's faces as the heavily laden train pulled out of the station. It was only as the train moved off and as she made her way to the ticket office to enquire when the next train was leaving that she paused to light a cigarette, finding it difficult to stop her hand from shaking.

Before too long another train arrived and she was able to resume her journey.

On July 18 John Starr, having been betrayed by the double agent Pierre Martin and arrested on the road between Dijon and Dole, was brutally interrogated at the SD Headquarters in Dijon. The next day he was taken to the Avenue Foch in Paris where the SD had their headquarters, and was surprised to see a British officer, Gilbert Norman, code named *Archambault*. Later he was dismayed to see on the desk of his interrogator a complete list of SOE training schools, together with the names of the instructors. This led Starr to wonder whether there was a mole in SOE.

Having discovered that Starr was a draughtsman, Hans Josef Kieffer, the head of interrogation, installed Starr in a room adjoining his own. Kieffer ordered Starr to copy maps and to draw pen portraits of himself and other SD and Gestapo officers. Starr had given the Germans his cover story; after listening to him, they said, 'They're all the same, the cover stories they send you out with.' Then they told Starr they knew the organisation he belonged to and started asking direct questions about the people he had met or been in contact with, where he intended to meet his courier, and where his radio operator was transmitting from.[11]

At first, according to Jean Overton Fuller, who interviewed Starr after the war for her book *The Starr Affair*, he told them nothing. Then, as things were getting pretty tough and he had more than accomplished his forty-eight hours silence with some to spare, he started to give them some information – just enough to keep them happy and only what the traitor Pierre Martin had already told them.

At this time there was a radio report to London from Harry Rée regarding Diana:

PAULETTE: I do not need her. Send her to another area. She is very efficient.

Cesar Report 10.8.43

Diana was dividing her time between the Hotel du Commerce and the Clerc house. However, after John Starr was arrested her position in the

Jura became increasingly untenable, and the breakup of the network *Prosper* had seriously affected her safety. The Germans were well aware of the presence of English agents in the area, and it was thought prudent for Diana to escape to the château as often as possible, where at least she would be safe for the moment. However, moving around the area and staying at various safe houses kept her one step ahead of the Germans.

She was being sent all over France – to Lyon, Besançon, and Montbeliard, even as far as Marseilles as a courier, activities much wider than those of an ordinary courier. She became the sole link between all of the agents in the Jura region and was always careful to be extra vigilant in Paris, which was a powder keg, alive with informers for the Gestapo. There was always the thought: could one's friends be trusted? She had been told not to talk on trains, even in the company of local *résistants*. Even local Frenchmen could not be trusted. There could be an informer working in the local café, and if somebody had hung a portrait of Petain then one could be fairly certain that the occupier was not a *résistant*.

Diana's work was physically demanding and arduous, made all the more difficult by the constant presence of German roadblocks. It is most probable she would have taken messages to Charles Skepper, her Lysander companion, in June, as he was running the *Monk* circuit in Marseilles at the time. She knew the south of France very well as she had lived there as a child. On one of her trips to Marseilles, Diana had another close escape. Her train was suddenly boarded by the German police in the process of one of their frequent checks, demanding to see the passengers' identification papers. Their harsh voices carried through the train: '*Vous … votre papiers, tout de suite.*'

Some people muttered under their breath, grumbling about *le damned Boche*. Diana was uncertain if her forged papers would pass the test, so knowing she had to act quickly, she squeezed her way through the train and locked herself in the nearest toilet, which luckily was vacant. Wartime trains were always crowded and it was inevitable somebody would soon be banging on the door. She prayed the soldiers would pass by; incredibly no one tried to enter or try the lock. She stayed there until the train slowed down at the next stop then she got off and took another train to Marseilles. In a moment of crisis she had kept her head. Her instructors would have been very pleased with her.

While Harry Rée had been working on the Swiss border, *Stockbroker* kept plugging along quietly with its sabotage tasks under the direction of the competent sub-agents he had left behind him. Diana had not seen Rée for a while due to the distance, but when he returned to the area in the company of Albert, the *résistant* she knew well, they discussed plans for an attack on Mouchard railway station in the arrondissement of Lons-le-Saunier and the tracks leading in and out of the town. An enemy train loaded with ammunition was going to pass through Mouchard and the *Maquis* decided they would derail it. Albert had arranged for the roads around St Amour to be watched for Germans – they could either be in trucks or on foot – while John Young was sending messages to London regarding the attack on Mouchard. The operation was scheduled for the next night. Diana had asked Rée if she could go along and observe. Her training report had noted that she had performed particularly well in the area of sabotage: weapons, explosives, dynamite and grenades. They were armed with .45 automatics with two magazines, a couple of pistols, even a sub-machine gun, plus enough *plastique* to detonate half the town. They had already made up the charges at the house of Jean Simon. It was just after midnight and the streets were quiet. The first train was not expected until some time around 4.00 a.m.

They approached the railway station quietly in their light, soft shoes without incident, and laid the charges, which had been tied with sisal and wrapped in newspapers, the detonators already in place; the fuses would be set nearer the time. This was Diana's first sabotage operation and she had helped in all of its steps. They set off across the fields to a small orchard that belonged to one of the *résistants* and waited with a bottle of *pastis,* talking quietly amongst themselves. Rée went back to set the timers and the rest followed. As Diana and Simon neared the station they saw a guard standing on the bridge across the railway yard, a rifle slung over his shoulder; then he started to move in their direction. There was no sign of Harry Rée. Simon, a finger to his lips, motioned to Diana to stay in the shadows while he crept up behind the German. There was no sound, just a muffled cry as Simon, one hand across the German's mouth, the other at his windpipe and with his knee in the German's back, lifted him off his feet, crushing his windpipe. Suddenly a man appeared, emerging from the shadows, a grenade in one hand. It was

Rée. He had been setting the fuses and was about to return to the others when he saw the German lighting a cigarette about to set foot on to the bridge.

The timers had been set for just over twenty minutes, just in time to return to the field and set course for home. A little while later, they heard the explosions, and just after that two further cracks a few seconds apart.

Young around this time was staying at the château and as things were too hot in St Amour, it was thought prudent for Diana to join him permanently. Too much had happened to arouse suspicion during this period: the increased activity of the Maquis in the Jura, her feeling of being followed, her scare on the train from Paris – she knew that the safest place for her to hide, and one that was well away from the town was the Château d'Andelot. This was also the site of one of the dropping grounds where she and her friends had waited patiently at night for the *parachutage* from the skies. In that magnificent sleepy haven, far away from the rest of St Amour, she was able to help Young with his transcripts in between occasionally walking down to the Clercs while keeping a strict eye out for Germans.

Inside the château broad stairs led to a vast echoing attic where Young would send his messages to London. Diana would have looked out of the window into the shadows of the night, remembering the beauty of the day, and now there was nothing, only a few twinkling lights piercing the darkness. During the day she would have stolen a look through the window and gazed down on to a panoramic view that stretched for miles, a view so peaceful, so tranquil, it must have been difficult to reconcile this vista with the country at war, to recognise that any moment the Germans might discover their hiding place. But it was a lonely existence except for the times she took messages to the Clercs. She would have walked in the grounds and hidden in the attic at night while Young sent his messages. The attic was far out of harm's way, and Diana would wait beside him, sometimes walking over to the window hoping they were safe. She would wait until an answer came back, sometimes not until the early hours of the following morning. It was dark and cold in the attic, even in the hot summer months, as there was little air. They could not show any lights at all, even though they were far away from prying eyes; it was a risk they could not take even for a moment.

They were still hunted, the Germans knowing that Diana and Young were at large somewhere in the area. There must have been times when she was a little afraid and must have wondered if she would survive. The thought of her mother and her brothers would have been on her mind, particularly in the moments when she was alone. England would surely have seemed far away. The only person apart from the Clercs who knew the whereabouts of Diana and Young was the caretaker, Marcel Bouvard, who lived in the castle and cooked their meals.

Elizabeth Nicholas, who visited the château in 1956, described the drive leading up to the château as steep and arduous. Diana, often in the company of Yvonne Clerc, would walk that steep climb back to the château. It must have taken great strength to have walked up nearly every day in the heat of summer, the two women carrying messages for John Young. Diana would say, 'When the war is over I will come back in a big American car and we will shoot up this road like a rocket!'[12]

In 2015 while researching this book I was driven to the château by the Janier-Dubry sisters, Claude and Christianne. It was quite difficult to find as they had not visited it before. It seemed a long way, the car climbing steadily up a long, winding road into the hills, around steep bends, and we spoke about how long it would have taken Diana and Yvonne on foot. The view was magnificent. It was a landscape of great strength, not dissimilar to what I imagined the Scottish Highlands to be. Lake Leman and the Swiss frontier lay far below. That day the lake was shrouded in a mist which swirled gently about its surface. Although it was the end of April, snow was still piled on either side of the road. I thought of Diana living so close to Switzerland and safety, a land which remained neutral during the war; to be within sight of security ...

We could see the château far above us, towering and beautiful, steeped in history. It must have reminded Diana of a Scottish keep. The approach was guarded by two tall, grey circular towers connected by a high stone wall. In this was set a heavy wooden door, which had once opened a passage across a drawbridge. There was an exquisite closed garden and to the right were stables entwined with vines, and beyond them a great terrace, the walls of the hill falling sheer beneath it. The property boasted a magnificent view – a vast panorama of rolling purple-green hills stretching for miles. Thoughts rushed through my mind: two English agents whose presence was known to the invaders but who had so far been undetected, their bravery, the isolation, the history, the abundance of birds and other wildlife, tragedy swirling around me ...

It was in August when the security of the château was compromised. St Amour had become even more dangerous. No one will ever know how the Germans discovered that the château was home to the two British agents; maybe someone talked, but in any event Diana and Young were warned, and by the time the Germans arrived they had flown. Unfortunately, M. Bouvard, the caretaker who had sheltered them as he had harboured John Starr, was arrested. He was to die in captivity.

John Young went straight to the sawmill at Clairvaux-le-lacs, where he hid out at the home of Raoul Janier-Dubry, head of the local resistance. By now Young wanted to return to England and had sent messages to this effect. He eagerly awaited a new operator. Diana went to the Val d'Epy, a tiny hamlet folded quietly in the rolling hills between Clairvaux and Lons-le-Saunier. A *résistant* friend of hers who owned an *epicurie*, Marie Raithouze, offered to put her up in her apartment above the shop. She let it be known that her cousin Marcelle who had been ill was staying with her to recover from an operation: 'She needs the good country air, *pouvre fille*.' Little did they know that Diana was as strong and tireless as anybody working in the Jura.

The grateful Diana wanted to help in the café and served some of the customers herself, although Madame Raithouze could see she was not used to such work. She spoke to author Elizabeth Nicholas of *Paulette* being gentle and brave and pleasant always: 'She helped me serve in the shop, *enfin,* one could see she was not used to such things. I could see she was refined and well educated, and she said working in the shop would prevent her from feeling bored.' It seems improbable that thoughts of boredom would have struck Diana at this time, as the countryside was in an uproar with Germans everywhere.

She stayed three weeks with Madame Raithouze. Whilst there the Germans came to search for her, but she had received advanced warning and had been hidden elsewhere, probably with one of the other Resistance families in the area. They questioned Madame Raithouze about an Englishwoman whom they believed to be concealed somewhere in the neighbourhood, and she replied she had never heard of such an individual: 'I swore that, on the head of my child; I knew that God would understand and forgive me.'

Madame Raithouze gave Elizabeth Nicholas a little scarf to hold, patterned with flowers.:

> That belonged to *Paulette*. She gave it to me when she left, so that I would remember her. *Pauvre fille*, in winter when it is cold in bed I wear it around my neck, and put my face in its folds. I wish it were possible to give back to her the warmth it gives me.

During this time the Germans, searching everywhere and determined to catch up with the two British agents known to be living in the area of the Jura, made a series of arrests. Diana laid low at Epy. Having changed her name and the way she was dressed as well as dyeing her hair to a bright shade of blond, she thought she had a reasonable chance of remaining at large. Madame Benoit Gonin, who was working with the Resistance and who happened to be a hairdresser, arranged to meet Diana and told her it would be a good idea to change the colour and style of her hair. Madame Gonin was also a friend of Monsieur and Madame Janier-Dubry, who owned the sawmill just outside the village of Clairvaux-le-lacs on the Rue Lons-le-Saunier and where John Young was sheltering. A short time after she had changed Diana's hair colour, Madame Gonin was visited by the Germans. They may have suspected her connections to the Resistance – to this day nobody really knows – but on that day the shop was full of waiting women and she was busy with a client.

Madame knew what the Germans wanted: where were the English spies? She left her client under the hairdryer and climbed up to the first floor, opened the door to the apartment and walked into the kitchen, the Germans following her. 'Sit down,' she said. Little did the Germans know that this apartment did not actually belong to her and her rooms were on the floor above. The room into which she had brought the Germans actually housed a Jewish man, and M. Gonin had been secretly hiding him, most of the time in a wardrobe![13] This brave and audacious move in the face of danger worked well. She offered the Germans a drink, which they declined; after they were soon satisfied that Diana was not hiding in the establishment, they went away.

One day following the incident one of the Resistance men came into the bistro and talked quietly with Marie Raithouze and Diana. He asked if it was possible for Diana to deliver a message for him in Lons. Because of her change in appearance she thought it would be safe to do this, but Madame Raithouze was apprehensive and warned Diana to be very careful. She was worried about Diana's English appearance, athough she was now a different woman from the *Paulette* of a few months ago. But typically Diana told her it would not take too long to bike into Lons; she was not afraid. 'I will be careful, *bien sur.*'

Diana biked to Lons-le-Saunier, a distance of several kilometres but not too far from Epy. It was dangerous because the Gestapo had their headquarters right in the middle of the town opposite the railway station. All went well and she reached Lons without any trouble, but little did she know the Gestapo were carrying out random checks in the area that day and were pulling people off the streets. She discovered this when she was parking her bike in the square. However, she had been trained for an event such as this. She knew she could not retreat so she remained calm. Diana was unlucky. The Germans quickly rounded up a group of people, of which she was one, and took them to Gestapo Headquarters. She was questioned and taken into a small room where her papers were checked. Her passport was still in the name of Juliette Rondeau.

What was she doing in Lons? How long had she been living in Epy?

She answered their questions politely. She was here to do some shopping for her aunt, who was very busy in the bistro. 'There was no one else to do it, M'sieur. I have been sick and I have had to cycle this distance slowly. My aunt will be wondering where I am ... she is expecting me back soon with the vegetables for our supper, you understand. She will worry. I have to help her as she has no one else and we have customers.'

The Germans could not fault her. They looked at the quietly spoken, fair woman with the blue eyes. 'We know resistance is very strong in this area and we know they have many helpers. How do we know you are not one of them?'

Diana looked at him with her level gaze. 'Oh M'sieur, I am not well enough to run around for the Resistance. I have not the energy ... just getting to this town has made me very tired.'

'Let's go through your story again, shall we, Mademoiselle?'

Diana sighed and rubbed her eyes.

'*Votre nom?*'

'Juliette Therese Rondeau.'

'*Date de naissance?*'

'*Je suis né le 31 Janvier de 1915.*'

'Where were you born?'

'Caen.'

The questions went on and she answered each: 'My parents are both dead, my father's name was Clement and my mother's Christine Martin. I went to school in Paris at the Sacre Coeur until 1932. Because we were poor I looked for work and tried to earn a little money as my mother was in poor health. I worked in the sales department of the *Printemps* in Paris and took up dress designing and hat modelling until 1936. In my spare time I studied Italian, Spanish and English and I taught those languages in order to save money for travel. In 1935 my mother died but she left me some money to fulfil my dreams of travelling. I visited Italy and the south of France.'

The Gestapo officer looked at her closely. 'We will give you the benefit of the doubt this time. However, because you were with that rabble over there' – and he pointed to the group of people who had been near her when they had been arrested – 'just to be sure we're going to keep you here overnight. Now, if you've been a good girl you've got nothing to worry about, have you?'

He pressed a buzzer on his desk and a German *Unteroffizier* came in, and saluted. Her interrogator spoke in rapid German.

'Keep an eye on this one, would you. She hasn't been cleared yet. Put her in Cell no. 17. If nothing else, that will teach her a lesson.'

Diana spent a cold night with little to eat. In an attempt to break her story, she was brought out and questioned once again, but she stuck to her account, remembering all she had been taught. She was very careful not to antagonise her interrogators, repeating her story politely but firmly. They could not shake her. Her slightly foreign French was not commented on by those whose French was less than perfect. In the end the Germans must have thought her to be exactly as she was – a pale, tired young woman recovering from an illness, shopping for her aunt, one of the crowd in the market square. They never realised that they had in their grasp the *Paulette* of the Resistance, and she was not passed on to more skilled interrogators. The following morning she was released unhurt but shaken.[14]

It is probable that Diana may have been followed on the way home from Lons, but again knowing how to detect a 'tail' would have successfully given them the slip. However, her arrest had badly frightened her, and she knew the chances of being caught again were too strong. There was no option but to leave the little hamlet of Epy and go to ground. And the place for that would be the Janier-Dubry sawmill at Clairvaux-le-lacs.

In mid-September Harry Rée returned to the Jura. Christiane Janier-Dubry spoke of the time he appeared in the area again under cover and met up with Diana. Christiane, a child at the time, always remembers Diana running out to greet him. 'Oh Harry,' she cried. 'Oh Harry!'[15] She was so pleased to see him. They discussed what was happening in the area. Over seventy people had been arrested, some of whom had belonged to the Abbe Schwander-Fouillette organisation in the Jura. Some had worked with Rée, others had been overlooked unaccountably. Some close friends of Rée's, the Gruets, in whose home he had waited for news of the attempt on Rommel's train, had been arrested. As usual, Rée warned Diana to be very careful.

In the weeks leading up to November John Young had received a signal from Baker Street announcing the imminent dispatch of another SOE officer and requesting the arrangement of a dropping zone (DZ) and reception. Rée had managed to warn London of the dangerous situation, and the drop did not materialise. Also there was no sign yet of the arrival of the agent. During the following weeks Young kept asking London to send more officers to the Jura network. While he had been in Switzerland Rée also had sent a number of messages through the British Legation asking for replacements.

But it was not until mid-November that London notified Young an SOE officer would be arriving in Clairvaux. Because of the precarious situation in the Jura, it was decided in London that the agent should be dropped not to one of the usual Jura grounds but elsewhere, and a similar signal was sent to a radio post originally established in the Sologne, south of Orléans.

However, the Germans had become increasingly confident at impersonating SOE agents in the field, and it was at the Avenue Foch in Paris, where Diana's old boss John Starr was now a prisoner, that *Obersturmbannführer* Hans Josef Kieffer decided to use this method to bring down the network in the Jura.

8

Betrayal

There can be no closer bond than that between the hider and the hidden. A British agent daily placed his life in the hands of local Frenchmen and their families whom he had never met before. Meanwhile, they harboured him in the knowledge that if their hospitality was ever revealed, conceivably by himself as a prisoner under torture, their lives and all that they owned would be forfeit.

- George Hiller

In early November 1943, while keeping a low profile and assisting Eric Cauchi, Diana and Young continued to arrange reception of arms. Then the Château d'Andelot cover was blown; no longer safe, Young and Diana left it for good. Young went straight to the sawmill at Clarvaux-le-lacs.

'*Gabriel* was first to arrive at Clairvaux,' says Christiane Voha:

He came before Diana. It was market day. My mother was pregnant with my brother at the time. This is what my father told me: 'In the market he had met his friend Paul Guyot, a *résistant* already in the SOE. Guyot told my father to go with him as he had something to show him, but my father replied that he didn't have the time. 'But you must come,' said Guyot, so my father accompanied his friend and that was the first time he met the radio operator, *Gabriel*. Guyot told my father that he must take him to his family and hide him and not to tell anybody. It is very possible that the Vichy *Milice* were in the market. They were always around poking their noses into things. For my father, it was a dangerous thing to do because he had two small children. So in order to avoid the *Milice* they took an alternative route home, going through the fields rather than the main road just in case they were seen by the Germans. As soon as they returned my father took him to my grandmother and she found a suitable place to hide him.

A short time later Diana, now known in the Resistance as *Marcelle,* joined Young at the sawmill factory belonging to the Janier-Dubry family, their final hideout. The family let it be known that their cousin Marcelle had come to recuperate in the country from a serious illness, a precaution still necessary even though this area was outwardly *résistant.* At first Diana laid low, leaving the house only to walk in the woods. 'She was happy here with us,' says Christiane. Her strongest memory is of Diana spending time with her and her sister, and helping her mother, Aimee:

> One day we were playing in the sawdust on the factory floor after the workers had left for the day, and my mother called for us to come to dinner. Diana picked us up and as I looked back, her beautiful black shoes had left footprints in the sawdust. I can see them to this day. I wish I could remember more but as I was only four at the time, it is not possible. Everything else has been told to us by our parents.

'She was always with us children to help our mother,' says Claude. 'I remember how lovely she was. She helped to care for us, taking us for walks. We loved her and we will never forget her.'

Very often Diana travelled in Raoul's green Samson car, a safe way of getting around as he was supplying wood and logs to the Germans. In return he asked the Germans for petrol so the family had all they needed. She loved to walk in the woods. She would smoke her favourite English cigarettes, but would be careful not to leave any trace. She would slip out often and walk for hours, sometimes in the company of Young. She was safe there, for the forest was thick. 'It was the only distraction they had,' says Christiane. 'There was always the thought too that if the *Boches* ever came for them they would have a few second's warning, and would be able to slip out of the house and down into the forest. But when it happened they had no opportunity.'

Meanwhile, back in England, in mid-November Baker Street finally notified Young that an SOE officer had been sent to France and would be arriving at Clairvaux-le-lacs. However, as mentioned, because of the precarious situation in the Jura, London had decided at the last moment that the agent should be dropped elsewhere and not to any grounds in the Jura. A signal was therefore sent to a radio post originally established in the Sologne, south of Orléans. Unknown to London, this radio post, known by the codename *Bertrand,* had been infiltrated by the Germans. Baker Street had no idea that an SOE officer, a Canadian named Frank Pickersgill, had been captured and that his radio was being used for receiving and conveying fake messages to London.[1] When *Obersturmbannführer* Kieffer saw the reports from the SD Dijon about Harry Rée's network in the Jura, he decided to use a similar method, using a captured British radio.

And so the Germans knew that an SOE agent was about to be dropped into Clairvaux. The agent's name was Andre Maugenet, a Frenchman who had escaped to England and been trained by SOE. When Young and Diana heard the signals from London informing them that the new radio operator would soon be on his way, they were thrilled – they thought he would be bringing with him messages from their families and probably important instructions pertaining to the imminent invasion.

The night of 15/16 November 1943 was cold with a bitter wind. A Hudson (a twin-engined RAF aircraft used to deliver and pick-up SOE personnel) piloted by Wing Commander Bob Hodges landed in the airfield north of Angers, the same one which had been used for numerous SOE operations. Five SOE men landed; ten were to be taken back to London. The arrivals were Victor Gerson, on his third mission as organiser of the 'VIC' escape line; Edward Levine, on his second trip to France to join the *Donkeyman* circuit; Jean Menesson, a young schoolmaster at the *Lycée Française* in Kensington, London; Paul Pardi, on his way to join Claude de Baissac, a thirty-five-year-old Mauritian, once described by Buckmaster as 'the most difficult of all my officers without any exception', and who was in charge of the *Scientist* circuit in the crucial Bordeaux area; and Andre Maugenet, code named *Benoit.*

Among those who were returning to England were Francis Cammaerts, *chef du réseaux* of the *Jockey* circuit; Denis Barrett, who had been dropped with agent Ben Cowburn near Argenton-sur-Creuse in April; Pierre Mulsant, who had been deputy for Cowburn at Troyes; and Charles Rechenmann of Tarbes.

All of the agents who had just landed were not to know that Henri Dericourt, the air operations man for France, had alerted the Gestapo, who were watching the passengers descend down the ladder and run to the safety of the trees surrounding the airfield. Dericourt greeted them, shook their hands and told the returning passengers to climb into the plane. These men had no idea that Hans Josef Kieffer of the Paris Gestapo was aware of their arrival and was going to allow some of them men to escape and others to be arrested.

The agents who had landed were allowed to disperse but were tailed by SD men and their V-men, informers for the Gestapo. Victor Gerson gave them the slip and disappeared, as did Edward Levene but he was eventually arrested in a Paris hotel. The three others, Jean Mennesson, Paul Pardi and Andre Maugenet were arrested on arrival at the Gare Montparnasse.

In discussions after the war about the events of that evening in November with author Jean Overton-Fuller, Dericourt admitted to betraying only four people, these three men and a Colonel Bonoteaux. His eyes had filled with tears as he said, 'You must think I am a monster. I am no monster.'[2] An ugly story was put around that the Germans had paid Dericourt four million francs for information about this pick-up on 16 November. Wing Commander Hugh Verity thought this sum was rather more than was needed for a chicken farm in Provence that he was trying to buy.[3]

All three men were taken immediately to the Paris *Sicherheitsdienst* headquarters of *Obersturmbannführer* Kieffer at the Avenue Foch.[4] Andre Maugenet was immediately interrogated. Initially he tried to brazen it out, but it was no use. His interrogators knew everything about his mission. No one will ever know for certain whether Maugenet gave way under interrogation or whether he endured brutal torture rather than betray his comrades. Cookridge says that he was tortured and quickly gave way, handing over the letter written by Young's wife and in the process divulging all. According to Michael Foot, 'Put under pressure, Maugenet (*Benoit*) seems to have talked; certainly there were deplorable consequences to *Stockbroker*.

Mennesson, on his second tour, kept silent, so did Pardi.' Authors like Cookridge and Eizabeth Nicholas were unwilling to pronounce a harsh judgment upon a man who found himself in such a situation. However, Maugenet quickly decided to cooperate with the Germans.[5]

Whatever the case, after his interrogation at Avenue Foch, Maugenet, or a German agent, possibly a French collaborator (Cookridge says an English- speaking 'V'-man), now assumed his identity. The man put on Maugenet's *Canadienne*, a leather jacket with a fur collar issued by SOE, and took his imitation crocodile-skin suitcase containing his personal belongings, a large sum of money and his forged identity papers in the name of 'Raoul Benoit', as well as the letter from John Young's wife. The documents had been produced in the SOE forgeries laboratory and were studied with great care at the Avenue Foch office.[6]

The Germans had every reason to be pleased with their success in impersonating SOE officers. It had worked when *Sonderführer* Richard Christmann had duped the *Prosper* team, and when SS *Scharführer* Holdorf played the part of Bertrand in the trap laid for *Madeleine*, Noor Inayat Khan, as well as earlier when *Sonderführer* Heinz Echert impersonated a Canadian officer in Normandy.

When the Clairvaux-le-lacs Resistance, headed by Raoul Janier-Dubry, heard the BBC message 'The Mississippi is the longest river in the world', repeated twice, this was interpreted as a good sign that the new agent would be arriving at last. This was the message they had been waiting for.

On 16 November Janier-Dubry was in his *bureau* (office) at the factory when he saw a car stop outside. A man got out, an unexpected visitor, and walked straight into the office. He greeted Janier-Dubry then said, '*Je suis Benoit*,' and proceeded to produce a message, purportedly from London, written in code on cigarette paper and concealed in a matchbox. It was proof enough, and Janier-Dubry was pleased that the new agent had finally arrived. He asked for the password, but *Benoit* was somewhat evasive. Raoul did not worry unduly and told him that his brother-in-law Henri Poli was not there and would be out all day. Instead he called a worker to get his sister Ida, as she would surely know the correct password.

When Ida said to *Benoit*: '*Faites-vous toujours des caisses cloutées?*' Do you always make hobnailed cases, he should have answered correctly: '*Cela dépend du prix que vous y mettez.*' It depends on the price you put on it.

Instead, he said nothing. Fumbling in his pocket, he produced a letter. 'This is for *Gabriel*.'

Even though he had failed to give the correct password, Ida took the letter as evidence that everything was all right, so she took him upstairs to where she lived with her husband and children. It was here that he met Diana and Young who, when he saw the letter, immediately recognised his wife's handwriting. Young told *Benoit* he had a problem with the SOE because three times he had asked for supplies: 'Everytime I ask for a dispatch of arms and explosives there is always a delay. They do not speak to us from London, they do nothing for me.'

'My father told me *Gabriel* was anxious all day,' says Christiane Voha, née Janier-Dubry. 'He seemed to have some doubts and paced the house, mentioning to my father that the new man from London knew very little of what was going on in London. His misgivings seemed to be directly related to the new agent *Benoit*, but in the end Young must have chosen to ignore them.'

At some time during the morning *Benoit* mentioned he had left his luggage at Lons and that it would be necessary to retrieve it. This seemed strange to both Young and Janier-Dubry. Why would he have to go back to Lons so soon, and why did he not bring the suitcase with him? However, as Janier-Dubry himself had to go into town to pick up his mother-in-law who had undergone an operation in the Lons hospital, everybody including Aimee, who was then seven months' pregnant with her third child, and the new agent piled into Raoul's car.

The two smaller children, Christiane, aged four, and Claude, aged around two, stayed at home in the care of a young Polish girl, Stanie, who was helping out in the household. She did not understand French and had no idea the family were *résistants*, so it was quite safe to have her working in the home. 'Stanie often looked after us,' says Christiane. 'She was very kind but had no idea how to do simple things like washing clothes and would wash the light and dark clothes together so the colours would run. This would annoy my mother as clothes were rationed during the war.'

Two days earlier Young had had a new photo taken in Lons for his *carte d'identité* and Diana wanted to pick this up. Also she had arranged to meet up with Henri Clerc; it would be here that she would introduce the new agent, *Benoit*. On the journey into Lons all went well and Diana and *Benoit* chatted together, *Benoit* explaining he would not stay in Clairvaux, instead preferring to stay in a hotel in Lons. As the car would be cramped on the way home from Lons, arrangements were made for Raoul, after having lunch at the Hotel de Strasbourg, to return with his mother-in-law and Diana and *Benoit* to stay in Lons and come back on the little *tacot* later.

Diana had arranged with Henri Clerc to meet up also for a drink at the Café Strasbourg, a meeting place and mail drop for the members of *Stockbroker* owned by the Mathys, who were also *résistants*. It was here that she introduced the new agent. Clerc admired her energy, her steady nerves as well as her poise and graciousness, and was not suspicious of *Benoit*. They talked amicably and *Benoit* asked how things were going in the region – were the Gestapo efficient? Then to Diana he said, 'Are you frightened?' 'No,' she answered. 'The Gestapo interpreter Schneider is on our side, and tips us off when any action is to be taken.'

Then they parted from Clerc, and Diana and *Benoit* took the *tacot* back to Clairvaux. It was getting dark as they made their way along the rue Le Saunier to the Janier-Dubry house. Diana walked rapidly, anxious to get back, but for some reason *Benoit* lagged behind. She had no reason to suspect anything was amiss and did not see the man whom she had been with all day, the man whom she had taken to meet other *résistants*, the man whom she trusted, flashing a torch behind him. She would have had no inclination that he was laying a trail for the Germans to follow. These men had been lying in wait for them to alight from the *tacot* and would no doubt have had a prearranged plan with *Benoit* to follow them all the way from Lons. Diana would have no inkling; no doubt her thoughts would have been full of the days ahead, the build-up to the invasion, and the imminent departure of John Young, who would soon be on his way home to England and who had become a dear friend.

They arrived home around 6.00 p.m. to find Young playing chess with Henri Poli. In the pretty, Swiss-style house of the Janier-Dubrys and the Juifs, who lived upstairs, all were busy, with Aimee and Edith preparing a big meal to welcome the new agent. Suddenly and without any warning the door was smashed open and German Field Police spilled into the room.

After visiting his mother in the house next door, Raoul was about to enter his own front door when he was pulled up short. Why were cars and people surrounding his house? What was a big crowd of *Geheime Feldpolizei* and SS doing at his place? He walked up to the door, perhaps thinking 'this cannot be happening'. All of a sudden with a sickening jar he felt a gun thrust into his back, the metal hitting against one of his ribs. Then a voice said quietly in German: 'Just walk into the room ... very quiet now and slowly.'

'Fais pas le con!' Don't be stupid. He said this jokingly, then just as quickly said, *'Oh, pardon!'* Then the gun was jabbed into his neck as the voice said, 'Now turn around'. He was pushed roughly into the kitchen, where he saw members of his family standing against a wall, their faces etched with fear. Germans waved weapons about, shouting. Outside more Germans, believed to be Gestapo or SD, dressed in civilian clothes and good quality yellow leather shoes, had climbed into the Juif house, where Mr Juif, his son Henri, *Benoit, Gabriel,* and Diana were covered by German carbines.

Suddenly *Benoit* produced a gun. Shock registered on the faces of the Janier-Dubrys. What was the new agent doing brandishing a gun at them? By this time the *Milice,* those unscrupulous Frenchmen who had thrown in their lot with the Germans, who were known to be even more vicious than the Germans themselves, were surrounding the factory so nobody could escape. Everybody was paralysed with shock; it had all happened so quickly. There was no possibility of escape as now the house was totally encircled. Meanwhile the children of the house – including Gilbert, the four-year-old Juif boy – cowered under the kitchen table.

Then a frantic search began for the radio transmitter and the crystals. There were shouts, threats, firearms going off, some through the living room ceiling; it was indiscriminate firing, aimed at breaking the resolve of the inhabitants. The first place they looked was in a *portmanteau* in the sitting room. No luck. But they would never find what they were searching for: the radio transmitter was not even in the house, and the crystals had been hanging on a coat hook covered by raincoats. Edith Juif, standing near the coat stand, sidled over to it, felt behind her and quietly palmed them. As she did this she murmured to one of the Germans: 'I must cover my baby, he will be cold.' For some reason no one took any notice as she sneaked into the bedroom of her two-year-old son and put them under his mattress.

Gabriel suddenly switched off the light. Just as he did so, a gun went off. Immediately one of the Germans standing in the middle of the room covering Aimee cocked his pistol and fired into the ceiling; another let off a shot under the table where Gilbert was cowering in fear. The children screamed and ran to their mothers. Gilbert would always remember that night when the gun went off, nearly killing him, and he would proudly show visitors the mark in the floor in the years to come.

In their fury and frustration, the Germans ransacked the whole house. They started with the children's room, searching for the radio transmitter and the crystals. 'My aunt Edith kept saying to the Germans, *"Je ne sais pas, Je ne sais pas."* She said *je ne sais pas* to everything!' remembers Claude Janier-Duby. 'The Germans were firing their bullets wildly around the room and Edith's daughter was sobbing, *"ils vont te tuer, Maman, on va te tuer ..."* They will kill you, Maman. It was a nightmare. After a time they stopped threatening her and went into another room. The crystals were safe.'

Outside the house there was a great commotion so the Germans went to investigate. Raoul was left temporarily unattended and was leaning against the door that led into his bedroom. Very quietly he opened it. When the Germans came back into the room they didn't notice the open bedroom door. Aimee silently mouthed the words 'Run for it!' But Raoul did not want to leave the family, so she opened the window urging him to 'Hop it!' He needed no further encouragement and jumped – a drop of approximately three metres down on to the terrace – and ran towards the little wood opposite the house. Aimee heard shouting and more shots being discharged, and she thought the noise of his fall must have been heard. Her heart sank – they must have shot her husband. But Raoul was a fit and healthy young man and he could run fast; the shots missed their mark. As he ran he could hear his heart beating fast and shouts of 'Hold them up!'

It was at this same time that Henri Poli, married to Raoul's sister, Ida, arrived back at the house. He was amazed to see it surrounded by cars and armed Germans. He had no idea what had happened and ventured in German to one: 'Be careful, your car is on the rail of the *tacot*.' When the man answered in German Poli understood immediately what had happened. He did not run, just continued to walk away nonchalantly, as if he was innocent. Out of sight of the Germans he went straight to the sawmill, from where he followed Raoul's path into the woods.

From the Juif house Diana, *Gabriel*, Edith and Gaston Juif, the false *Benoit* and the Gestapo came into the kitchen. To add to the melee,

Ida Poli entered covered by a German brandishing a gun; followed also by a friend and fellow *résistant,* M. Claisse, who owned a café in Clairvaux near the local *église.* Claisse had sensed something was wrong at the Janier-Dubry house, and, speaking a little German, thought it was a good chance to see if he could be of some help. He pretended to be surprised when he came into the kitchen: '*Oh … Bitte,* I wanted to stay up with you Raoul, but I see you have guests so I will leave.' One of the Germans said: 'Sit down!'

As the Germans talked amongst themselves M. Claisee leaned forward, trying to hear what they were saying. While this was going on, Diana, who was standing against the kitchen wall, dropped *Gabriel's* photo into a wooden case nearby. When Raoul's mother came into the kitchen she had to hold on to a chair to prevent her falling over. She asked for a drink of water, saying, 'I am going to faint.'

By now people who were coming past the house were arrested immediately. They too were brought into the overcrowded kitchen, and one of them, M. Vincent, was very anxious because he was carrying some black market butter in his bag, which he was going to offer the Janier-Dubrys. This provided an unexpectedly comical situation. M. Vincent was immediately ordered to tip his bag upside down on to the table. '*Vide!* Empty!' M. Vincent was so nervous that he tipped the butter out and then put it back into his bag, and carried on doing it … in and out, in and out. The Germans also arrested M. Raymond Paget, a *résistant* and friend of the Janier-Dubrys who previously had sheltered *Gabriel* and Diana.

By now some of the German cars had driven away, while others remained in surveillance outside the house. Out of sight of the Germans one more guest arrived at the house, the *résistant* Jean Simon, who had come to celebrate the arrival of *Benoit* with a bottle of champagne. In the past he had always been careful when approaching the house, but in this instance, seeing the cars outside and hearing all the noise, he entered by way of the terrace then hid the champagne and his automatic in a pile of wood. Then he walked around to the back of the house and knocked on the window of the room where Raoul's grandmother slept. 'Open Aimee, it's me, Jean!' The window opened suddenly, and Aimee, who had gone into the room to check on her mother-in-law, said: 'Jean, go away, quickly! *Filez!*' Then she closed the shutters abruptly so that he had no chance to enter. He did not need a second warning so, like Raoul, Jean leapt over the balcony on to the sawdust below and, sliding down the steep ravine into the forest, ran towards the woods. No shouts followed him so for the moment he was safe. He successfully made his way to Clairvaux and warned his comrades, who immediately organised the removal of the radio set.

While all this had been going on Raoul also headed for the village of Clairvaux. However, hearing shouting as he approached, he ran on to Cogna, the next village. M. Courbet, a *résistant* friend lived there, but he found the Courbet house shut up. By now it was late, after 11.00 p.m., but after banging on the door for some minutes M. Courbet opened his door. Raoul was out of breath, but managed to gasp: 'Mon dieu – vite, vite, the Gestapo is at home. You must let the other *résistants* know. Raise the alarm quickly!'

M. Courbet was shaking so much he could not get his feet into his shoes, and when he finally did he could not tie his shoelaces properly. Raoul had to repeat his instructions three times. '*Mon dieu! Allez*! I cannot run any more. When I am better, I will follow you.'

Back at the Janier-Dubry house old M. Janier-Dubry had escaped to a neighbour as the Germans had forgotten about him for the moment; he was able to stay there for the rest of the night. By this time Aimee was in a state of shock. She remained in the kitchen, stirring a pot on the stove, and did not move from there. In the middle of the drama her youngest daughter, Claude, wanted to go to the toilet so took her potty into the middle of the room, sat on it and used it as she had always done. For the rest of her life Ida Poli would always have the memory of Claude sitting on the chamber pot in the midst of devastation and tragedy.

The Germans roughly pushed everybody to the door: Ida, then M. Paget, *Gabriel*, Diana and Gaston Juif. Aimee Janier-Dubry begged them not to take M. Paget: 'Please don't take M'sieur Paget, he is innocent,' she said. But the Germans took no notice and pushed everybody into the cars outside; that is, all except Gaston Juif, who was standing on the balcony. He had turned around and muttered 'I must get a coat' and had gone back into the house. Then the car took off without him! Incredibly, at that precise moment the Germans had forgotten about him. M. Juif had had a very lucky escape.

'In the end it was all for nothing,' said Christiane. 'The *Boches* never even looked at *Gabriel's* raincoat. They left, saying, "We will be seeing you again."'

Some time after those who had been arrested and driven away to be interrogated at Lons-le-Saunier, Raoul, in the company of the local hairdresser and *résistant*, Suzanne Benoit-Gonin, returned to pick up the radio transmitter. The coast was clear and it was imperative to remove the device before the Germans returned. Across the road from the house was the local *gendarmerie*, and Raoul banged on the door. M. Daubigney, head of the *gendarmerie*, needed no persuasion in giving his gun to Raoul in case he needed it when entering the factory. Raoul was joined by M. Courbet, who by this time had managed to tie his shoelaces, and followed Raoul, Jean Simon and Gut Grancher, the chief of *Libre Jura*. Grancher, having hidden arms in the Pont de Poitte cemetery, in the next village to Clairvaux, wanted to return with men and arms and fight the Gestapo to save the two *Anglais*. But they were too late. Young and Diana had been taken away.

Two members of the Janier-Dubry family, Henri Poli and Gaston Juif, had been forgotten by the Gestapo. Whether they had been in hiding or simply overlooked was not known at this stage. When Poli learned his wife Ida had been taken, he was more determined than ever to get even with the Gestapo. By this time they were outside the Janier-Dubry house, and when Aimee heard their voices outside she was amazed. 'What are you doing? Are you mad? Go away, quickly. The Gestapo may come back any time.' Her caution was warranted because they did come – not that night but every day for over a week.

Raoul, Poli and Juif quickly removed the radio transmitter and Diana's valise with her papers and personal possessions, as well as *Gabriel*'s luggage that have been left behind. Then they went to *la clouterie,* the nail factory, woke everybody up and gave them the transmitter to hide. It was then they heard that Raymond Paget, the black marketeer, had been one of those arrested.

'Those German swine even took Diana's perfume ... they looked at her jewellery and said, "Oh, it's too cheap", but they took it anyway,' said Christiane Voha. 'They said everything they took was of no value. Huh ... a beautiful red stone in a setting of solid gold which she gave to my mother ... *Mon dieu*, thank goodness they didn't take it. Diana had said to my mother, "I give you this, Aimee. The Germans aren't going to have it." Maybe it was a premonition. Maybe Diana thought it could be the last time she would see my mother. Perhaps she was sad, I do not know, but I think maybe this is so.'

Diana had also left behind a cigarette holder, which was overlooked by the Germans, or perhaps they just didn't bother with it.[7]

It is thought by Christiane that Diana's papers may have included courier information for London. On subsequent visits to the house the Gestapo ransacked the rooms, taking personal belongings, perfume, jewellery, linen, etc. On each visit, stand-over tactics were employed, with ugly threats of imprisonment and deportation if the radio transmitter did not turn up. But each time they were met with the same answer: *'Je ne sais pas, je ne sais pas ou il est.'*

The day after the arrests the Germans, again in the company of the hated *Milice*, arrived early in the morning to burn down the factory and to kill old M. Janier-Dubry, Raoul's father. He remained calm and invited them in: 'Come in, come in. You have arrived just in time. We are drinking wine and eating *tarte*. Why don't you join us? I am old enough to be a dead man!'[8]

Maybe it was his forced calmness, the heroic welcoming gesture of an old man, but the factory was not burnt down. 'Perhaps the Germans drank too much wine, I do not know, but my grandfather was not taken,' says Christiane. But overriding the euphoria of Janier-Dubry senior's escape was always the sense of tragedy, the sadness of the arrests and the very real uncertainty as to whether his loved ones would return.

The transmitter and crystals and other arms were never found by the Germans, which surely saved the lives of the remaining Janier-Dubry family. Unknown to the Gestapo, they had been hidden in a bag buried deep in hay. Henri and Ida had a nanny goat for milk that fed on this hay, but in the earth nearby was a bag full of *plastique* that wasn't touched by the goat, and in this same bag was the radio transmitter; there were also grenades hidden in the factory but these too went undiscovered.

On their visits to the Janier-Dubry house the Germans continued to question Aimee as to the whereabouts of her husband. She would always answer in the negative, saying she never saw him as he had another woman. For days afterwards she was so traumatised by the arrests and the whole experience that she was unable to change out of her clothes. Not only was she fearful for the safety of her husband, her children and the rest of the family, but she knew that if he were found and arrested, Raoul would be taken to a concentration camp from which he would never return.

Henri Clerc, who was still in hiding, had not heard about the arrests but the day following the arrests a message purporting to be from Diana had been telephoned to his sister's house, asking him to meet Diana at the Café Montmorot. Clerc's sister had passed this message on, but some instinct made him uneasy. It was the curious sense of danger developed so often in clandestine work. However, he decided to go anyway, and in the company of his sister went to the rendezvous, exercising extreme caution. When he walked into the café the first people he saw were his friend and fellow *résistant*, Leon Mathy, flanked by two unmistakable Gestapo men. Not a flicker of recognition showed on Mathy's face as Clerc sat down, gave his order, drank it slowly, got up, paid and left. An hour later he was in the hills with the *Maquis*.

Elizabeth Nicholas questioned Clerc about that time in November when the arrests had taken place. She mentioned the Alsatian, Schneider, the Gestapo interpreter, whom Diana had referred to as the one who 'was on their side and tipped them off when any action was to be taken'; after the war, Schneider was given the *Légion d'honneur*. He remembered Diana and Gabriel and the November of 1943 very well. Schneider told Nicholas that he had had a drink with Diana on the day she was arrested. However he had that evening been summoned to Gestapo Headquarters and asked if he knew a Paulette; he had replied he knew many. The Germans said, 'the *Paulette* of the Resistance?' and he had replied, no, he did not know that *Paulette*. In fact, at the time the Gestapo must have known, through the false *Benoit*, that he had been playing a game with them.

Nicholas asked Clerc if he was sure Schneider was on their side and Clerc answered without hesitation: 'I owe it to him that my wife is alive today, and our child. It was he who got word to her after I had been forced into hiding that she too was about to be arrested. There can be no doubt where his allegiance lay.'

Whilst in hiding from the Germans, Raoul hoped that somehow the factory could be kept going, as his staff of around twenty workers needed the money to support their families. He had left money to pay their wages, but when the Germans looted the house they had stolen all the money – except for one thing, that is. Before the arrests they had taken the precaution of hiding some very good wine, which was not in the house. If the Germans did come Raoul knew they would without doubt take every bottle of wine they found.

Although the Germans were still looking for Janier-Dubry, some nights he even managed to continue work at the factory as there was much for him to do. He was not apprehended, and when the hue and cry had died down he managed a couple of visits to the house, especially when his son, Jean-Louis, was born two months after the arrests. In July 1944, when he knew the country would soon be liberated, he decided to go fishing in the hope there would be few remaining Germans in the area. However, the enemy had made a bridge over the river that was still heavily defended, but he thought he would risk it anyway. Just as he pulled up a trout, two Germans appeared. Very quickly he gave them the fish. They asked for his *carte d'identité*, studied it for a minute, and then thanked him for the fish, which in reality should have been thrown back as it was very small. He carried on fishing, thanking God for the reprieve. Raoul managed to stay hidden from the Germans until the war was over.

Ida Poli, who knew little of the clandestine involvements of her father, husband and brother-in-law, was kept in prison for the duration of the war.

The reactions of those left behind – the friends Diana had made for nearly five months – can only be imagined.

Lons-le-Saunier was liberated the same day as Paris, on 25 August 1944.

It was as a result of the treachery of the double agent, Pierre Martin, that Henri Clerc's father had also been arrested. Fortunately he survived his imprisonment, but his health was gravely impaired and he died a few years after the Liberation.

Yvonne Clerc also just managed to avoid being arrested:

One day I was approached by a German who made no secret of his intentions towards me, so I immediately hid with a friend. But the Germans then told my husband that if I did not go along with what they wanted they would take my daughter who at that time was in school. She was only three and a half years old. So my friend went to the school and told the teacher it was imperative she remove my daughter because the Germans were going to come for her. The teacher immediately handed the little girl over. It was not a moment too soon. Soon after the Germans arrived and told the teacher to hand over the Clerc child. The teacher replied she was not in school and she didn't know when she would be returning. They then questioned the children but they were wonderful; none of them told the Germans anything. They must have been very afraid, but they never mentioned that the little Clerc child had been at school that day.

If the child had been taken by the Germans, Henri Clerc would have done anything to save her.

Some questions remain: why didn't John Young act on his suspicions about the new agent? For example, there was the lingering suspicion as to why the false *Benoit* had to go back to Lons to collect his suitcase. Surely he would have brought it with him? And was it the true or the false Maugenet who came to the Janier-Dubry house? After the war, British authorities were reluctant to reveal the results of the investigation into the case, but the French authorities strove to catch up with Maugenet, who had spent the rest of the war as a 'guest' of his captors. In 1945 he disappeared. Nine years later his trail was taken up in Canada, and in 1955 the French government began extradition proceedings in Ottawa. By then he had disappeared again and was believed to have gone to South America. He was never traced.

According to Henri Clerc this is what happened:

He had stayed in touch closely with Diana, even when she was hiding out at the Janier-Dubry sawmill and had had a drink with her in Lons on the very day she was taken. The false *Benoit* had spent the evening before he went to meet Diana and Young with Clerc and Schneider, the Gestapo interpreter. Although Clerc was in hiding, *Benoit* had known how to get hold of him. The only explanation for this is that information would have had to be given to him by the true Maugenet, obviously under duress. It was strange that Clerc himself had not been arrested, but this may have been the result of poor police work by the Germans, or perhaps they thought he was more useful to them if left at liberty. For example, a known agent can be spotted he may be able to lead them to other unknown agents; but if he is arrested his colleagues disperse, and it must be assumed that another agent will take his place. The aim of a counter-espionage organisation is to leave known agents at liberty as long as possible so that they can be kept under observation and eventually Réeled in. By then Schneider knew he was living on borrowed time; his own position was severely compromised. Schneider and Clerc then speculated about the two *Benoits* – the false or the true. Clerc told Elizabeth Nicholas that 'it was not a pretty business. What Schneider did was no easy thing; evidently he had sometimes to stick a dagger into the heart of a comrade. He was an invaluable link in the chain, to safeguard it he had to sacrifice others. That is not pretty, nor is it easy.'

It is rumoured that it was the true *Benoit* who had that night dined with the Gestapo officers, and who had been seen drinking and laughing and singing with them. In 1958, Elizabeth Nicholas says that it was believed *Benoit* came from the Anti-Communist Bureau in Paris. But this was never proved. At the end of the war the people of Lons-le-Saunier had read in the papers that Maugenet, whom everybody believed was the true *Benoit,* was wanted for questioning by the French authorities. However, when Eric Cauchi produced a photograph sent from London of the true *Benoit*, Clerc then realised that he was not the man he had spoken to that day in Lons.

According to Foot there is even an ugly rumour that Maugenet did not need to be impersonated, as he did the job himself. Nothing in his file confirms this. Possibly this is the incident the double agent Roger Bardet referred to in a confession he made as to his work as an *Abwehr* agent. In it he says that the *Abwehr* had loaned him to the SD in order to facilitate the penetration of an unnamed resistance organisation by impersonating an agent newly arrived from England.[9] A difficulty of linking the loaning of Bardet with the betrayal of Young and Diana is that Bardet was barely half Maugenet's age and unlike him in appearance; but the letter from Mrs Young would have been introduction enough.

There is some debate over all this. The most likely explanation is that Andre Maugenet died in Gross-Rosen Concentration Camp in Poland. His name is on the Valencay Memorial and the Gross-Rosen plaque. There is a book published in Polish by the Gross-Rosen museum that includes his photo. No actual date or cause of death is given but it was probably around September 1944. Of the other 20 SOE agents nearly all were executed, so the same may have happened to Andre Maugenet. But there is no definite evidence of his actual demise – this is the best-guess scenario based on available evidence.

Inside the Avenue Foch

Courage in battle is at least helped by the presence of others, and perhaps by the fear of shaming oneself in front of them, or it may be summoned by the sight of a comrade in need of rescue, but Resistance men and women were for much of the time alone with their fears, often in the hands of their perverted enemies. That is when character is most severely tested, and we who have not experienced it can only imagine how great the strain can be.

- R. V. Jones

Poor youth: how quickly it passes.

- Old Greek saying

After hearing of the Clairvaux raid Harry Rée reported to London the capture of Diana and Young through his Berne Legation link. He himself was now in grave danger. Mass arrests occurred throughout the Franche-Comté with the rounding up of members of the Resistance. Rée was continually on the run, moving from place to place almost every night.

Diana and Young were driven to Gestapo Headquarters at Lons-le-Saunier, and once inside were immediately interrogated. It is noted that considerable pressure was put on Young as the clandestine radio operator for the region to disclose the whereabouts of his radio set. The Germans were anxious to get hold of this as they would be able to play more of the 'radio games' that had already taken place in Paris and in Holland. Young was tortured to reveal the whereabouts of his radio but refused to divulge any information. In a cell close by Diana could hear his screams. She was questioned closely and answered politely but firmly that she had nothing to say. As far as can be ascertained, she was not tortured. After one night at Lons they were transferred to 84 Avenue Foch in Paris the next day.

The Avenue Foch is a broad avenue in one of the best parts of Paris, lined with chestnut and plane trees and beautiful ornate buildings. The *Sicherheitsdienst* had requisitioned Nos 72, 82 and 84; No. 84 was one of three houses acquired in the grand residential boulevard connecting to the Arc de Triomphe. The Germans used it for various operations, including counter-intelligence and the orchestration of the 'wireless game' they played with SOE. It is one of a few places in Paris synonymous with the secret police.

Some of the serving officers in the SD at this time were Helmut Knochen, the *Befehlshaber der Sicherheitspolizei* (Head of the Sipo) in Paris for most of the war; Karl Boemelburg, head of counter-espionage section IV, a tall, elderly, heavy-drinking homosexual, supposedly friendly with Henri Dericourt, his subordinate; Hans Josef Kieffer, a former police inspector at Karlsruhe, the only man connected with the repression of SOE in France who had had much relevant pre-war experience; and Josef Goetz, a former teacher who handled IVF, Kieffer's wireless sub-section, with a considerable degree of skill. These men served as the main German interrogators in the Avenue Foch. Kieffer would deal with the SOE agents from the Jura.

On arrival Diana and Young, handcuffed together, were shuffled out of the police van and bundled into the building before being taken upstairs to be interrogated. As they were taken into an office, Diana was shocked to see her former boss, John Starr, apparently walking around free.

Young was put in a cell with Starr for one night and told him they had been expecting a new agent, *Benoit*, to join them, and that the man who came, 'identifying' himself by handing over a letter from Young's wife back in England, later came back with the Gestapo to arrest them.

John Starr saw Young and Diana brought in. The Germans said to Young as they passed him: 'Here's your old chief!' They were obviously shocked, but it was not until Young was put into Starr's cell that he was able to hear what had happened. Starr saw Diana only briefly in the Avenue Foch but he saw much of John Young. This very unusual procedure – two recently arrested SOE men from the same circuit sharing the same cell because of shortage of space – seemed to Young most significant and sinister. There could be only one explanation, a bug. Both Young and Starr thought the situation dangerous. Of course it was very tempting to talk but knowing there was probably a concealed microphone somewhere in the room, they hardly dared say a word.

After he had been arrested Starr had been asked by Kieffer to fill in the F Section circuits on a map of France. Initially he did not agree to do this, but after talking it over with his cell mates they all agreed it might be an opportunity to learn things that could prove useful to Baker Street if he were able to escape and make his way back to London. Starr agreed and was established in a small room at 84 Avenue Foch. By day he worked at his drawings and lettering, where he saw and was seen by many of the captured agents who were brought there. During his time there he came into contact with a British officer who often sat reading a book and listened to music on a radio – someone obviously at ease in these surroundings. This was Gilbert Norman, code named *Archambaud*. It was Norman who had told Starr he had learned that not only had the Germans been able to make copies of the messages in transit between France and London, but they were also operating the radio sets of some of the captured wireless operators. However, the worst Starr learned was that London was continuing to answer the incoming messages, which of course fell straight into the hands of the SD.[1]

According to Starr, Norman's purpose in accepting the position at Avenue Foch was to collect intelligence to bring to London in the event he managed to escape – especially the information that the Germans were working the radios of captured British agents. To Starr this was a strange situation, but to Norman's credit he did make an attempt to escape with this knowledge, together with Noor Inayat Khan and Colonel Leon Faye, only to be brought down by his and Faye's reluctance to abandon Noor when they were trapped on the roof of the Avenue Foch (their attempt to jump to freedom was interrupted by the unfortunate timing of an air raid; guards below threatened to shoot and they were immediately returned to their cells; Starr had then given his word of honour not to escape again).

Young told Starr how he had been arrested and about the man who had been sent out from London as a replacement, code named *Benoit*, who was obviously in the pay of the Gestapo and who had tried to make him reveal where he had left his radio transmitter. He showed Starr his backside, which was all the colours of the rainbow, and said he had been beaten savagely with a belt. He had suffered so much he had been afraid that if they began again the next day he would break down and tell them where his radio set was.[2]

Resistance members and SOE were pragmatic about the odds of an agent surviving torture without revealing something. Unlike in Hollywood movies, where the hero unflinchingly endures pain at the hands of his enemies without uttering a word, in the real world of espionage few were able to hold their tongues forever. No one could predict if they would break under torture, but most would, if not completely then partially. For many the immediate consequences for their comrades would not be huge.

Agent 'Tommy' Yeo-Thomas, 'the White Rabbit', said the first fifteen minutes of torture were the worst; but he added that if an agent could manage to get through the first five minutes, he had it made. The most terrible torture always happened at the beginning of proceedings, but after three days even that became easier to bear: 'The body seemed to become accustomed to it.'

Others said they recited poems to themselves, lines they had learned years before in school, Shakespeare's sonnets or verses from the Bible, or counted up to one hundred and then started again. Prospective agents were aware of all this before they embarked. And they *were* afraid. Brave men were always afraid, otherwise they tended to do foolish things, taking unnecessary risks that endangered not only their own lives, but also the lives of others.[3]

After that night in the cell Young was taken for interrogation. During that same morning according to Starr, he was taken down to the head of the wireless section at No. 84, Josef Goetz, a tall man with glasses. Goetz had been a schoolteacher in Hamburg who had been selected for the *Sicherheitsdienst* because of his ability with languages. He greeted Starr with: 'Well, were you pleased to see your friend?'

'Not in this place.'

'I expect you had a good talk.'

'No, it wasn't intresting for us.'

'What? Didn't you want to know what he's done with the radio set? It's your responsibility, as his chief.'

'I didn't ask him, and he didn't tell me. Do you really believe that we should be foolish enough to fall for a trap like that?'[4]

Young never revealed where the radio set was and Starr is sure he never gave the Germans any information at all.[5]

The following night Young was moved and was put into the next cell to Starr. Eventually, Starr felt they were no longer under surveillance and tapped through the wall in Morse, telling Young that an escape involving him and Noor Inayat Khan, as well as Colonel Faye, was being planned, and that he could have a screwdriver with which he could use to get out his own bars if he wanted to come too. Incredibly, Young replied that he had given his word of honour to Ernst Vogt, a part-Swiss former bank clerk and 'now Kieffer's interrogator and interpreter, who spoke both English and French, not to attempt to escape.

After 19 November Vogt lost sight of his prisoners.[6]

It has been noted in several books that Diana was tortured to reveal information, most probably about the whereabouts of the radio transmitter, her friends in the Resistance, and other intelligence. It is also on record, though unsubstantiated, that she said nothing. She answered the questions politely but firmly; she had nothing to say.

She was ushered into Kieffer's office, where he sat writing at his desk. He waved her to a seat in front of him. Light streamed in through the window and she could dimly hear the sound of traffic passing somewhere in the street below them. For a few moments Kieffer carried on writing. Then he looked up and appeared to be studying her. 'Ah ... you are *Paulette* of the Resistance,' he said in not particularly good English. Diana said nothing. Then he got up and offered her a cigarette.

'No, thank you.'

'Do you smoke, Mademoiselle?'

'Oui, but no thank you, M'sieur.'

'Well, we will get down to business then. I will get straight to the point. We know all about you and your organisation in the Jura. After all, as you have seen we have your boss here. I hope you will be sensible and cooperate as your friends have done. Tell me ... your boss, Major Buckmaster. Did he interview you in the Hotel Victoria in Northumberland Avenue in London or was it in Baker Street itself?'

Diana looked up at him. 'I have nothing to say.'

'Did you go to Arisaig in the Scottish Highlands before your final school at Beaulieu? Or perhaps it was one of the other country schools? The House in the Woods, perhaps, even Boarmans? Oh, by the way, is Parks the butler still at Orchard Court? You see, it is foolish to be stubborn. We know everything.'

She tried not to show surprise. They indeed knew a lot. She smiled politely. 'If that is so, then you don't need any help from me, do you, Major?'

'Oh come, come my dear. As you can see we know a lot about your SOE. But there are still some things we need answers to. I hope you will help us.'

Diana drew a deep breath. '*Je regrette*, but as I have already said, I cannot possibly help you.'

Kieffer drew on his cigarette and looked at the patently English girl in front of him. He wondered why she had been sent to France with her too obvious English looks, but there was courage and determination in those blue eyes. She would be difficult to break.

'We know everything about your circuit in the Jura but want to establish one or two points which have puzzled us. Did you know there is a double agent working for us in that area?'

Her hand tightened on the side of the chair. '*Je ne sais pas.*'

'All right, but I want you to think about this. We need to know the whereabouts of the radio at Clairvaux. If you tell us where it is we will make your time here much more pleasant. Your friends in this building have already cooperated with us and consequently are enjoying certain privileges as a result.'

'I have nothing to say.'

Kieffer pressed a buzzer on his desk and spoke in rapid German.

'Take her back to her cell immediately.'

'That will be all for now, Mam'selle. We will be seeing each other again. I ask you to think over carefully what I have said.'

Diana was escorted out and returned to her cell forthwith. This was to form the pattern of many meetings with Kieffer, but he was unable to break her. I would think from all I have heard from the people who knew her, trained with her and worked with her, that this would be in keeping with her character. As Diana said several times: 'I do not think I will talk. They can do what they want.' Also, no further arrests were made in Clairvaux, suggesting that neither she nor John Young talked during interrogation.

When the Germans realised they would get nothing out of her, she was transferred to the civilian prison at Fresnes, near Paris, on 5 December 1943. While she had been at the Avenue Foch she had inscribed her name and number on the walls of the prison cell, discovered by the Allies in 1944 after they liberated the city.

During training agents had been told to expect the worst at the hands of their German captors. They were told to try to withhold names and addresses for about forty-eight hours to enable meetings to be cancelled and contacts to flee. There was also the 'L' pill, which may or may not be on their person at the time of their arrest, but could be used if the owner so wished. 'In reality this advice was poor,' says historian Nigel West:

The Germans were extraordinarily well informed about almost everything to do with F Section and the SD interrogators at 84–86 Avenue Foch and their Gestapo counterparts at 11 Rue Saussaies exploited the fear and expectation of torture quite subtly; in fact some of the key figures of the German side, such as the resourceful Hugo Bleicher of the *Abwehr* or Ernst Vogt were never accused of having maltreated any of their prisoners. In most cases physical abuse was not necessary to obtain cooperation, and John Starr, who was present for much of the time, testified after the war that he was not aware of any prisoners having been manhandled in the Avenue Foch while he was resident there, but the fear of it was often very strong in prisoners who had just been brought in. Sometimes they had had bad experiences in the provincial headquarters where they underwent their first interrogations. This had led them to expect still worse things when they came up to the Avenue Foch. All the windows on the top floor were fastened after Pierre Brossolette, an RF Section Agent, had jumped out of one of these windows.[7]

After the war a report dated 9 October 1943 was found when British officials were given access to Avenue Foch. This report reached the desk of Vera Atkins, who at the time was struggling to find out the whereabouts of her lost agents. An intelligence officer in Paris reported:

I had visited the torture chamber at Avenue Foch where inter alia Kieffer had an office. I found a moving inscription from men and women who knew they had lost everything, except their honour.

Names underneath are those present in the cells. Their ultimate fate is unknown to me but I was informed during the last few days before the departure of the Germans that several people had been taken downstairs into the courtyard, placed aginst the wall and shot.

The officer then gave a list of names he had found, which included S/O D. H. Rowden, 4193 WAAF OFF. 22.11.43, 5.12.43 and A/S/O Nora Baker.[8] He added, 'The dates are, I understand, those of the arrival and departure of the various people at Avenue Foch.'

The only prisoner with whom Starr was ever alone was John Young, on two occasions. The first was when Young had just been brought in and was put in Starr's cell for the night. As has already been noted, they had hardly said a word to each other. The second occasion was at Christmas when Kieffer had brought them in a tray with whisky and gin, had joined them for a drink and wished them the compliments of the season, then left. As before, Starr and Young were very careful what they said to each other. As Jean Overton-Fuller comments:

Kieffer was in a way quite friendly to Starr. On Sunday mornings he would come round to each of the prisoners' cells in turn, open the door and give biscuits, chocolate and cigarettes to the inmates, exchanging a few words. The food was excellent since the prisoners had the same as the Germans.[9]

Captured agents were usually offered a 50 per cent chance of life if they talked, and such bargains were sometimes kept. 'The broad truth about spies of all nationalities who fell into enemy hands was that they were kept alive as long as they could serve a purpose, and shot when their usefulness expired,' says Max Hastings:

The emotive word 'murdered' is often used by post-war writers when mentioning SOE agents, especially women, killed by the Germans. In truth, all of them knew that if taken death would almost certainly be their fate, legitimised by the laws of war. Every captured agent who wanted to live struggled with the decision as to how much he or she might reveal without becoming a traitor, and some misjudged the answer. (*Secret War*)

Half a century later, Francis Cammaerts, the leader of the *Jockey* circuit, looked back at these events: 'Those who tried to play games with the Germans were bound to lose. We were amateurs, they were professionals, and there was no hope of outsmarting them. They were skilful manipulators of information and made it appear they knew more than they did.' As for 'the parole nonsense', the reluctance to break a promise given under such circumstances, it was, he thinks, 'unspeakably stupid':

> It is a myth that Allied agents and Resistance workers who fell into German hands seldom talked. Almost every prisoner of any nationality gave away a little or much, with or without undergoing torture. The Gestapo employed Latvian, Dutch and indeed French collaborators to conduct the torture of prisoners, while German officers asked the questions.[10]

After the war Ernst Vogt, whom Jean Overton-Fuller had managed to track down, told her that as soon as he saw the file on Starr sent up from Dijon, he realised the interrogators had wasted five weeks while he spun them a fairy story about how he was an independent who had nothing to do with SOE at all; that even at Avenue Foch he gave nothing away. Starr was eventually transferred to a concentration camp, where he managed to survive the war. However, many captured agents who passed through Avenue Foch questioned his loyalty. When he returned to England after the war, Vera Atkins was cool to him and an investigation was launched into his exact relationship with the Germans. However, no charges were laid and he lived the rest of his life in France with his wife and children.

Vogt backed this up by telling Jean Overton-Fuller:

> Bob denounced no one, and no one was arrested following his arrest. He was one of the rare officers of the French Section whose arrest had no unpleasant consequences for his colleagues or for other agents of the French Section. Not a single paper, not a single address, was found on Bob permitting the German police to make an arrest.[11]

One wonders if the word of a Gestapo officer after the war is over can be taken as gospel.

Fresnes Prison, known to the French as the *maison de correction de Fresnes,* located some ten miles or so from the heart of Paris, was the biggest criminal prison in Europe. In 1943 it was in the hands of the Germans and at this time was home to *résistants* and Allied prisoners, most of whom were agents and spies. It was a huge labyrinth of cells, corridors, kitchens, dungeons and chapels. The food was to be very much worse than the Avenue Foch, which hadn't been at all bad. Diana was in the women's section, and when she arrived she was given just one dirty blanket and a coarse, grey sheet. Then she gave her name shown on her identity disk: 'Diana Rowden, aged 28, single, Church of England, English, born in London in 1915'. She was then strip-searched by two glowering SS women and made to stand facing the wall. When that humiliation was completed, the women accompanied her along a fearful underground passage that seemed to stretch for miles. '*Schnell, schnell!*' they shouted at her as they pushed her along the passage. Suddenly she saw steps leading into daylight. Before her were many lines of cells in a huge gallery. She was led into one of these, which contained just a bunk with a straw palliase, a small table, and a bucket in a corner.

It was a soul-destroying existence in Fresnes. Only the strong survived. The months turned into years for some people, and for Diana the days turned into weeks. Food was very bad, with just the barest minimum to sustain life. In the morning prisoners had a mug of something resembling coffee, in reality the weak notorious *ersatz* imitation, and if they were lucky a piece of dry black bread. Lunch was a small bowl of a watery substance with one or two vegetable peelings floating therein; there was a complete absence of meat or actual vegetables.

Day became night and night became day. Many nights the sounds of women's screams broke the deathly silence. It became a pattern that Diana eventually came to expect. Then dawn would come and the new day would start again. Each day was the same. With the advance of winter, small circles of ice appeared on the window of her dirty cell. She would glance down into the yard below and watch as small circles of prisoners took their daily exercise outside in the yard. The nights were the worst: there was no electric light and the cell was plunged in an intense darkness. Even Diana, a woman of great strength and one who on many occasions had been used to a lonely existence, must have had moments of desperation.

There were three divisions in Fresnes composed of three cell-blocks, each of five floors. The first was for male German deserters; the second was for male political prisoners, Frenchmen and those who worked for the underground resistance movements; the third was mixed, male and female, also for political prisoners. The top floor housed women German prisoners, whose cell doors were left open when the RAF bombers came so they could get away if bombs fell. When the RAF did fly over loud cheers could be heard from the prisoners, who rushed to the windows of their cells to try to watch them.

The prisoners communicated by tapping on the walls of their cells. 'There was a very old system of central heating in the prison which was not operating, but they could communicate by the ducts or by knocking against the walls using a very elementary code,' said George Abbott, an SOE agent in Fresnes in 1943:

'A' was one dot, 'B' two dots, two taps, and so on. You could hear these sounds and you could even hear the voices but I never communicated with anybody. What guarantee did I have that the chap next door to me was not a stool pigeon? Time was measured by the sounds you could hear outside. For instance Saturdays and Sundays were far worse than the weekdays because there were practically no sounds outside. However, on Sunday afternoon you could hear the crowd shouting in the stadium in Fresnes but there was no sound in the prison except prisoners trying to communicate between themselves.

Peter Churchill, who had run the *Spindle* network in the French Riviera, was also a prisoner in Fresnes.[12] Together with Odette Sansom, his courier, he had been arrested by Hugo Bleicher, alias Colonel Henri of the German *Abwehr*, in April 1943 and was now one of many captured SOE agents in Fresnes prison. In *The Spirit in the Cage* he describes being taken out of his cell in early November 1943 where he joined a group of men and women, including Diana, on the ground floor. Churchill is in error here as to dates because Diana had not been arrested then, and was certainly not in Fresnes in early November. To his delight, he quickly spotted the smiling grey face of Odette, who managed to whisper that they were going to have their fingerprints taken: 'We shall be together. I've fixed it.' They were taken to the rue des Saussaies, a large, bleak grey building of the Ministry of the Interior, a building which Elizabeth Nicholas described as gaunt and forbidding when she visited in 1955.

Churchill found himself in a large open pen where the whole group had been herded together under the watchful eye of a guard. He managed to slip up close to Odette. As she spoke to him with her back to the sentry, a girl he had never seen before, one who was patently English to her fingertips, stood between him and the guard so that he could not see Churchill's mouth moving. Despite Churchill's anxiety not to miss a second of this golden opportunity to speak with Odettte, he was nevertheless instinctively conscious of this girl's unselfish act, which included a delicacy of feeling that made her turn about and face the German so as not to intrude on their privacy. Churchill could not imagine what this refined creature was doing in their midst. He asked Odette who she was.

'Diana Rowden, one of us,' replied Odette.

Elizabeth Nicholas also portrays this aspect of Diana's selfless character when writing about this meeting between Churchill and Odette at the rue de Saussaies: 'In this passage I sensed something of the quality of Diana Rowden, which was soon to be made clear to me in all its splendour. I was to be shown other aspects of this instinctive courtesy, this gentle consideration in circumstances of great stress, for others.'[13]

After talking with Odette for some time and after having their fingerprints taken, Churchill and the rest of the group of SOE agents were photographed for the records, then they returned to Fresnes in the usual overcrowded Black Maria.

It was at Fresnes that Diana was to come face to face with Ida Poli of the Janier-Dubry family, who had been arrested with her and John Young on 16 November. After being incarcerated at Ravensbrück Concentration Camp until the camp was liberated, she told her family of seeing Diana's 'white strained face at Fresnes'. She did not see her again and so did not know she had been moved eventually to the prison in Karlsruhe; at that stage after the war the Janier-Dubry family still hoped that somehow Diana would survive and return some day to the Jura.

Christmas for Diana, her first and only Christmas in prison camp, came and went. The prisoners tried to make the best of it, some of them singing Christmas carols in their cells. There were visits from the prison chaplain, and a free Red Cross parcel given to all of them.

Those in solitary confinement ate their delicacies in silent loneliness. No doubt Diana thought of her mother, wondering if she had been told of her arrest. She would have asked God to comfort her mother and the rest of her family, and prayed for her friends, who like herself had been captured or were in prison, and she would have asked God to give her strength for what lay ahead.

1944 arrived with snow, sleet and freezing winds cloaking Fresnes in an atmosphere of desolation, adding to the bleakness of the prisoners' lives. Then slowly early spring arrived and with it the hope that the war would soon finish, that surely the invasion would be underway before too long. On the morning of 12 May Diana heard her cell door unlock and one of the wardresses march in: '*Raus! Raus!*' Pack your things, *Fraulein* Rowden, you are leaving us.'

So this was it. She took a deep breath and said calmly: 'Where am I going?'

'You are to go to Germany. Be ready to leave in an hour.'

Diana packed her few remaining possessions and looked around the cell. The time had come. She walked over to the window and looked down for the last time on to the courtyard below, watching some of the prisoners do their early morning exercise. She would face whatever was in store for her as she had done all through her life – with God's help.

Karlsruhe, close to the French-German border, seemed an unlikely place for any prisoners to have been taken. However, on her return to England from Ravensbrück Concentration Camp, Odette Sansom would relate to Vera that she had travelled to Karlsruhe with seven other SOE women. She didn't know the women but after looking through photographs and jogging her memory for names, she confidently identified six of the seven. They were Diana Rowden, Eliane Plewman, Yolande Beekman, who had worked for the *Musician* circuit and who had been arrested in January 1944, Madeleine Damerment, a devout Catholic who had escaped from France and who had been involved in the rescue of escaped Allied prisoners, and Vera Leigh, formerly a dress designer who had helped downed Allied airmen escape before she herself escaped from France in 1942. After training in SOE for three months, Vera Leigh had returned to France and become a friend of Julienne Aisner, ex-mistress of Dericourt, the Air Movements officer. To complete the seven were Odette Sansom, who had worked with Peter Churchill in the *Spindle* organisation, and Andrée Borrel, aged twenty, one of the youngest women to be sent into France. No one knew at that stage that all except Odette were doomed to die.

There was one other woman prisoner with the other group going to Karlsruhe, 'Jewish looking, small and slight', according to Odette. When Vera Atkins was trying to establish which SOE women agents had gone to Karlsruhe, she at first thought this young woman was likely to be Noor Inayat Khan. But she was not Noor. Although recruited in London, she was from the F Section *Juggler* circuit. Her name was Sonya Olschanesky, a German Jew.

These eight women were all going to Germany together. They talked, eagerly and yet cautiously, while they were left alone. They wondered if it was a good or bad sign that they were moving on. At this stage no one knew about the mass killings taking place in the camps. They exchanged questions and news about people believed to be captured, about information gathered from the outside. Odette was horrified by the appearance of some of them. She noticed Diana Rowden looked grey and haggard, a different person from the woman Odette had seen in the rue des Saussaies at the start of her captivity.

On 12 May 1944 Diana was taken from her cell in Fresnes and transported once again to Avenue Foch (called '*Avenue Boche* by the French) with her seven travelling companions. The women enjoyed a surprisingly comfortable day. Like Diana, most of them had been here before during their interrogations before being sent on to Fresnes, but it is unlikely they would have seen much of the headquarters of the *Sicherheitsdienst*, at this time the headquarters for the whole of France. F Section prisoners were kept on the fifth floor, in twelve attic rooms directly above Kieffer's fourth-floor office, with its Louis XV furniture; on the same floor was a bathroom and a guardroom with many books. Kieffer's secretary, Katya, was rumoured to be his mistress.[14]

Kieffer liked to bring his prize prisoners down to his rooms and talk to them about the English public schools and the English officer class. Kieffer had asked Brian Stonehouse who was the heir to the British throne and 'what does the English officer class think of Churchill?'

After the war Vera Atkins entered Kieffer's office and noted the chandeliers and the views over grassy lawns where a German officer arrived each day on horseback in full army riding gear. 'Kieffer was not a remarkable figure,' she said. 'He did not impress his prisoners with any great sophistication or even with any particular love of Hitler. Rather he gave the impression of being a somewhat bluff professional policeman. He did not even speak good English or French and always used a translator. Yet he had certainly won the trust of many of his prisoners.'

Many SOE prisoners who were returned from the concentration camps told Vera that Kieffer let it be known that he had personally secured Berlin's authority that F Section agents should not be killed. Even those fortunate individuals who had returned from the concentration camps did not believe that Kieffer really expected or knew that they had been sent there. When Noor Khan, who never trusted Kieffer and had no time for him at all, was sent to a camp, John Starr remarked that he believed Kieffer had sent Nora to an ordinary German prison to stop her trying to escape again. He was sure Kieffer would not have sent her to a concentration camp.[15]

It was a beautiful spring day in Paris, and the women prisoners looked through the windows of the room in the Avenue Foch down to the street and saw people walking past and heard the dim murmur of traffic. It was just a glimpse of ordinary life, one they had not seen for a long time. Odette requested they be served tea, and the Germans complied. Someone produced a lipstick and powder that she had in her possession, and as they were passed around the girls smiled at each other, delighting in these simple luxuries that they had not seen for a very long time. They spent the rest of the time reminiscing and sharing their stories. The talk was of their mutual experiences at Avenue Foch and the inevitable questions as to what was going to happen to them.

Diana was delighted to see Eliane Plewman, her friend from training school days. They greeted each other and were able to say a few words together before they were all hustled upstairs into one of the rooms. Suddenly they were left alone and were able to speak with freedom. The need for silence had passed, as they knew this was the last port of call in the journey to Germany, and that they would in all probably not return. All members of French Section, they spoke bravely of things that had happened during their time in France. All of them spoke of the prison at Fresnes and the cold and deprivations, then of England and those days, seemingly long ago, of gaiety and friendship and freedom.

Some time later Hans Kieffer came into the room and offered the women some chocolate. Some writers have written it was John Starr who did this. It is known that Starr had been given some chocolate by Kieffer, who as a non-smoker was a chocolate eater, and on Sunday mornings would unlock the cells at Avenue Foch and offer either chocolate or sweets to everybody – except the SOE operator Rabinovitch, who had been a radio operator for Peter Churchill's *Spindle* organisation, either because he was a Jew or because he was known to be uncompromisingly aggressive.

At this moment the women's appearance at Avenue Foch prior to transport to Karlsruhe was a sign of the expected invasion. It was a double-edged sword; once allied trooops landed in France, prisoners could become an encumbrance. For the Avenue Foch staff to have to take them along with them in a possible retreat would be inconvenient. It is known that Kieffer lived in Karlsruhe and it may be that he thought it could be a place where they could be kept safely without him losing access to them.

In the middle of the afternoon Kieffer made a further visit and announced what they already knew: that they were en route for Germany, and at 6.30 that evening their train would leave from the Gare de l'Est. Surprisingly he asked if there were any requests. The redoubtable *Odette* spoke for all of them: 'We would like some tea, please, some real English tea in teacups. Not as it is made in France or in Germany, but in the English manner: one spoonful for each person and one for the pot. And with milk and sugar, please.'

For a moment Kieffer looked nonplussed and slightly amazed, then he said, 'I will see what can be done.' Then he left the room.

A short while later, a woman came in with a tray on which was placed a teapot and seven beautiful Sevres china cups, one for each of them. After Odette poured the tea she asked the woman to fetch more hot water. The tea, the cosmetics, the sun lighting up the room, and the unquestioned treat and the calming effect of the tea succeeded in raising the women's spirits. Now they could face whatever lay ahead.

Odette Sansom was to remark later that she had been impressed by the bravery of the women. Although some of them cried, most of them were optimistic. She remembered an air of apprehension, the knowledge of not knowing what lay ahead. And she herself was especially fearful as she was the only one condemned to death.

At 6.00 p.m. an SS officer came into the room with some uniformed men. The time had come to leave for Germany, he announced. 'You are to be handcuffed in pairs and if there is any trouble, any attempt to escape, we will not hesitate to shoot. You will be taken in a coach with windows and you are forbidden to raise your hands or to indicate to passers by that you are anything other than normal travellers.' He stood aside and indicated the door: 'Come, we will begin.'

That evening, handcuffed in pairs and under heavy guard, the eight women were taken to the Gare de l'Est and put on a train for Germany.[16]

10

Karlsruhe Prison

You, whose mind is often tormented with anguish, take heart.
You are not forgotten by your brothers outside ... The shackles
that bind the limbs cannot imprison the soul. Some day all this
will come to an end and you will be free.

- A written message from a Bishop to prisoners
at Fresnes Prison

What was happening back in England amidst all this change? Had
Diana's mother been notified that her daughter was missing? At
that stage it was thought prudent at SOE headquarters not to notify
Mrs Rowden of her daughter's arrest, even though Harry Rée had
reported back to London that both Diana and John Young had been
arrested. A copy of a letter on file says that Diana had asked before
she left England for her mother not to be notified if she went missing
until the last possible moment, and it was not until 3 October 1944,
almost a year after the arrests, that Mrs Rowden, having had no news,
wrote to the War Office enquiring as to her daughter's whereabouts.

'Good news' letters were sent out from time to time to agents'
families when they were in the field, but in the event of Baker
Street receiving confirmation of agents who had been captured or
in the event of the worst case scenario, next-of-kin were always
informed at least of the bare circumstances of death when this was
established. There were times when it wasn't always possible to
notify families directly, for various reasons: staff shortage, security,
time constraints, and, of course, in the case of many agents who had
died in captivity or action, it was not until after the cessation of war

that Baker Street was able to confirm the fate of an agent; so many ends were left loose.

'This is not easy to understand or to excuse,' said Michael Foot,

... and it has caused justified bitterness, of which Elizabeth Nicholas' *Death Be Not Proud* is an example. Any infantry battalion or air force squadron commander worth his salt made a point of writing to the next-of-kin of his officers, at least, within hours of their becoming casualties. But in SOE this was much more difficult. In F Section Buckmaster wrote many letters in his own hand to relatives on Allied soil, when he was quite sure it was safe to do so, but in many other cases he felt he had to keep silent till the war was over, and then demobilisation put him out of touch with detailed inquiries.

One or two points can be urged in favour of silence. Certain news about the arrest or death of agents was usually difficult, frequently impossible to obtain; and it was thought less cruel to let families dally with false surmise than to inflict on them rumours of suffering that might prove untrue. There were obvious security objections in wartime to letting anybody outside the umbrella of the Official Secrets Act know about the fate of a secret agent; it might be fatal to an agent under arrest if a hint of his true identity leaked back to the Germans, and thus destroyed a cover story. (*SOE in France.*)

A letter from Vera Atkins to Mrs Rowden read:

As you know she went to France in June 1943 to assist a British Liaison officer working with the French Resistance movement in the Jura. She was very keen on this work and the only aspect of it which troubled her considerably was the thought of the anxiety which you would suffer if you lacked all news. We agreed to write to you and she asked us that should anything happen to her we should not let you know until the last possible moment ...

On 12 May 1944, Diana, in a party of eight women including Sonia Olschanesky, the *Juggler* courier who had worked for SOE but had never been trained by the organisation, and their guards, began their journey to Karlsruhe civilian prison in the Rhine Valley, in Germany.

The women were all handcuffed together, a ridiculous precaution as they were unarmed and helpless, and their captors, at least six in number, were armed men, The Karlsruhe arrangement suited Kieffer because, as mentioned earlier, his family lived there. Because of this arrangement under the pretence that he needed to make further enquiries of the prisoners, he was often able to stay with his family, never in fact calling on the women in prison.

It was a beautiful spring evening when they left the Avenue Foch. Paris was crowded with people walking in the warm evening. Cafés were crowded, couples walked hand in hand along the boulevards. The women must have breathed in the warm air and looked at the people who were walking free in the most beautiful city in the world, and wondered: would they too one day be free or was this to be the last time?

At the Gare de l'Est two second-class compartments had been reserved and the eight prisoners separated into two groups. According to Odette, they were guarded by SS. The windows were guarded, and some eight to ten SS filled the corridor – all this security for eight helpless women. Yolande Beekman and Odette faced Andrée Borrel and Vera Leigh. The other four girls, Diana, Sonia, Madeleine and Eliane, were in the other compartment, similarly guarded.

The city of Paris and its outlying suburbs were soon left behind, the train travelling east through open countryside. One of the SS men guarding Odette pointed to a heap of rubble as they passed through a station: 'That is the work of your RAF. They have also destroyed my mother's house in Dortmund. I only wish that an accident could happen to the train, as it would give me great pleasure to crush your skull under my heel and save the German hangman a job.'

Odette replied, 'You are a man under orders and it is your duty to deliver all of us, alive and well, to Germany. If an accident were to happen, your first care should be the safety of your prisoners. I frankly do not think you are very clever.'

He called her a dirty name.

The hours passed and the prisoners dozed as best they could, their heads on each other's shoulders. The train jolted on through the night and eventually the first colours of dawn showed through the grimy windows of the train. One of the guards said in a guttural tone, 'That is the Rhine that we are passing through now.'

Odette asked the SS man where they were going, and he replied with obvious satisfaction: 'You are going to Karlsruhe where you will be killed. I am very pleased it was decided to kill you in Germany and not in France. It means I get forty-eight hours unexpected leave and I can go and see *meine liebste Mutti,* my dearest mother.'[1]

When they arrived at the station at Karlsruhe, the girls noticed that the people looked well dressed but their faces were drawn and pale and many looked up to the sky as if they expected at any moment the RAF to drop bombs. The girls were locked into an office on the station platform and requested their handcuffs be unlocked so they could use the lavatories privately, but this was refused. After a little while they were taken out and put in pairs into taxis and driven to Karlsruhe prison. Finally their handcuffs were unlocked and the women separated.

Karlsruhe Jail in the *Riefstahlstrasse* was a massive granite building surrounded by a central courtyard. The women's wing was located on the east side. The prison was divided into two: the main part in *Akademiestrasse* 11, and in the second, female political prisoners were in a wing of *Gefangnis* 11, the men's jail in the *Riefstahlstrasse*. It was here that the British and French women were held. By the time of their arrival in May 1944, the main women's prison had been overcrowded as many prisoners had been transferred there from France ahead of the German retreat.

George Kaenemund was a political prisoner in Karlsruhe who was in the reception office of the prison when the special intake of women prisoners arrived. It was his job to record their names. When in 1945 he was questioned by Vera Atkins, who had been trying to find her missing girls, he remembered only four of the women's names, but got the spelling and the date wrong. He remembered the name of Churchill (this would be Odette Sansom who was going under the name Churchill), Leigt (Vera Leigh), Plumeau, likely to be Eliane Plewman, and Martini, Madeleine Damerment.

The women were all subjected to a degrading search conducted by wardresses before being allotted cells. These were narrow rooms at ground level with spyholes in the door. Each room had a toilet, a folding table, two seats and two beds made of planks laid together with straw paliasses. There was a cupboard and some hooks for clothes. The cells had been designed for two, but there could be as many as four prisoners in one cell. There was also a small shelf, which could hold a cup of tea. Each cell had two bunks and one high-barred, tiny meshed window very high up under a sloping buttress so that all one could see was the sky high above. The SOE girls were now as far away as possible from one another, and a new pattern of life began. Diana, who was to share a cell with two German women, political prisoners convicted of minor crimes, found herself in an overcrowded, airless prison. As time went on she became friendly with her cell mates, who were impressed by her cheerfulness and courage.

The prison was noisy with banging doors, shouting male voices, keys clanging, and always a smell of disinfectant and stale food, but compared to a concentration camp, not uncivilised. One of the political woman prisoners, Elise Johe, would joke about what they would choose to eat if they were back at home.

At 6.30 a.m. the prisoners were wakened by a bell, and they washed, made the beds and cleaned the cell. The hatch was then opened and food was pushed through. Frau Theresia Becker was the chief prison wardress at the women's prison. She was tall and thin, aged around fifty, with a sparrow's face. At 8.30 a.m. she made her inspection. Whilst this was in progress, the women had to stand in the corridor stating the offence for which they had been imprisoned. While this was happening they would perhaps be able to speak to the other prisoners or pass on messages. Later in the morning they were able to exercise for half an hour in the prison yard. The women formed two circles, with the SOE women in the outer ring. If it rained the exercise was cancelled.

The rest of the day was devoted to work; peeling potatoes, grinding coffee or sewing. Lunch took place between 11.30 and 12.00 p.m., coffee was distributed at 4.00 p.m., and supper was offered between 6.00 and 7.00 p.m. Bedtime and lights out was at 8.00 p.m. The food consisted mainly of bread, sometimes mouldy but more than adequate, black coffee, thin soup, salad or vegetables, with a small ration of margarine every other day. On Sundays they had stew or noodles. Sometimes there were small luxuries like fresh milk, butter and sausage. Surprisingly, on this diet Madeleine Damerment put on weight.

After the war, when Vera Atkins was as aforementioned searching for her lost women agents, she showed Theresia Becker (whom she had tracked down) photographs of the women Odette Sansom had told her were on the train to Karlsruhe. Immediately Becker said that they had all been in the prison. When asked if she could remember the women's names she recalled only one: *Martine*. This was Madeleine Damerment's alias.

'Their admission to the prison was, of course, most irregular,' she told Vera Atkins. 'The women had been admitted under the "protective custody" order, which applied to political prisoners and spies. I had no authority to take such prisoners into a civilian jail. It was highly unusual and against the rules.' Becker had protested to her seniors and it was agreed that she should have to keep the women for a maximum of two weeks only. Keeping such prisoners meant a lot of extra work as they had to be exercised separately and the prison was short-staffed. Protective custody prisoners could not associate with one another and therefore could not be taken to the basement during air raids; the girls were exercised singly by walking up and down in the courtyard. Once it was noticed that the SOE girls moved faster than the others and ran together in the outer circle, where they were able to talk occasionally, that exercise was immediately stopped. In the mornings and afternoons the prisoners worked, some of them peeling potatoes, and others like Yolande Beekman did darning, patching and embroidery for Frau Becker. Every three weeks all the women prisoners were escorted for showers. During heavy raids the women were all locked in their cells – they showed great courage, as they had to. They were known to have cheered up their cell mates, all of whom spoke of them afterwards with the greatest admiration.

When Vera Atkins was shown around the prison by wardress Becker after the war, she was able to glean the layout of the prison. Becker led her up some stone steps on the right of the gatehouse, then down a corridor and around three sides of the courtyard anti-clockwise, where they passed line after line of male cells. A white gate opened into the women's section and the warder's office where Becker kept the prisoners' possessions. She saw the room where the girls had lined up, peeling potatoes. Vera also met Hedwig Muller, who had been in the same cell as Madeleine Damerment. Muller had been arrested by the Gestapo in May 1944 for joking about the Führer to her boyfriend.

The girls forged deep friendships in Karlsruhe prison. It was possible that sometimes they felt safe, for just a little while – that perhaps the war would soon be over; after all, the second front would be coming. Lisa Graf, a political prisoner, when asked if the girls might have stayed safely in the jail until the end of the war had Becker not so rigorously observed the prison rules, answered:

> Maybe, maybe not. I thought at the time when I saw those girls, they are not going to come back. And so, I thought, I will fix them all now in my mind. *Martine* [Damerment] told me all about the other girls ... we were all *copines*. When they were in the courtyard below I was at the window and Madame Greiner, one of the guards, would come and tell me the name of each and everything they were wearing and when they were leaving. I caught glimpses of them sometimes. In the shower I had a few words with Odette, I remember. She told me some girls were leaving. I remember her face. If I think now I do not see the faces of the others, you know.

'If I think now I do not see the faces of the others, you know.'

Once more Becker approached the prison governor with a request for instructions. The governor accordingly wrote to the head of *Abteilung IV.3* of the K Gestapo whose deputy had signed the instructions to the prison. *Abteilung IV* under Dr Farber was responsible for counter-espionage and anti-sabotage, as well as for all measures against the State. Accordingly, a letter was sent to RSHA Berlin asking what was to be done about these women, and eventually a teleprint message concerning four of the women was received by the head of the Karlsruhe Gestapo, Gmeiner, instructing him to arrange for their execution at a convenient camp. Roesner, the head of Section 3 just mentioned as responsible for counter-espionage and anti-sabotage, was ordered to make the necessary arrangements. He chose Natzweiler. Gmeiner agreed. He was a former member of the notorious *Einsatzkommando* unit on the Russian front, a man who loved order, and had no mercy. He telegraphed to the RSHA for instructions.

The women might have stayed in the prison until the war was over had it not been for the officious Becker, who it seemed could not get it out of her head that their position in the prison was irregular: 'In her efforts to get their position regularised, this busy-body of a jailkeeper drew the attention of the local Gestapo to their existence.'[2]

Finally, in July orders were y received from the *Reichssicherheits-hauptamt* (RHSA) in Berlin for Diana, Andrée Borrel, Vera Leigh, and

Sonia Olchanezky to be taken to Natzweiler concentration camp. Horst Kopkow was the Berlin counter-intelligence chief, and Hans Kieffer of Avenue Foch, who had interrogated Diana, answered directly to Kopkow. It was Kopkow who ordered the 'special treatment' for the agents and who signed every protective custody order for spies. Kopkow was fastidious, and always required 'receipts' for bodies when executions had taken place, except when the cases were *Nicht und Nebel*, those prisoners destined to disappear into the fog, in which case special secret procedures were enforced. His department also had a secret section, or *Nachrichtendienst*, which handled highly secret matters.

The Karlsruhe Gestapo handled women's cases with 'special care'. If women were to be sent anywhere the chief, Joseph Gmeiner, would send one of his women office staff along on the transport to deal with the female prisoners' 'special needs'.

In early July Lisa Graf, the political prisoner, had climbed up the sloping buttress to the window's edge and seen Andrée Borrel in the courtyard below. Andrée suddenly looked towards Lisa's window and signalled 'goodbye'.

When author Sarah Helm visited Karlsruhe prison to research her biography on Vera Atkins, she noted the scratches on the whitewashed walls, which were of solid granite one foot thick, were still there. These were the same walls where the women had passed messages in Morse to each other with their forks and spoons.

Lisa Graf, in a statement to Vera Atkins, wrote:

Towards 5 July 1944 four women prisoners left in the morning in a transport for an unknown destination. They were:

1) *Denise*, a young woman with black hair, blue eyes, pale skin, wearing a grey coat and short blue socks, with navy blue shoes that had rubber soles.

2) A young pretty blonde woman with black eyes, who people said was a Jewish dancer. If my memory is right people called her Dany. She was wearing a dark green, stripey dress and white espadrilles and must have been about twenty years old.

3) A young woman about thirty years old, fair, with blue eyes dressed in beige and in her hair she wore a little green ribbon.

4) Somebody aged about twenty-five with blond-red hair and grey eyes and she was wearing a grey coat with white espadrilles.

In 1946, in answer to a question put to her by Vera Atkins, Becker said she could not be certain as to the exact date the girls had been taken from the prison but that Mrs Churchill had left in July 1944 and the rest soon after. She was sure that all the other women, apart from Mrs Churchill, had left together in one group sometime in August. Vera asked to see the prison records, but Becker said that the French had destroyed all the records of Karlsruhe prison. 'They made a fire,' she said. It was Major 'Bill' Barkworth, an SAS intelligence officer, who found these records. Vera had made a note on her report: 'While they are all very anxious to be helpful, their information cannot be relied upon.'[3]

So near and yet so far.

Years later, author Sarah Helm spoke to Theresia Becker's nephew, Franz Becker. 'I remember the story about the girls going up the chimney,' he said. He went on to say that his aunt had told him these girls were spies and that's why they were in prison. They were then suddenly taken away and had left behind clothes and some other little personal possessions:

> My aunt was worried about what should be done with them; she liked to do things by the book. She wanted to send the things on to the girls but she didn't know where they had been taken. So she called up the chief and said these things should be sent on to the girls. But she was told it was no good. They had gone up the chimney.[4]

Whilst in Germany Vera Atkins also tracked down a German woman, Lili Simon, who had been a Gestapo secretary. She told Vera she had gone on a journey with several women prisoners with a colleague named Max Wassmer, who was in charge of transport. This is what she told Vera:

> I met the four prisoners with their luggage in the hall of the station in Karlsruhe. They were handcuffed two together. We took the express train as far as Strasbourg and then got a local train. During the journey the prisoners asked where they were going and Wassmer said they were being taken to a camp and that they would be expected to work. They talked about how they would be glad to get away from peeling potatoes

now they had left Karlsruhe prison. The surrounding country was lovely and the women enjoyed it and looked forward to working.

Lili was ordered to leave the train at Shirmeck and return to Karlsruhe: 'I did not know they were being taken to a camp in order to be executed.'

Evidence collected from people like Hedwig Muller and Lisa Graf suggests that whilst in Karlsruhe the girls were not ill treated; they were put into separate cells that they shared with one or two German prisoners – most of them political rather than criminal prisoners. There was little doubt that Hedwig Muller, Else Sauer and Nina Hagen struck up a real friendship with them and did everything possible to help them by sharing food parcels, sending laundry out with theirs to be washed, and so on. Nevertheless they had a hard time, and the last survivors became very anxious when the first four girls had been taken away.

'In the first group,' said Muller, 'there had been a girl called Diana.' She had only heard the name. 'And there was a dark southerner, who had left in the first group, and there was also an older woman, more stocky in appearance.' Then Muller suddenly recalled this older woman was named Simone. Vera Leigh's alias was *Simone,* so it was likely it was Leigh that she was referring to.

In my research into the time Diana spent at Karlsruhe, I read that one of the women who had been incarcerated at Karlsruhe had told her jailers that she was a lieutenant in the British Army and had demanded to be brought before a proper court martial. At the time my first thought was that this would be typical of Diana, but then I read the woman was Andrée Borrel – also a very strong and determined woman. Actually, this is an indication of the character of both girls. It also points to the fact that at one time at least one of the four women had not been tried. It is noted that the woman defended herself most energetically.

A guard told Vera Atkins it was in July that the women prisoners left Karlsruhe:

They were collected from the prison in a large green covered truck which looked like a hearse. I think that the number collected was seven. Odette Churchill was not part of this transfer as she was due to leave about a fortnight later for Ravensbrück. The departure of these women took place between four and five in the morning. It was already light at this time, because part of my duties consisted in looking after the blackout and I had already taken this down.

11

Natzweiler – Camp of Hell

For God proved them, and found them worthy for Himself.
As gold in the furnace, hath he tried them.

-- *Wisdom of Solomon*

A note about the Romans – they used to think the souls of the
departed stayed near their tombs.

- Jack Higgins, *Night of the Fox*

After Paris was liberated in August 1944, Maurice Buckmaster, who had
been promoted to full colonel, went to France at the end of September
in the company of Major Bourne-Paterson to start his victory tour of
F Section circuits, codenamed the 'Judex Mission'. Essentially this was
an intelligence exercise to find the number of British agents who had
not returned, either missing or dead, and to categorise the list of arms
and ammunitions still remaining in the country. The Judex Mission
is looked back on as being more of a political demonstration, and its
strategic or tactical value was low.

Others who served in SOE, like Nicholas Bodington, had been
dispatched to lecture Allied forces on conditions in France. Vera
Atkins had elected to stay put initially in Baker Street, as she felt
keenly that she could not desert the men and women who had not
yet returned. It was three months since the Normandy landings and
some of the agents had already started to trickle home from the
concentration camps. Of the four hundred or so F Section agents
sent into the field, more than a hundred were still missing, sixteen of
them women. Vera was determined to account for every one of them.

In November she set up a base where agents could make contact when they came in from the field. This was at the Hotel Cecil in the rue St Didier; gradually agents such as Francis Cammearts, Lise de Baissac, and Pearl Witherington who had fought with the *Maquisards* returned there. However, there were many unaccounted for. When Vera could do no more in Paris she returned to England to her office in Baker Street to carry on her investigations.

On 3 October Mrs Rowden, who by now would have been expecting to hear some news of her daughter, wrote to Major Mackenzie of the War Office: 'It always seems such a long time between letters and when are are a week or two late it seems a life time! Actually it is 16 months only since I saw my daughter, and it seems much longer owing to being unable to send and receive letters to and from her.'

Over the following months there followed an emotionally charged and strained exchange of letters. In the interests of a balanced portrayal, this exchange is reproduced at length here. The first letter in response, from Major I. K. Mackenzie, sent from the War Office, reads as follows:

Dear Mrs Rowden,

I much regret to inform you that we have recently been out of touch with your daughter, and I am afraid that under the circumstances we must consider her as missing. I very much regret giving you such bad news, as I know the anxiety it is bound to cause you, but I have every reason to believe that your daughter is a prisoner of war and will eventually be all right.

I would like to suggest that you call to see me at the above address at 2.30 on Monday, 23rd October, and in the meantime would impress upon you in the interests of your daughter's own security that you make no enquiries about her except through me.

Once again, may I say how extremely sorry I am to give you such worrying news.

Mrs Rowden's pained reply soon arrived:

Oct 18th '44
Dear Major Mackenzie,

Thank you for your letter of 15th October with its very bad news. It certainly is as Diana herself would have put it – a very bad show. I do hope that she may have gone into hiding and turn up again soon; in fact I've been expecting her home daily lately. However, you believe she is a prisoner of war and will eventually be all right.

I hope this will prove so. I need not say what a blow and shock it is.

I am staying here with a sister and doing a three weeks cure in bed for heart trouble, and so fear I shall be unable to come and see you on Monday 23rd Oct; in fact I shall not be available or leave here until about Nov 6th. Any day convenient to you after that would suit me. I think I must continue the treatment and get it over as quickly as possible, as it is useless to postpone it as I've already done so three months ago and the result has been bad. Should you get any further news I should be very grateful to have it.

Thank you again for your sympathy and kindness.

P. S. I will of course make no enquiries about my daughter excepting through you.

On file, dated 27 October 1944, there is a memo from Major Mackenzie, Administration, stating that 'it would appear that a female agent named PAULETTE who went to the field on 16.6.43 by Lysander to work in the JURA was reported on 28.11.43 as having been arrested with our organizer GABRIEL, since when we have no further news of her.

'We should be very interested to have further details on the woman mentioned in your memorandum. Our agent is about 28 years of age. Held a commission in the WAAF in the name of DIANA HOPE ROWDEN (Number 4193) and transferred to this organization in March 1943.

It would seem that by now Mrs Rowden was perplexed and growing slightly angry, as on 10 November 1944 she again wrote to Major Mackenzie:

Dear Major Mackenzie,

I am back in London again and would be much obliged if you could explain to me the fact that on Sept 25th you wrote to me that you had again had good news of my daughter

D. H. Rowden – and that in your letter of 15th Oct you told me that she was missing and you believed prisoner of war.

From what I gathered from my elder son, M. E. A. Rowden, you had known that she was in prison quite a long time ago and it was only when she was evacuated probably to Germany that you lost touch?

I am rather muddled about it all I'm afraid.

Another letter, written by Mrs Rowden to Vera Atkins, said she had not given up hope and was starting her own search:

I should like to know what name Diana was going under as that may help my search for her. A friend of a cousin of mine who went out with Mrs Churchill to Russia wanted to get information from Russia for me from either Stalin or Molotov, who she knew personally!

There followed an invitation to Mrs Rowden by Major Mackenzie to call on him on 16 November when they could discuss the situation, but unfortunately there is no record as to what took place.

The next correspondence is dated 1 May 1945 from Vera Atkins to Mrs Rowden, wherein she apologises that neither she nor Major Mackenzie were available to see her and asks her to make an appointment before calling. She also says that they were still without news of her daughter:

I can tell you however quite definitely that she has not been in any of the camps so far overrun. We have reason to believe that she may be in a camp which is about to be overrun by the Russians and therefore we are hoping for news shortly. Whatever it is you may be certain that we will get into touch with you at once.

A further letter to Vera dated 7 May 1945 mentions that Mrs Rowden was sorry she was unable to see anyone when she called:

My son came on 72 hours leave unexpectedly and as I have bad heart disease he thought it safer to accompany me as the Dr says I must if possible be spared any sudden shock. It looks as if news should soon come through now from the camps now that hostilities are at an end in Europe.

On 11 May 1945 Vera replied:

11 May 1945
Dear Mrs Rowden,
  I have just heard that your daughter was seen in July last to be in good health. She was then being moved to Germany together with a number of other English women and their morale was evidently good. I know that this has been a very hard winter and many things may have happened but I do feel reasonably hopeful that when news comes it will be good.

Yours sincerely,
Flt/O. V. M. Atkins

There followed on 20 December 1945 a letter from Vera Atkins to Mrs Rowden advising her that the branch of the War Office through which she had been dealing with was closing down and that the financial side of her daughter's affairs had been handed over to the Air Ministry Pay Office with effect from 1 May 1945:

Everything possible has been done and will indeed continue to be done to obtain further news but I am sorry to say that there is at present nothing to add to the information which we have already passed to you. The various branches dealing with search have been fully briefed and specialist officers are searching any available records in Germany.

  Whilst it is greatly feared, in view of the absence of any news of her since the cessation of hostilities, that the chances of her being alive are now extremely remote, it is proposed to allow some further time to elapse before the grave step of officially recording her death is taken. If and when it is finally decided that there can unhappily no longer be any alternative but to record her death, you will be notified by the Casualty Branch to whom all future enquiries regarding her position should be addressed.

  In the meantime every effort will continue to be made to find out her ultimate fate.

On 22 December 1945 another letter to Mrs Rowden from Vera gave her a much fuller account of Diana's wartime activities in France, including the fact that she had been working in the Jura:

She was very keen on this work and the only aspect of it which troubled her considerably was the thought of the anxiety which you would suffer if you lacked all news. We agreed to write to you and she asked us that should anything happen to her we should not let you know until the last possible moment. We now know that she was unhappily arrested towards the end of November 1943. For various reasons we did not hear of this until the spring of 1944. We knew that the invasion was about to take place and we hoped that she might be found in France when that country was liberated. Unfortunately this was not the case.

We now know that she was imprisoned in Fresnes near Paris from where she was moved in the company of several British women in the middle of May 1944. They were sent to the prison of Karlsruhe where they remained until approximately 25 July 1944. At that time they were all in good spirits and in good health. We know that she, in the company of others, was moved away from Karlsruhe in the general direction of that part of Germany now occupied by the Russians. We have made enquiries through every channel to try and find out her subsequent fate but unfortunately without results. For a long time we were not unduly worried as we felt that there was a reasonable hope that she was alive and that we would eventually succeed in contacting her. With the passage of time and in view of the improved communications with the Russian zone, I am sorry to say that we have now practically abandoned hope. Investigations will continue in order to ascertain her fate.

I wish to assure you that all who knew her share in your anxiety and I am deeply distressed at having to give you such bad news.

On Diana's personal file a confirmation letter from Air Ministry to the War Office, dated 11 April 1946, confirmed that Diana had been killed at Natzweiler on approximately 25 July 1944. A further letter to the War Office, dated 26 April, states that 'S/O D.H. Rowden and A/S.O. N. Inayat-Khan were killed in the camp at Natzweiler on 6 July 1944, and not 25 July 1944 as previously stated. Death was caused by an overdose of a narcotic and the bodies were immediately cremated.'

In response, Mrs Rowden wrote a letter to the Junior Officer Commander, presumably attached to the Air Ministry, thanking her for her letter of 29 April and giving details of her daughter's fate. She thanked her and her staff for the sympathy conveyed, explaining she was trying to find consolation in what she had learned. She 'would be obliged if the official certificate of death could be sent to her solicitors, Sir Arthur C. Morgan of Messrs Park Nelson & Co, 11 Essex Street, The Strand, W.C.2'.

Major M. Mott at the War Office had now taken over the correspondence regarding the victims' families. On 24 May 1946 he advised Mrs Rowden that

the responsible Camp officials, who are in Allied custody, will shortly be tried as war criminals, and that the charge is specifically, inter alia, complicity in the murder of Miss Rowden.

In the ordinary course of events therefore it would be inevitable that in any press publicity concerning the trials mention would be made of her by name. In view of the distressing circumstances in which she was killed, we are most anxious to spare you any further pain which such publicity might entail and should you so desire, I should be only too willing to endeavour to arrange for the suppression of her name from any reports which may be published.

Mrs Rowden replied immediately to the new War Office correspondent:

27th May 1946
Dear Major Mott,
    Thank you for your letter which I received this morning.
    I appreciate your kindness in offering to endeavour to have my daughter's name suppressed in any press-publicity concerning the trial of the camp officials. I feel, however, that it is not necessary. My pain is too deep and my loss too great to mind seeing it in print. I am convinced that the only possible further pain I could suffer would be if the camp officials are let off.

Reports from Vera Atkins to the War Office give full details of the names of the women who had been killed at Natzweiler, including

Vera Leigh, Andrée Borrel and Diana Rowden. At that stage, April 1946, it was thought by Vera Atkins that the fourth woman killed at Natzweiler was Noor Inayat-Khan:

> I have so far only been able to interrogate one of the SS who was present at the execution and he denies having been there. It is possible that when the others become available for interrogation I may be able to obtain a sworn statement from them. It will, however be appreciated that such statements are not readily given as in most cases they would constitute a death warrant for the man who was present at the murder. It is however certain beyond any reasonable doubt that four women met their death as described above in the camp of NATZWEILER on the evening of the 6 July 1944 and that the women have now been properly identified as:

> Diana ROWDEN
> Nora INAYAT-KHAN
> Vera LEIGH
> Andrée BorrelL
> [Against the name of Nora Inayat-Khan is the word 'NO!']

In the period between 1941 and 1944 some 12,000 prisoners, most of them Jews and French Resistance fighters were in the camp at Natzweiler – the only camp on French soil. It was a labour camp and those who were too sick or unable to work were put to death. Others, particularly 'N *und* N' prisoners and Jews, were sent to the quarry to be worked to death. The *Night und Nebel* order, the idea of making people disappear, had come from a decree issued by Hitler's Chief of Staff, Field Marshal Wilhelm Keitel, on 12 December 1941. As Sarah Helm details,

> While it had been intended to deal with civilian resisters, either in Germany or in German-occupied countries, the aim was to deter others by treating 'N *und* N' prisoners abominably and then killing them off so nobody would know what had happened to them. Although some SS chiefs chose not to apply the decree to spies by the end of the war hundreds of thousands 'N *und* N' prisoners had indeed 'disappeared' into specially designated secret camps. Natzweiler was one of the best-kept secrets of all.[1]

Among the missing on the SOE lists were agents Brian Stonehouse and Robert Sheppard. They were lucky, having survived imprisonment in several camps, and eventually they trickled back to England, emaciated and ill. They told of the almost daily event of carrying the bloody and emaciated corpses of those workers who had not survived the day. They told Vera Atkins of the names of some of the most sadistic guards at Natzweiler – Zeuss, Nietsch, and Ermenstraub, who flogged their prisoners to death. Vera stored these names in her mind in preparation for the coming war crimes trials.

'They wanted us to be beasts and they nearly, very reached it,' said Robert Sheppard. 'They would say things like "*Du bist der Britische Offizier?*" Ah, a British officer? Put him in the shit. But the worst part is the daily life, when you wake up in the morning and you don't know if you're going to be alive in the evening ... With friends like Brian, although we were miserable, we were starving, we always wanted to keep dignified in front of everybody.'

Some time before four and five on the morning of 6 July 1944, not quite two months after they arrived in Karlsruhe, four of the women are awakened and told to get themselves ready for a journey. They are taken to the reception room where their personal possessions – parcels, a small suitcase, a fur coat – are returned to them, and then they are handed over to two Gestapo men, Christian Ott and Max Wassmer. They are headed for the concentration camp *einem ZZ-Lager zugefuhrt*, to a camp at Struthof. Germans are sticklers for keeping impeccable records and this is later noted by Vera Atkins when she visits the camp in 1945.

A large green, covered truck makes its way through the town of Strasbourg, then up a long winding road into the mountains of the Vosges. This is Alsace, fought over for centuries on the border between France and Germany. The four women are prisoners of the German Reich. Their names are:

Andrée Borrell, of the First Aid Nursing Yeomany (FANY). She has been a prisoner since the 25 June 1943.

Section Officer Diana Rowden, of the WAAF. She was arrested on 18 November 1943.

Vera Leigh, also of the FANY. She was arrested in Paris on the 19 November 1943.

The fourth girl is Sonya Olschanezky, whose identity is yet to be discovered by Vera Atkins. She was arrested in January 1944 and

SOE knows little about her. This is due to the fact that she was never trained in England but recruited in the field.

As their journey takes them higher into the mountains, the smell of pine drifts into the truck. At first sight the beauty of the mountains and the trees rising on either side of the road is entrancing, like something out of a fairytale, and as they climb higher into the mountains the passengers in the truck glimpse old castles and monasteries.

Now the road twists and winds its way as it passes through small villages surrounded by dark green pine trees and dense woodland. The truck slows as it nears the picturesque town of Shirmeck, then passes through the village of Rothau. Through the gaps in the truck the women glimpse half-timbered houses with red and pink geraniums in full bloom in wooden window boxes. From somewhere down in a valley a bell tolls from an ancient church, and they glimpse villagers in wooden clogs going about their business.

'Where are we going?' asks one of the girls to their guards.

'We're taking you to a place where you will do agricultural work, a camp where you'll work on a farm.'

They look at each other, hope in their eyes.

A farm!

The French province of Natzweiler in the Bas-Rhin Department is an isolated hamlet some sixty-five kilometres south-west of Strasbourg. The mountain La Roche Louise lies directly above it. Before the war this area was a much-loved ski resort. Enthusiastic skiers would ski down the Louise to the nearby Hotel Le Struthof, stop off for refreshment and then continue down into the valleys. To Hitler in 1940 the northern slope of the Louise was a suitable place for a concentration camp. It was perfectly positioned: a lonely area around 900 metres high, often swept by icy winds and heavy snow in winter. The camp was built by several hundred prisoners, who laid out the site in terraces, one above the other. Down in the valley in the town of Schirmeck there was already a camp for prisoners. It was reserved for opponents of the Nazi regime and for those guilty of having resisted the Germanisation of Alsace after Hitler's annexation of the area. The prisoners built the camp in atrocious conditions, the object being to kill off as many as possible.

At last the truck comes to a stop. The guards get out and tell the girls to disembark. Max Wassmer gestures to the girls: '*Komme ... we will take you to the Kommandant.*' Blinking in the sudden harsh light, they climb slowly down and gaze around them. They have no reason to feel afraid. They have not been roughly treated on their journey. Then … a glimpse of buildings below built on tiers, steps leading down to buildings, guard towers, rows of green, timbered huts, men with skeletal frames and shaved heads, a mass of staring faces; there is no birdsong, no wildlife.

The women see rows and rows of male prisoners. They have no idea why these men are here or what their nationalities are. They seem to be a mixture of races: Danes, Norwegians, Frenchmen, Dutch and Belgians, large numbers of Russians, Poles, and many hundreds of Jews. All are wearing labels: a blue triangle for homosexuals, green for felons, black for work dodgers, violet for Jehovah's Witnesses, yellow for Jews. And then there are *Nacht und Nebel* prisoners, those destined to disappear into the night and fog. They wear round yellow labels with three black circles with 'N *und* N' written on their backs. These prisoners are not allowed to communicate with any other prisoners; they are kept in a separate compound and can be shot at any given moment.

A man, tall and emaciated with very dark eyes and the long fingers of an artist, looks up from his work on the outskirts of the prison compound. With his friend Robert Sheppard, Brian Stonehouse is engaged in laying a pipeline just inside the wire on the east side of the camp. Sheppard, code named *Patrice,* had been parachuted into France on 31 May 1942 with another French agent, Robert Boiteux. The two men are British SOE agents. Stonehouse will always remember 6 July 1944, not only because it was just before the failed attempt on Hitler's life, but because of what he saw. The images will never leave him.

He notices four women carrying various parcels, one carrying a not very good fur coat. There is one tall girl with very fair, heavy hair; he can see it is not its natural colour as the roots of her hair are dark. She is wearing a black coat, French wood-soled shoes and a fur coat on her arm. Another girl is short with very black oily hair, aged between twenty and twenty-five years and wearing a tweed coat and skirt. The third girl is of medium height, rather stocky with shortish fair hair tied with a multi-coloured ribbon, and aged about twenty-eight. She is wearing a grey flannel, short fingertip-length swagger coat with a grey skirt, which he remembers thinking looked very English. The fourth woman of the party has shortish brown hair and is wearing a brownish tweed coat and skirt; she is more petite than the blonde in grey, and older.

He notices that none of the women are wearing makeup and all are pale and tired looking. They walk straight ahead down the long, steep *Lagerstrasse* holding their heads high, carrying their little packages, almost as if they have come to stay the night at a transit camp. After all, they have nothing to fear.

He remembers clearly all these things. They are imprinted indelibly on his mind. One day – a long time in the future – he will draw from memory the images of that day …

Never will he forget what he saw that day in July.

In the afternoon thick fog suddenly descended on Natzweiler. The outside work parties returned early and there was a distribution of soup. Obviously something was up in the camp, as everywhere SS men were running around. All prisoners were consigned to their barracks and nobody was allowed outside or to stand in front of the windows. Clearly something was about to happen that should not be seen. Floris Bakels, a Dutch prisoner, was lying on his upper berth and gazing out on to the terraces, the granite steps of the *Lagerstreet*:

> All was deserted. Then I noticed two heavily armed SS on the sloping *Lagerstreet* and behind them – four girls. Four summery girls with lovely long hair and gently swaying skirts, some with bare arms, all with bare legs. They looked around. They seemed like angels from heaven. And behind them two more SS men. I followed them with stinging eyes, one moment invisible behind a barrack, the next re-appearing far down below, finally disappearing in the direction of the bunker. The next day we heard it all on the network of connections via privileged prisoners who had connections with even more important *Huftlinge* working in the bunker and the crematorium. We had seen four English or French girls.[2]

A French prisoner who was working in the kitchens, Roger Linet, could see from their appearance when the women passed that they had not come from a camp. To him they seemed young; they were fairly well groomed, their clothes pristine, their hair neatly brushed and each had a case in her hand: 'They looked fairly normal.

I remember the fair one because she stood out from the rest as being very English-looking, particularly as she was wearing a green ribbon in her hair. I learned later that this was Diana Rowden, a fearless courier, who carried messages all over France.' Although many of the prisoners could not help but remember the arrival of the women, none of them in the future, after the war, would be able to describe their faces. Only one man could do that – the tall man with the dark eyes, Brian Stonehouse.

Major Van Lanschot, a Dutch resistance leader, later said there was no doubt they were 'first class': 'It was the first time the prisoners had seen women in Natzweiler and everybody could not help but talk quietly amongst themselves and wonder what was the reason why they had been brought in. The general opinion was they were too good to start a *Puff* (a brothel).'

Walter Shultz, a Polish prisoner and the camp interrogator, was told that the women were to be 'employed in the officers' mess'.

A new rumour rushes through the camp. It comes from the kommandant's office. In a room in the crematorium beds are being prepared. Maybe there's going to be a brothel after all.

The women walk into the office of the camp kommandant, Fritz Hartjenstein. There are several other camp officials present in the office, including Joseph Gmeiner, chief of the Karlsruhe Gestapo, and a Karlsruhe official named Hermann Rosner, who hunts down infiltrators, commandos or parachutists. He would boast at the bar that he once took a tank into the Warsaw Ghetto at the height of the uprising. It is Rosner who tells the jailers to write in the register: *fr fuss*, 'special cases', which are used to describe the manner in which SOE prisoners leave the prison. Sometimes the words in the register just say '*Einem K. Z*'. Max Wassmer hands over the women together with a copy of the movement order and the *Vollzugszettel*, the execution order received from the RSHA, the Head Office of the Reich Security in Berlin. Wassmer then leaves having requested that the Karlsruhe Gestapo be informed when the execution has taken place.

Neither Gmeiner, Rosner or Wassmer or any member of the Gestapo have bothered to take any steps to find out whether these women have been legally tried and condemned to death. Has anyone acquainted them with their impending fate, in case they wish to appeal or lodge a protest? Do they know why they are here?

Magnus Wochner is head of the Political Department. One man, believed to be with Christian Ott or Max Wasmer from the Criminal Department in Karlsruhe, says to Wochner: 'I have got the four women here who are to be executed.' Wochner says: 'It is nothing to do with me; take them somewhere else.'

Suddenly the prisoners see the women coming out of Harjenstein's office accompanied by camp officials. They are transferred to his big open car and are given a tour of the camp. It is almost as though they are on parade.

There are more than 6,000 men in the camp, brave *résistants*, many of the bravest in Europe – and they can do nothing to help these women. They are not allowed anywhere near them. An order is barked out: 'All prisoners are to be in their barracks by 8.00 p.m. You are required to shut your windows and all blinds are to be drawn.'

The camp's dental surgeon, Kurt Aus Dem Brugh, in the company of the camp adjutant, *Obersturmführer* Johannes Otto, sees the women in the orderly room who are busy unpacking their kit. One is brushing her hair. Brugh asks Otto what are these women doing in the camp? Otto replies they are English, possibly spies, and that they have come from Karlsruhe prison. Orders are that they are to stay for the night in the prison inside the camp before moving on the next morning. Brugh offers a cigarette to the blonde woman who is standing near him. In evidence at the Natzweiler trial in May 1946, Brugh will remember that he did not converse with the women, most of whom, especially the blond, are very quiet. Around 5.00 p.m. that evening the women are led around the back of the prison block, entering from the rear entrance, which faces the forest and down the mountain. Accompanied by SS men, the women are taken to the *zellenbau* by Walter Schultz and are confined in one cell. The key is turned in the lock. The guards talk among themselves; one of them, Nietsch, says to Schultz, 'Nice things, eh?'

By this time the whole camp knows the real reason why the women have been brought to the camp. The only people who don't know are the women themselves. No one can warn them. The 6,000 prisoners can do nothing but watch as these good-looking young women, who should have had their lives ahead of them, walk past the prisoners to certain death.

The camp doctor, Werner Rohde, is in the officer's mess when Dr Plaza, Otto and Straub rush into his room and tell him about the arrival of the women 'spies'. Straub says that to hang women – Englishwomen and Frenchwomen – would lead to a great 'to-do'. He says it will create '*ein grosses theater*. We will have to find another way.' The doctors propose another way: to inject the women with a lethal substance, but they are not sure if they have the necessary quantities in stock.

Since their arrival Franz Berg, the crematorium stoker, has been busy making sure everyone knows as much as possible about the women. He passes the word around right down to the barracks on the lower terraces that there are British women among the group. Several prisoners are successful in managing to talk to the women. One of these is Georges Boogaerts, and when the guards are distracted, he calls across to them in their cells. Like Albert Guerisse, alias Patrick O'Leary, who after the fall of Dunkirk had run one of the most successful escape lines for Allied prisoners of war, Boogaerts is a Belgian doctor and is in charge of the prisoners' hospital. The windows of the hospital block look directly on to the prison block, a distance of some twenty-five yards. He manages to make his way from barrack to barrack until he is in the hut nearest to the prison. From there he is able to call out: 'Hello, are you English girls?' All of a sudden a face of a girl appears behind the bars of the window of the gaol. She says to him, 'Yes, I am English.'

Boogaerts says, 'Well, why are you here?'

Then the face disappears.

By whistling and whispering as loudly as he dares, he manages to get the attention of another of the women. A window is opened and a few hurried words are passed between him and the girls. One of the women with dark hair calls herself *Denise*. Her real name is Andrée Borrel. Boogaerts is successful in throwing some cigarettes through the window. Having found out that the women are British and French, he tells his friend Albert Guerisse. He is sure Guerisse will want to talk with the girls. Later that day he is told by the Dutch doctor that he is allowed to speak with one of the women in the hut opposite. At 7.00 p.m. that evening he goes to the hut, whistles and sees a woman appear at a window in her cell. He calls out: 'I am a British officer. Who are you?'

She replies: 'I am British.' She wishes O'Leary the best of luck. Although not confirmed, this is likely to have been Diana, as apart from Vera Leigh she is the only English girl of the four.

O'Leary wants to keep on talking but he is interrupted with a warning that the SS is present. If overheard, he will be shot on sight. He can do no more.

Franz Berg, the stoker, remembers that 'during the afternoon between their arrival in the crematorium cells and their murder, a French prisoner was able to speak to them: 'He told a German prisoner from Cologne, who told me that they had said they had been held in prison for more than a year, and that they had come from Karlsruhe. I also remember having heard that one of the two Frenchwomen was the mother of two children.'

Brian Stonehouse remembers seeing the *Rapportführer*, one of the SS men who had taken the four women down the camp steps when they arrived. The prisoners called him 'Fernandel' because he looked like the comic French actor of that name. He was walking up the steps in the middle of the camp from the crematorium carrying the fur coat Stonehouse had seen on the arm of one of the women.

Later, Berg brings four portions of food down from the kitchen at the top of the camp – thin soup and bread – for the women's last supper. It is his duty as *Kapo* of the bunker to personally fetch food for the people he has in his bunker. Everybody knows that in the evening people are going to be executed. But on this occasion Berg is not allowed inside the cell to distribute the food. This is done by the senior *Blockführer*, Nietsch. Shortly after this meal, at 8.00 p.m. the women are moved into the single cells – small, airless cubes with low ceilings where it is impossible to stand. One of the girls asks Berg for a pillow. At his trial Berg will tell the court he thought it was Vera Leigh.

Later that evening, Peter Straub tells Berg to heat the crematorium to the maximum heat by 9.30 p.m. and then to disappear. Berg is used to this sort of work; he is used to burning bodies about three times a week. The doctor is going to come down to give some injections.

At some time during the evening Dr Boogaerts notices an SS medical orderly going into the hospital block to borrow a syringe. Another prisoner, Rauson, hears a rumour from the *Kapo* in his own barrack, a man named Duchanek, who had heard it from Berg that injection is the method to be used. The order comes again to all prisoners: 'Stay in your blocks at the risk of being shot!' Following orders, all prisoners are in their barracks by 8.00 p.m. and their shutters are closed. Night sentries are on guard in the watchtowers. The only movement is inside the crematorium, where Berg is stoking the oven.

One of the medical orderlies, *Unterscharführer* Emil Bruttel, was in the dispensary near the crematoriunm and is rung up by Dr Plaza to check how many capsules of Evipan are in stock. Bruttel tells him there is just enough for the normal requirements of the operating theatre. Ten minutes later Plaza phones again: 'Look in the medical stores and see if we have any Phenol, and if so, how much.' Bruttel phones back to say that there is about 80 c.c. Plaza then rings a third time and orders Bruttel to be ready with Eugen Forster, another orderly, for work. He is told to bring the phenol and a 10 c.c. syringe as well as one or two strong needles. Bruttel and Forster are then told to come to the camp entrance. Bruttel takes the Phenol with him, about which he knows nothing and which is contained in a dark brown bottle with a glass stopper, while Forster takes the syringe and the needles; then they head to where they have arranged to meet.

By now it is very dark. They meet Dr Plaza, Dr Rohde, Adjutant Ganninger and some of the *Blockführers* of the camp staff, among whom are Nietsch and Ehrmanntraut. They are told to hurry into the camp; the gate is closed behind them. A block leader goes ahead with an oil lantern used for security reasons. While walking to the crematorium Bruttel learns from the officers' conversation that four women have been arrested in Paris and condemned to death as spies. He gets the impression that the doctors are reluctant to carry the necessary instruments themselves to the place of execution, and that they feel they will gain more courage and confidence by the presence of a number of people for an act which is evidently highly distasteful.

There is no way back for Bruttel and Forster. They did not carry security lanterns, and to go through the blacked-out camp without any identifying light is certain suicide as the guards will shoot instantly.

The group is observed as they make their way down the *Lagerstrasse* – the same path as the women had followed earlier in the day. Albert Guerisse peers between his curtains, watches the group carrying torches on the way down and identifies the two SS doctors – one in uniform and one in civilian clothes – and several other SS staff and officers.

It is obvious that the plan of execution has already been drawn up by the officers before entering the camp. In the crematorium the light in the oven room has already been put out so that one cannot see into a little room where there are several beds. It is here that Bruttel and

Forster learn the details of the plan from the explanations given by the doctors to Ganninger.

Nietsch and Ehrmanntraut are dispatched to fetch the women separately from the cells.

At 9.30 p.m. Straub makes his way back to the crematorium and checks that the furnace has been heated to the desired temperature. He then sends Berg back to his room with orders not to come out again. The group with the doctors who had been walking down the *Lagerstrasse* now arrives inside the crematorium; Berg will say later at trial that Harjenstein is among the group.

Berg goes to his room where Georg Fuhrmann and a Russian from Leningrad, named Alex, are seated on their bunks. A few minutes later the camp Adjutant, Otto, Nietsch and the kommandant look into his room. Berg pretends to be asleep. Through a fanlight over the door it is possible to see the corridor outside. Fuhrmann, who occupies the highest bunk, is able to look through this without standing up. He whispers that 'they' are bringing a woman along the corridor. They hear low voices in the next room and then Fuhrmann can see figures dragging something on the floor that is below his angle of vision through the fanlight. At the same time the men can hear the noise of heavy breathing and low groaning. Fuhrmann sees another two women, and again they all hear the same noises and groans as the insensible women are dragged away.

The fourth woman, however, remains in the corridor. Berg hears her say '*Pourquoi?*' A voice that he recognises as that of the doctor, who is in civilian clothes, says '*pour typhus*'.

When the four women are brought from the cells they are first made to sit on a bench in the corridor that leads from the oven to the dissecting room. They are told by Ganninger, who speaks a little French, to undress for medical examination. This they refuse to do unless a woman doctor is called. They are told they will be given injections against illness. The first woman is then taken by Straub into the room where the doctors are and injected in the upper arm. He then helps the first woman back to the bench, where she sits down next to the others who are still waiting. The same procedure is followed with the second woman. When Straub arrives back with the second woman after she has been injected he finds that the first is sitting 'stiff and stupefied'. The process continues until all four have been injected and are sitting in this stupefied condition. It is then, according to Schulz, that they are taken to the room next to the crematorium. Here they are laid down and their clothes are taken off by Nietsch and Ermenstraub.

At the trial Dr Rohde will testify that after their injections, three of the women are easily undressed. However, the SS *Scharführer* has difficulty undressing the fourth woman as rigor mortis has already set in. He is therefore unable to take off the pullover she is wearing and has to 'tear it open'. Rohde yells at him and tells him the bodies will have to be undressed in a decent manner.

Once undressed, the women are dragged along the remaining length of the corridor to the oven and then placed inside it. The usual practice is to place a body on a transporter and then push it into the oven. Normally bodies are laid out alternatively; the first goes in feet first and the next head first.

Under interrogation after the war, Berg reported that at least one woman was conscious when she was put in the oven. His account was related to Vera Atkins as well as the court. He said that once the women had been dragged through the corridor, 'From the noise of the crematorium oven doors I can state definitely that in each case the groaning women were placed immediately in the crematorium oven.'

More than one witness talked of a struggle when the fourth woman was shoved into the fire. Bruttel described what happened:

As the last body was being placed in the oven a mistake appeared to have occurred, since the body threatened to slide out of the oven again. The possiblility of death not having occurred appears completely out of the question. He said as far as he could tell, after the injections death occurred within five seconds with the accompaniment of twiching.

This differed from Schultz's testimony: 'When the last woman was half way in the oven she had come to her senses and struggled. As there were sufficient men there they were able to push her into the oven, but not before she had resisted and scratched Straub's face.' Straub also claimed she had shouted *'Vive la France!'*

Another witness, Emile Hoffmann, the military musician from Luxembourg, testified to having heard the same cry. Prisoner Rauson said the whole camp was listening and watching, peeping though gaps in curtains as these things were happening: 'That evening we were listening carefully as we suspected foul play. I myself heard some screams and I now suppose that the women, still unconscious from the injections but alive, when put in the oven must have recovered consciousness and screamed.'

The next morning, in the course of his duties Berg has to clear the ashes out of the crematorium oven. He finds a pink woman's stocking garter on the floor near the oven; and on top of a pile of coffins he discovers a cardboard box with several empty glass ampoules, about two and a half centimetres long, labelled 'Evipan'.

Emil Bruttel walks back with the doctors up to the officers' mess, listening to the doctors discussing what has happened over and over again, saying that they had intended to use the drug Evipan but because of the small amounts in stock they had resorted to Phenol. They repeatedly tell each other that the reason the women were killed is because they were spies. And they describe their method of killing as more humane than shooting or hanging.

Schultz notices that Straub's face has been severely scratched, and Straub recounts: 'I have been in Auschwitz for a long time, in my time about four million people have gone up the chimney, but I have never experienced anything like this before. I am finished.'

That night there is a party in the officer's mess.

Author Floris Bakel wrote of that time in Natzweiler:

Christmas 1943

I walked down to the plateau next to the crematorium beyond which stretched enormous woods. I had a magnificent view of the valley, which was full of a violet haze. As I stood there in solitude, slowly regaining my sense of self, far away beneath the haze in the hidden church bells started pealing. Not long after a huge silver cross appeared to me in the sky to the north, where Holland lay. 'The people who lived in darkness saw a great light; and light dawned on the dwellers in the land of death's dark shadow." I did not imagine this. It was reality, so help me God Almighty.[3]

12

The Trial

The part played by the women members of SOE, who were infiltrated into enemy-occupied countries, was by no means insignificant. To them is due all honour.
– Sir Hartley Shawcross, Attorney General

As Allied armies began to push through France in August 1944, the Supreme Headquarters Allied Expeditonary Force (SHAEF) had sent specialist officers to gather political intelligence about the German occupation of France, and in particular about its war crimes. One of these officers was Prince Yurka Galitzine, the son of a White Russian prince and an English mother. He was part of a small Allied Combat Propaganda mission, a group of French and American officers to France, and his job was to report in detail on what the retreating German army had left behind. They were in Alsace in November when Strasbourg was liberated. However, nothing could prepare him for what he was to discover on a lonely hilltop in the Vosges Mountains: the remains of the concentration camp known as Struthof-Natzweiler, which had been evacuated in October with its prisoners driven eastwards ahead of the Allied advance to camps in Germany. The actual liberation had taken place on 22 November by French troops operating with the US Seventh Army.

Galitzine had heard that not only had there been British men imprisoned at Natzweiler but possibly three British women, as well, who had been seen in the camp:

It was rather like a sort of tourist trip to start because it was so beautiful, just seeing the woods and the mountains. We didn't really know what to expect. I mean I had heard that there was a camp up there and I imagined it was going to be a sort of either a tented camp or rather like a barracks ...

Amazingly, the records of the camp were intact and had been left behind in the administration building after the staff had vacated the camp. On carefully going through all the records Galitzine was able to put together a record of killings, medical experiments carried out on live prisoners, conditions on slave labour on starvation rations, and brutal punishments carried out by sadistic criminals. He had gathered enough evidence to write that 'one day three women spies were brought to the camp and shot in the sandpit. They were described as being one Englishwoman and two Frenchwomen.

The first thing that really hit me was the smell, which in fact you could tell quite a long way before you got to the camp. I suppose the best description is almost like a knacker's yard; a sort of deserted knacker's yard with coffins lying about the broken urns with human ashes lying around, piles of filthy clothes which smelt to high heaven.

Galitzine's report was not believed. It was not until other camps such as Bergen-Belsen and Dachau had been liberated the following April that the world learned of the appalling atrocities that had taken place in Hitler's Third Reich. His report also mentioned that one of the English prisoners had left behind some drawings he had made while in Natzweiler: he had given them to one of the civilian foremen employed by a local firm of stonemasons contracted to the Germans to supervise the slave prisoners who worked in the quarries. The drawings had been signed by 'BJ Stonehouse'.

Outraged that his report had not been believed, Galitzine, a former journalist with the *Daily Express*, leaked the story. By the autumn of 1945 word of his findings reached an SAS intelligence officer named Major Eric 'Bill' Barkworth, head of the SAS war crimes investigation team. He and his men had already taken part in two operations in the Vosges in September 1944 in which some of Barkworth's men went missing, believed killed. When the SAS team officially disbanded, Galitzine managed to keep the team going so they could track down the murderers and bring them to trial. The trail eventually brought them to Natzweiler-Struthof.

Vera Atkins was already aware of Galitzine's intelligence report on Natzweiler, and in December 1945 the two met up at Galitzine's Eaton Square address. She found a tall, striking young man with impeccable English public school manners. For his part he saw an attractive woman in WAAF uniform, determined to find out what he could tell her about her lost SOE women. He was somewhat surprised at her visit: 'She asked me straight away if I had been to Natzweiler and if I had heard anything about the [SOE] women, and she produced a list with photos of eight or ten women. I said: "No, but I do remember in the report I wrote somebody had told me that three British women had been killed there."

He agreed the case should be followed up and that he would support her efforts. Vera then obtained a temporary commission as a squadron officer in the WAAF, which would authorise her to deal with the military in the various zones. Galitzine also helped her to get the War Office to agree to attach her to the War Crimes Investigation Unit in the British Zone. She had just three months to complete her investigations as the judicial process was already underway.

One of the first agents to return home was Brian Stonehouse, who in the company of his friends Bob Sheppard and Pat O'Leary had been liberated by the Americans from Dachau concentration camp. When returning prisoners were liberated and their identifications established, special military transport was laid on to bring these people home. Vera made a point of meeting every one of the F Section agents personally. Brian Stonehouse and Bob Sheppard arrived back at RAF Northolt and Vera was waiting for them with a car. She remembered exactly what they were wearing:

They had decked themselves out rather tastefully in fact with American boots with trousers tucked into them and loose jackets and I should think about five yards of blue silk material, dotted white, wound around them as scarves, which they had pinched from the *Industrihof,* which was the workshops attached to the camp, and one of these was donated to me. Close-shaven heads, hollow-cheeked, very bright-eyed. Both of them tall, needless to say, slim. Brian, very dark brown eyes, long sensitive face. Bob, fair, blue-eyed, round, amused robust face. With these two no emotion other than joy. Brian I had reserved a room for in Chelsea Cloisters ...

A short time later, Vera Atkins wrote the following letter to Stonehouse C/, the Intelligence Group Secretariat at the HQ Control Commission for Germany in Lubeck:

> I was so pleased to hear of your promotion and posting to a job which sounds interesting.
>
> I saw Pat O'Leary the other day, who tells me that you know of three women who were sent to Natzweiler in Aug 1944 and who were murdered shortly after their arrival. Can you give me any details of them? As you know the smallest scraps of information are often very useful. If you know of anyone else who could help in identifying them I should be glad if you would give me their name.

Vera met up with Brian and asked him to make a statement in the form of an affidavit. He was able to describe the four women who had been brought in under custody, and even managed to sketch them from memory. Vera thought it likely that the fourth girl, small and dark, was probably Noor Inayat Khan.

More than forty years later, Stonehouse remembered vividly that July day, the day when the women arrived in the camp for over 5,000 men: 'We thought: what on earth are these women doing here, because they didn't look starved, they were well dressed – you know, sort of from the real world.'

In due course the woman whom Vera thought was Noor Inayat Khan turned out to be Sonia Olschanezky, who had been admitted to Natzweiler the same day as the other three women. She was the fiancée of SOE agent Jacques Weil, second-in-command of SOE circuit *Juggler*, allied to the *Prosper* network also based in the Paris region. After the two circuits had been penetrated and broken, in May 1943, Weil had escaped to Switzerland but Sonia had continued to work on her own until she was arrested in January of 1944.

Of the agents who eventually made it back home, many found it difficult to adjust to civilian life after the war. Olaf Réed-Olsen, who had taken part in the demolition of the heavy water plant in Norway, struggled with his sleep for two years following the raid.

Now that Vera had been given a temporary commission as squadron officer in the WAAF, Galitzine lobbied on her behalf; the War Office gave her three months' attachment to Lieutenant-Colonel Gerald

Draper's legal section of the War Crimes Investigation Unit at Bad Oeynhausen in Germany. She made a great impression on everybody who met her, one of whom was Draper. He described her as

> ... a remarkable woman. I don't think I have met anybody like her, or am likely to do so again. She arrived as a very composed, very self-contained, self-assured person with a sense that she conveyed immense reserves of mental ability and purpose. A quiet-spoken woman, who managed to convey to those she addressed the sense of purpose; she was there to do something, and nothing, but nothing, was going to deter her. (*Secret Hunters*)

Draper recalled she was also a woman whom it was almost impossible to ruffle. She would discuss appalling things that had happened to the women agents with a degree of detachment, concentrating on the technical details of how it had happened and how the mission had led to their capture: 'I thought she was a charming lady, and a very efficient one.'

It was not until investigations into war crimes in 1945 and 1946, led by Major Barkworth of the SAS War Crimes Investigation Team and assisted by Vera Atkins, that full details emerged of the four women's fate at Natzweiler. Because of the sheer weight of evidence, it was agreed that a specific trial should be held, culminating with a British military tribunal at Wuppertal in Germany.

On 27 April 1946 Yurka Galitzine briefed Barkworth and Vera on preparations for the trial and explained that there was now great pressure from the War Office to expedite all war crimes investigations, and therefore the Natzweiler trial was being rushed through even though not all the accused had yet been traced. A young trainee solicitor, Major Anthony Hunt, had been appointed to prosecute the case. Vera felt that the women could rightly be classed as 'spies' since there was no other category for military persons operating in civilian clothes in enemy-occupied territory. But she was determined that the defence should not therefore claim lawful execution. To this end, she had secured the agreement of the court that the names of the dead be withheld from publication on the grounds that this would spare the anguish of their next-of-kin. However, the victims' families had no objection to publicising the names. Mrs Rowden had written to say Diana's name could be publicised.

Vera Leigh's half-brother had actually stated he thought it 'preferable' for the full story to be published. Furthermore, as each of the families knew by then that their loved ones had died at Natzweiler, suppressing names in newspapers was redundant. On the eve of the Natzweiler trial Vera's anxiety about publicity was intense. Everything had been done in London to try to keep 'this disgusting business' out of the papers, as Major Norman Mott, formerly of SOE's security directorate and now handling residual affairs of SOE while it was closing down, put it.

During his investigations, Gerald Draper interrogated Peter Straub, the camp executioner. He described Straub as 'an extremely unattractive member of the SS concentration camp staff of Natzweiler'. However, Straub talked quite openly about what had happened, taking refuge in the fact that as a minion he was only obeying orders. (This defense was not going to wash with the judges at the trial.)

'I recall Vera being particularly concerned as to whether or not the four women had been injected before they were thrown in the oven and we believed that Straub had been the person who had disposed of them into the furnace,' said Draper. He recounted:

We proceeded to talk about the method of disposing of these agents and then spoke about the other executions that he'd carried out by hanging. We discussed the height of the stool on which the wretched victims stood before it was kicked away. And he was not sufficiently intelligent to realise the drift of my question until he appreciated that I was establishing that he had let them die by slow strangulation as opposed to a prolonged drop to break the neck.

At the end of this interview he referred to the number of 'pieces' he had disposed of in a day and with that I said, 'You leave this room on your hands and knees like an animal. You are not fit to stand and talk to human beings on your legs.' I seem to recall at that stage it was the first and last time I ever saw Vera Atkins show the slightest form of distress.

The station hotel at Hamburg along with the Hotel Bahnhof served as bases for the prosecution team. In the days leading up to the case Vera and Odette Sansom, who six months earlier had become the first woman to be awarded the George Cross, were to be the prosecution's star witnesses.

Vera had discovered certain documents, personal records of Karlsruhe prison relating to three of the deceased women. She had looked through the register of names and seen the column 'taken to' against the name Diana Rowden, which stated she had been taken to *'einem KZ'*, short for *Konzentrationslager*. Natzweiler documents had shown that four women had been sent to a concentration camp on 7 July, but they also had a note attached which said effectively 'Collected on 6 July', and throughout the documents continued to describe these deceased as 'In Protective Custody'. The young trainee solicitor appointed as prosecutor for the case, Major Anthony Hunt, pointed out that persons under sentence of death would hardly be described as in 'protective custody' before both and after the day they were actually killed.

The trial took place on Wednesday, 29 May 1946. President of the military court was Brigadier the Hon. J. B. G. Henesay of the Grenadier Guards; the other four members were Majors Cooke, Whitfield, King and Turnhill. The Judge Advocate was A. A. H. Marlowe, KC, MP. Major Hunt acted as counsel for the prosecution and ten German lawyers acted as counsel for the ten defendants, Dr Grobel acting as lead counsel for the defence on account of his fluency in English.

Addressing the court and the jury in the opening speech for the prosecution, Major Hunt emphasised that they were

> ... about to hear the story of the killing of four women, and the facts of the story for sheer barbarity are without parallel in the history of civilization. I feel sure the court will pay considerable attention as to whether or not these women were dead when put into the crematorium oven. There is a considerable weight of evidence to show that life was not extinct at that time ...

The authoritative book on the trial, *The Natzweiler Trial*, makes for harrowing reading. In the introduction A. M. Webb writes:

> Perhaps no war crime committed during the 1939–45 War can be equal to that committed in the Concentration Camp at Struthof-Natzweiler near Schirmeck in Alsace on 6 July 1944 for which nine of the camp officials or staff were tried by a British

Military Court for the Trial of War Criminals at Wuppertal at the end of May, 1946. This crime was the cold-blooded killing of four women by injection followed by cremation, in circumstances which gave rise to suspicions whether or not the victims were dead or even unconscious when they were put into the crematorium oven. The defence was, broadly, that this was a lawful, and indeed a humane, execution of spies, duly tried and sentenced to death.

Webb makes a specific point:

The victims were carefully kept in ignorance of their fate. On the journey to Natzweiler they were told they were going to do agricultural work, and at Natzweiler no official appraised them of their fate. Even as they were given the injections, when one of the women asked why she was being injected she was told it was for typhus.

The case for the prosecution was that such a killing at such a time and in such circumstances raised a strong presumption that those who took part in it knew that it was illegal and was in violation of the laws and usages of war. Certainly one member of the party seems to have felt this: Wochner, the head of the political department which handled prisoners such as these, was notably agitated as a result of this execution.

Vera Atkins was the first to take the stand to give evidence for the prosecution. She named three of the four women, except Sonia Olchanezky, whose identity at the time of the trial was unknown. Vera stated she was an intelligence officer who had worked for SOE from March 1941 until the end of July 1944. It was through Odette Sansom, who had been on a journey from Paris to Karlsruhe with seven other women prisoners, that Vera had been able to recognise from descriptions given to her by Odette six of the seven names. In the course of her employment at SOE she had seen them when they first joined, during their training and before they left for the field:

During the course of investigations in Karlsruhe I was able to establish that the four who had left were Denise Borrel, Vera Leigh and Diana Rowden, and a fourth women whose identity

I was and am unable to ascertain. From questioning former prisoners in the camp at Natzweiler, I was able to establish that these four women were seen in the camp there. It became known on a certain date in July that four women had been injected and cremated in Natzweiler.

Major Hunt asked Vera if there was anything on the records from the prison at Karlsruhe to show that the prisoners had been tried or sentenced to death.

Vera answered: 'No.'

'Are they described there as in protective custody on and after the date of their death?'

'Yes.'

When the defending counsel, Dr Grobel, asked Vera if the girls had been in uniform, she replied that they were members of the FANY, the First Aid Nursing Yeomanry, which is a recognized auxiliary service whose members retain civilian status.

'Did these women who retain the status of civilians wear uniform when on duty?'

'In England, yes.'

'In France, during the execution of their duties, they did not wear uniform?'

'No, it was impossible.'

Vera went on to tell the court that the women were not engaged in espionage against the German Army. It was not an intelligence mission.

Dr Grobel argued in court that international law allowed for the execution of irregular combatants, and he invited the court to 'consider this case from the point of view that it was a normal and simple execution of spies', to which Vera retorted that 'the girls were not spies'.

Vera also told the court that certain documents had been handed to her by the prison director of Karlsruhe relating to seven of the eight women who were at one time held at Karlsruhe. Three of these papers were in connection with Borrel, Leigh and Rowden. She was also able to tell the court that the document contained Gestapo instructions to the prison that they should be taken into protective custody. It was also established that the date the prisoners left Karlsruhe was 6 July 1944.

As the trial progressed, prisoners who had been in the camp were questioned on whether they had seen the girls mentioned and how many were present. Some said there were three girls, others said four. There were also discrepancies with the time of day: some said 3.00 p.m., others 5.00 p.m. Some said they carried rugs, or just one rug; some said they all carried fur coats; one said they carried boxes, another suitcases. The one thing they all agreed on was that the girls were all well dressed. The French prisoner mentioned earlier who was working in the kitchens when they passed by, Roger Linet, had said 'they seemed young. They were fairly well groomed, their clothes were not rubbish, their hair was brushed and each had a case in her hand'.

The affidavit of Brian Stonehouse was introduced in court as evidence for the prosecution:

AFFIDAVIT OF BRIAN JULIAN WARRY STONEHOUSE of 513 Chelsea Cloisters, SW3 make oath and say as follows:

During the month of July I was working on the outskirts of the prison compound engaged in laying a pipeline with other prisoners just inside the wire on the east side of the camp.

My attention was drawn to a group of four women accompanied by two SS men, one officer and one NCO, whom I believed to be the *Rapportführer*, a man whom we had nicknamed 'Fernandel' owing to his likeness to the French actor.

The four women were carrying various parcels and one was carrying, what I remember thinking at the time, was a not very good fur coat. There was one tall girl with very fair heavy hair. I could see that it was not its natural colour as the roots of her hair were dark. She was wearing a black coat, French wooden-soled shoes and was carrying a fur coat on her arm. Another girl had very black oily hair, and wore stockings, aged about 20 to 25 years, was short and was wearing a tweed coat and skirt. A third girl was middle height, rather stocky, with shortish fair hair tied with a multi-coloured ribbon, aged about 28. She was wearing a grey flannel short 'finger tip' length swagger coat with a grey skirt which I remember thinking looked very English. The fourth woman of the party was wearing a brownish tweed coat and skirt. She was more petite than the blonde in grey and older, having shortish brown hair. None of the four women were wearing make-up and all were looking pale and tired.

As this was the first time that I had seen women at this camp the occurrence clearly stamped itself in my mind.

The whole party moved down the path on which I was working and passed me within a few feet so that I was able to observe them very closely. They went down the full length of the path and turned to the left towards the crematorium building where they disappeared from my view.

Later that evening all the prisoners were confined to their huts before the usual time, and by then rumours were flying round the camp that the four women whom I had seen were English and came from Fresnes, and further that the reason for our confinement was that the women were to be executed that evening.

I cannot remember with any certainty the further events of that night.

At some time during either the evening of the day on which I saw the women or the day after, I remember seeing the SS NCO whom we called Fernandel walking up the steps in the middle of the Camp from the crematorium carrying the fur coat which I had seen on the arm of one of the women.

Other witnesses for the prosecution included Pat O'Leary, formerly Albert Guerisse, and by now a lieutenant-commander, who had witnessed the arrival at Natzweiler of the four women. Recalling the further events of that day, he told the court that around 9.00 a.m. on the day of the execution an order was given that none of the prisoners in the camp were to be allowed out of their huts or to be seen at the hut windows. To the question of whether he saw any of these women again, he answered that he had gone to the window of his hut and witnessed the four women going to the cematorium, one after another; a little later from his window he 'could watch flames coming out of the chimney of the crematorium'.

After the trial O'Leary said that it was the policy of the Germans after 1943 not to try war criminals in order that there should be no death sentences to carry out. It was suggested by the defence that these women might have been tried *in absentia* on the material provided by their several interrogations, or by some 'strange court' or even early in the morning of 6 July at Karlsruhe. But there was no evidence of any of these suggested trials, and certainly a trial *in absentia* would have been a nullity and incapable of supporting a valid sentence.

Medical orderly Emil Bruttel told the court that 'the plan had been that once a woman had been brought into the injection room she would be made to lie on a bed and a doctor would then administer an intravenous injection in her arm. In each case 10 c.c. of phenol was used.'

There was some discrepancy as to which doctor administered the injections. Dr Rohde said he gave the first injection but was so upset by having to perform the task that Dr Plaza had to take over. Others said that Rohde gave two injections and Plaza the other two so as to share the responsibility.

On the fourth day of the trial, Saturday, 1 June 1946, the closing speeches of the defence and those for the prosecution were made. In the summing up the judge advocate told the jury:

> The case for the prosecution is that the four women were killed in Struthof-Natzweiler Camp probably on 6 July and the charge against each of the accused is that he was concerned in the killing. It is necessary for you to arrive at some conclusion as to whether these women were spies or not. You have heard, in that connection, the evidence of Squadron Officer Atkins, who has explained to you what the duties of these women were, which was mainly, as I understand it, to establish communication with the Resistance Forces in France and to keep communication between those forces and London ... There is a very considerable amount of evidence produced by the prosecution from which you would be justified in drawing the conclusion that there was no trial.
>
> One is bound to say that if someone comes up to you and says: 'Go and kill somebody else over there', you will naturally want to know why: you do not just go blindly and do it.
>
> You should give considerable attention as to whether or not these women were dead when put into the crematorium oven. There is a considerable weight of evidence to show that life was

not extinct at the time. You have to consider was this a lawful execution? The defence says that the killing was justified on the grounds that these women were spies and that they were entitled to be dealt with as such. It is perfectly true that a person who takes part in a judicial execution, as it is known in our law, is, of course, exculpated from any criminal responsibility, as in the case of a public hangman.

Rule 162 of the Hague Convention says that if you are satisfied they were not spies then the further tasks which are ahead of you are considerably simplified. Article 30 of the Geneva Convention says that a spy, even when taken in the act, must not be punished without a previous trial, and in connection with that it is summed up in Para 37 of the amended Chapter XIV of the Manual of Military Law, which says, 'Whether he belongs to the regular army or to an irregular corps, is an inhabitant or a deserter, their duty is the same: they are responsible for his person and must leave the decision of his fate to competent authority. No law authorises them to have him shot without trial and international law forbids summary execution absolutely.'

In considering their findings, the military tribunal applied a crucial principle: that while an accused might not have been responsible for the orders to execute the girls, he could nevertheless be found guilty due to a precedent adopted by all the Allied Military Tribunals. This essentially stated that someone who was present but did nothing to prevent a war crime taking place had a share in the responsibility for it. The individual cases for the defendants were a convoluted web and involved a mixture of accusing one another, claiming that they were simply carrying out orders, or asserting that they were not there at the time. Dr Grobel in his closing speech on behalf of all the defence lawyers agreed with the counsel for the prosecution that 'the case of these women was extraordinary in world history'. He quoted Article 30 of the Geneva Convention that the execution of spies was permitted as long as a sentence preceded the execution. He argued that the Convention did not explain how such a sentence should have been passed and went on to stress that international law gave no conditions as to how spies should be executed.

Sir Hartley Shawcross, the Attorney-General, reminded the court that human memory was short:

> The horror and revulsion which men felt at the atrocious crimes which accompanied the war tend to fade and disappear. It is right that the personal liability of those who commit the individual crimes, consequential though these may sometimes be upon the ruthless policy of the leaders they have chosen to set up and inherent to the totalitarian state which they have helped to create, should not only be firmly enforced but clearly remembered.
>
> The horror through which the world passed in those dark years was not just a nightmare which cannot recur, but is something against which the collective conscience and alert vigilance of mankind, asserting the rule of law in international affairs as in municipal ones, must protect us.
>
> The Natzweiler men who stood in the dock were the minor henchmen of those who stood in the Nuremberg Dock. Yet the record of what they did is perhaps more poignant and more vividly illustrative of the utter pitilessness and cruelty of the Nazi system than is the Nuremberg record in all its massivity. The fact that it was a doctor, Werner Rohde, who had sworn the Hippocratic Oath and of whom his old professor said 'he was a good student in the best meaning of the word', who was the accused and held most culpable in this case, is a measure of the tragedy of totalitarian Germany and, indeed of our civilization.

Consquently the tribunal found that the killing of the four women constituted a war crime. The sentences given caused some surprise among relatives and friends of the four women, as they were perceived as relatively light in some cases:

> Peter Straub, NCO in Political Department, responsible for arranging executions and for operation of the cells and crematorium – guilty, thirteen years imprisonment.
>
> Magnus Wochner, head of the Political Department and Gestapo liaison officer between criminal police and state police in the camp – guilty, sentenced to ten years imprisonment.
>
> Friedrich 'Fritz' Hartjenstein, camp kommandant – guilty, death sentence [later commuted to life imprisonment].

Franz Berg, former kapo, trustee prisoner, responsible to Straub for crematorium operation – guilty, five years imprisonment.

Werner Rohde, camp doctor – guilty, sentenced to death [hanged in October 1946].

Dr Kurt aus dem Bruch, camp dentist – not guilty.

Wolfgang Zeuss, responsible for maintaining order among the inmates and for the day-to-day economic functioning of the camp – not guilty.

Emil Meier, camp guard commander – not guilty.

Fritz Harjenstein was again sentenced to death in February 1947 by a French tribunal at Rastatt for other crimes. The sentence was not immediately carried out and he was kept in prison until another trial by the French, at Metz in June and July 1954. Once again he received the death sentence, but this too was commuted to life imprisonment. He died in prison of a heart attack in October 1954.

Further trials were to find Franz Berg and Peter Straub again guilty of other war crimes. This time both received the death penalty and were hanged in October 1946.

In 1954 and 1955 Wolfgang Zeus was twice sentenced by the French to death for other war crimes. Although he was then released by the French, he was deported to West Germany where he was investigated for murders at Dachau. In June 1960 he was sentenced to life imprisonment with hard labour.

Two former SS officers at Natzweiler who were implicated in the executions did not stand trial. Heinrich Ganninger, adjutant and deputy camp commandant, was arrested, but before trial he committed suicide by cutting his own throat in Wuppertal prison in April 1946 shortly after questioning by Major Barkworth of the SAS War Crimes Investigation team. He had also been facing prosecution for his earlier service and actions at Auschwitz.

Another potential accused was Dr Heinrich Plaza, the camp doctor who had been in the process of handing over to Dr Rohde. However, Plaza could not be traced at the time of the Natzweiler trial. After the war he resurfaced and worked openly as a doctor in Perach, Altotting in Bavaria. He was sentenced to death *in absentia* by the French in 1954, but an investigation by the West German authorities was terminated in 1952 on account of Plaza's advanced multiple sclerosis. Despite the claimed severity of this condition, he did not die until 1968.

On the sentencing Vera pointed out to Major Norman Mott, then in charge of residual SOE affairs while the office was closing down,

I was at Wuppertal during the entire time of the trial and I am satisfied that the sentences were perfectly fair. It should be borne in mind that the people in the dock were not all directly concerned with the killing, and a number of those directly concerned with the killing were not in the dock. Many of the accused would be tried on other counts, when their sentences would certainly be death.

She was to be proved correct.

13

Footprints in the Sawdust

At the time I said these four names should be given to the world and put high on the gallery of fame with Edith Cavell.
— 'Star Diary', 2 October 1946

After the war a marble plaque was erected on the wall of St Paul's Church, Knightsbridge, commemorating the names of fifty-two members of the FANY, 'who gave their lives for King and country' in the 1939–45 war. Diana Rowden is among them. It is close to the one-time vicarage that served as the headquarters of the First Aid Nursing Yeomanry.

On 31 July 1945 two posthumous awards were awarded to Diana, the *Croix de Guerre* and Member of the Order of the British Empire, as well as her being 'Mentioned in Despatches' in appreciation for all she had done in her service to her country. Maurice Buckmaster had written:

> Her organiser was arrested a month after her arrival, but in spite of the fact that she was seriously compromised by this and other arrests in the area, Rowden remained in the area and continued her work. She was obliged to lie low for some time but she insisted on carrying on. [She] performed excellent work as a courier but was eventually arrested at the end of November 1943.

Incredibly, it was not until 1946 that Mrs Rowden learned that her daughter had been awarded the two decorations. Because she had heard virtually nothing of her daughter's service, she was under the impression that Diana had failed. Noor Inayat Khan, Yolande Beekman and Eliane Plewman had been awarded posthumous *Croix de Guerres*. When researching Diana's life, Elizabeh Nicholas thought that surely Diana too had been decorated, but she had said nothing to Mrs Rowden in case she was mistaken. Nicholas asked the FANY if they would approach the military attaché at the French Embassy in London to enquire if Diana had been awarded a *Croix de Guerre*. They took action and the embassy replied that Diana had indeed been awarded a *Croix de Guerre*; they could not understand why it had not been given to her next-of-kin. There was no explanation for this from the British side, and it was not until October 1955 that Mrs Rowden finally received the decoration which had been awarded to her daughter in January 1946.

The story of Diana's belated award became known in the village where Mrs Rowden lived and was picked up not only by the local paper but by the *London Star* on 26 November 1955: 'Through a confusion in the records it was not until this week that Mrs Rowden learned of the award of the *Croix de Guerre* to her daughter in 1946.' 'A confusion in the records' is one way of describing a disgraceful turn of affairs. Dame Irene Ward, MP and a penfriend of Elizabeth Nicholas, decided not to let the matter rest. She made enquiries as to how this had happened, and when the answer came it was indeed incredible. In 1942 the committee on the 'Grant of Honours, Decorations and Medals in Time of War' recommended that posthumous awards conferred on British service personnel by foreign governments should not be accepted. The reason given was that some foreign governments issued posthumous awards much more freely than did the British government, and if they had accepted posthumous awards made by foreign governments they would have been 'unable to reciprocate'. Dame Irene was later informed that the British had returned to the French government all citations and insignia which they had been asked to send to the next-of-kin of RAF and WAAF officers whose death had been presumed. The *Croix de Guerre* for Section Officer Rowden was amongst those returned.

One question remained: if Diana's award had been sent back to the French, why were Eliane Plewman's and Yolande Beekman's conferred? Their families had been informed about the awards and Mrs Rowden was not. By this time Elizabeth Nicholas was fuming and made no bones about calling the whole thing a 'miserable, squalid affair'.

Mrs Rowden had not been bitter but she had been saddened that some of the women who had shared danger with her daughter had received the *Croix de Guerre* whilst Diana had got nothing.

The full recommendation for the Award of the MBE to Diana Hope Rowden is as follows:

This officer was landed in France by Lysander in June 1943 as courier to a circuit in the JURA. Her commanding officer was arrested a month after her arrival, but in spite of the fact that she was seriously compromised by this and arrests in the area, ROWDEN carried on her work in cooperation with the W/T operator of the organisation. For four months she worked untiringly travelling long distances in dangerous territory in order to maintain liaison between the various groups of the circuit. She was constantly sought after by the Gestapo and was eventually arrested towards the end of November 1943. After spending some time in prison in France she was deported to Germany.

For her courage, self-sacrifice and devotion to duty, it is recommended that this officer be appointed a Member of the Order of the British Empire.

(sgd) C. McV. GUBBINS
Major-General
14.9.45

In writing about the agents after the war, Churchill wrote the following:

From the knowledge I had of their hazardous work, I should say that they were among the most illustrious of any who served this country in the dark years of the war.

I felt a total dedication to those agents of SOE, 480 in all, whose average life in the field narrowed down to a mere three weeks, as we later discovered. Some were picked up as they landed; many were betrayed by German sympathisers; others were never heard from after they bailed out; but they were all magnificent.

It is now acknowledged that SOE's administrative winding-up was bungled – many inquiries which ought to have been pursued were allowed to drop. Some weren't even taken up. However, in fairness to the organization, when it was disbanded in January 1946 by Cabinet decision, the small winding-up staff that was left had other things to do besides following up casualties, and it was thought more important to resettle the thousands of survivors from all over the world than to investigate the affairs of the hundreds of dead. Jean Overton-Fuller makes a valid point that much suffering was caused to many people, left long years in ignorance by secret authorities unwilling to admit they had made mistakes or too busy with other affairs to rectify them. 'The trouble was that time pressure and staff shortage were always severe, and the security blanket thick; so many ends were left loose,' she wrote. 'This is not easy to understand or to excuse; and it has caused justified bitterness.'[1]

One or two points can be urged in favour of silence. Reliable news about the arrest or death of agents was usually difficult and frequently impossible to obtain, and it was thought less cruel to let families dally with false surmise than to inflict on them rumours of suffering which might prove untrue. Obviously there were security objections in wartime to letting anybody outside the umbrella of the Official Secrets Act know about the fate of a secret agent; it might have been fatal to an agent under arrest if a hint of his or her true identity leaked back to the Germans, thus destroying the cover story. A further point worth remembering was that the press was not always reliable in their reportage.

An article in 'The Star Diary' about Vera Leigh, dated 2 October 1946, referred to the fact that the names of the victims of the Natzweiler trial had been withheld. It continued:

> At the time I said that these four names should be given to the world and put high in the gallery of fame with Edith Cavell ... Now one of the four can be so honoured; her name appears in the *London Gazette* today with the posthumous award of the King's Commendation for brave conduct.

However, had the names of all four girls – Diana, Andrée Borrel, Vera Leigh and Sonia Olshanezky – been published at the time of the Natzweiler trial, the impact of publication at that time would have been much greater than after – the impact then being small in comparison.

After the names were released to the public, other newspapers such as *The Evening News* took up the topic:

> Miss Vera Leigh, a British girl in a Paris fashion house before the war, was burned alive in a crematorium at Natzweiler with [sic] Andrée Borrel and [sic] Diana Rowden ... Miss Rowden, wireless operator, went long distances in dangerous country to maintain liaison with various groups and once escaped after being arrested ...

These newspaper reports in the months after the war made harrowing reading for the unsuspecting British public, many of whom no doubt had thought that surely all the stories of atrocity, barbarism and evil had come to an end. The horrific facts, written in cold bold type as told in the report of the Natzweiler trial and subsequently published in 1949 by William Hodge, would have shocked even the most emotionless readers. However, what about the victims' families? We know that Mrs Rowden was too traumatised to even discuss her daughter's death, that in fact for a long time afterwards she took to her bed unable to communicate with the outside world.

The names of the murdered women at the Natzweiler trial had been suppressed by the Press as it was thought that to publish them would cause distress to the next-of-kin, who had asked that they should be withheld. The Press agreed, and those words redacted in the reports in 1946 were not made public until 1948 at the time of the unveiling of the FANY memorial. A year later, in 1949, all the details were given to the Press. As Elizabeth Nicholas wrote: 'These [sic] men had treated the murders as casually as an incident in the day's work.'

Most of the captured SOE agents had passed through the interrogation centre at Paris Gestapo HQ, at 84 Avenue Foch. When Vera Atkins found out that Kieffer, the Paris Gestapo chief, was being held by the French, she was able to interrogate him. She remembered their meeting in the dining room at the Villa Degler:

> I had the oportunity of a prolonged and quiet conversation with Kieffer and he started by informing me that of course he always had a great concern for our people, for whom he had the

greatest admiration, and in particular some of the women and some of the men, whose names he mentioned to me. And he felt that he had a very clear conscience in that they must all have survived. So I quietly told him what exactly he had done, about sending them on with their records, and selecting Karlsruhe for the women for his own convenience, since he happened to live there. It was nice for him to have an excuse to return from Paris whenever he felt like it, and when I told him the fate of one or two he pretended to cry. And I think that I have rarely felt as angry or disgusted as I did at the sight of this man who produced tears. And I remember saying, 'Kieffer, if one of us is going to cry, it's going to be me, and you will please stop this comedy.'[2]

It was in March 1949 that Mrs Rowden wrote to her brother-in-law, Henry Wells Rowden, with whom she had been previously been unacquainted.

Diana, aged 29, was foully murdered by the Germans at Natzweiler Concentration Camp on 6th July, 1944. I only heard of this in May '46, and bought this place on her account in late '45, having been told that she was missing, and would probably be liberated near Christmas '45, and would want a quiet spot to convalesce. The shock of her awful fate was dreadful to me and to her 2 brothers. She was an intelligence officer in the WAAF and worked at the Air Ministry and was Mentioned in Dispatches and was courageous to a degree. The whole ghastly affair does not bear thinking about. She volunteered for special secret service work and flew into France in '43 and did wonderful work in preparing for D-Day. Letters from British officers who saw her in various prisons said her dignity and courage and her kindness to her fellow-victims was wonderful. There is a plaque outside St Paul's, Knightsbridge – put up to her and her fellow heroines, and also another in the French Institute. Life without her is like a day without sunshine, as she was so gay, so happy-natured and spread happiness wherever she went.

George Miller, whom Vera had also interviewed for French Section, later wrote: 'She speaks with a kind of quiet, firm authority that makes it clear why no one can refuse her anything she requires. The woman knew she could master anyone in trousers. But she had a vulnerable side too.' When author Rita Kramer asked Vera if she had noticed whether Wuppertal was a zoo (the Natzweiler trial had been held in the zoological gardens at Wuppertal) she answered that she was too churned up to notice: 'It was just a building. It could have been a zoo or it could have been the Grand Hotel.'

Years later, Vera told of the strain talking about those grim days. 'I don't think anyone realises it is a considerable strain talking about all this. One has to think back over fifty years and when I talk about those people it brings back a whole lot of other things and it is not a subject I particularly enjoy. And you know, since '45 in all those years I have never been without somebody who was writing. Never. I do it,' she said quietly, 'as a sort of moral duty.'

In Lons-le-Saunier in the immediate aftermath of the war, the families of those who had been thrown into concentration camps or simply disappeared wondered what had happened to their loved ones. The people of the Jura who had known and worked with Diana and John Young wondered what had happened to them, and hoped for a long time, like the Janier-Dubrys, that somehow Diana had survived – that one day she would turn up or get in touch.

Odette Mathy, whose parents had belonged to the Resistance and who had owned the café in Lons-le-Saunier, the same café where the false *Benoit* had met members of the Resistance the day of the *arrestation*, wondered about Diana's fate when she returned home. Diana had been a frequent visitor to her parent's home in Lons. Odette was one of the lucky ones who had miraculously survived the atrocious conditions of camp life. When Elizabeth Nicholas called on her in the 1950s, Odette told her that Diana had come to the Mathys' house with an Englishman 'who in reality was a spy'. Soon after the Gestapo had come for Odette and her parents; they never returned from deportation.

Odette also recalled seeing Diana some time in February 1944 at Fresnes but was unable to speak with her. Two months later she left for Ravensbrück: 'I still remember her very well in spite of the fact that I was only 18 at the time. She was a great friend and we took part in several missions together.' When Rita Kramer also visited Odette and her husband, also a concentration camp survivor, during the 1980s, she saw two photos: one of a dark-haired handsome man, '*Gabriel*', and the other of a half-smiling young woman, under which was the name '*Marcelle*', one of Diana's code names and one for which she was known in the field. Across the bottom was written '*Arretes par la Gestapo le 18 Novembre 1943*'.

In the latter part of the 1950s Professor Michael Foot was asked to write SOE's official history, and to defend its actions and their results against the charges which had been brought against it by Dame Irene Ward and the Conservative government of the time. One of the subjects raised in the House was one of incompetency and the fact that too many of SOE's women agents were amateurs. However, Foot was able to respond that so too were many of the SD and Gestapo staff they were up against. Although Hans Kieffer had been a police inspector before the war, and Josef Goetz a teacher, most of the other SS staff were more likely to have had careers as some kind of criminals before the war than as professionals in counter-espionage. On the other hand, many of F Section's so-called amateurs had turned out to be the most successful agents, and they had been drawn from civilian life rather than from the ranks of the military.

An interesting comment was made by Elizabeth Nicholas. She was told by a Frenchman, who had worked for SOE in the Jura area and had been trained in England with Maugenet, that he had been captured on landing and taken to Lons-le-Saunier. (If so, it could only be Mennesson or Paul Pardi, as they were with Albert Maugenet and all three were captured on landing.) 'He was the one disagreeable Frenchman I had met out of all the people who had known Diana,' wrote Elizabeth. 'He was bitter about his experiences with SOE and said several times it was idiotic to suppose that any Englishman could possibly teach anything to a Frenchman who had already learnt much about clandestine activity in the hard school of reality.' (*Death be not Proud*.)

In Dec 1943 – unfortunately too late, and six months after the tragic exodus of Diana and the three other agents – Buckmaster invited Squadron Leader Hugh Verity of Special Duties 161 Squadron to discuss a telegram from another network. This accused Henri Dericourt, in charge of F Section's receptions on the ground, of liaison with the German counter-espionage people in Paris. At that stage Verity thought it unthinkable that Dericourt could be a traitor. They were good friends and Verity felt there was no reason to distrust him. But both Buckmaster and Verity agreed that despite their incredulity they could not ignore the risk that there might be some truth in the accusation. They agreed that they had to get Dericourt back to London for interrogation, and meanwhile that they should not risk the lives of any more agents by sending them out to his receptions. Buckmaster called in F Section's operations officer, Major Gerry Morel, 'who always had a pale face';[3] when told of their suspicions his pale face turned even paler. He volunteered to kidnap Dericourt himself at gunpoint if necessary. Dericourt, it is reputed, was paid £5,000 for every agent he betrayed.[4] Dericourt was therefore recalled to London, where he stayed until after the war.

When told of the mendacity of Dericourt after the war, Gilbert Norman, alias *Archambauld*, who was accused postwar of throwing in his hands with the Germans when he was at Avenue Foch, said: 'I can sleep at peace because I know I was not responsible for the arrest of *Prosper*.'

However, the question of whether agents such as Norman had turned traitor dogged Vera Atkins, When she interviewed Kieffer at the time of the war crimes trials in Germany, she found him to be frank when she asked specifically for names of prisoners whom he had 'turned' and persuaded to work for him; and yet he looked uncomfortable. Some 'more or less helped, though not necessarily voluntarily,' he said. 'Most were made to feel they had nothing to lose because we knew so much already ... *Archambaud* [Gilbert Norman] had helped a lot,' he said eventually. 'In the end there were many who helped because they felt they had no choice.'

'The French Section had no traitors then?' asked Vera, now prompting Kieffer to volunteer the information she was sure he had. 'There was nobody who willingly betrayed us?'

'You know yourself there was one. You recalled him to London – *Gilbert* [Henri Dericourt]. He was Boemelburg's agent,' referring to his boss, Karl Boemelburg, head of the *Sicherheitsdienst* in France. 'For Boemelburg in fact he was more than an agent. He was a friend going back a very long time. And he alone dealt with him. He was Boemelburg's's forty-eighth agent.'[5]

Within months of the end of the war, the SOE was ordered to be dissolved at the behest of the Foreign Office and SOE's rival, MI6, the Secret Intelligence Service. The defunct organisation's most secret files, including all the wireless messages exchanged between SOE's London headquarters and its agents in the field, were entrusted to the Foreign Office for safekeeping. Each bundle of records was meticulously marked 'Important Historical Records. Never to be destroyed'. However, less than a year after they had been handed over to the Foreign Office for safekeeping, all those records were burned. Was it because SIS did not wish future historians to assign SOE credit they did not feel the organisation deserved? Or was it to destroy forever any traces of the violence perpetrated by MI6 upon its wartime rival service?

However, far more strange was the remark Vera Atkins had made to Elizabeth Nicholas about F Section records. As she recalls Vera's remark: '[She said] French Section records had always been diffuse, and that she herself had gutted them when the Section was being disbanded, that professional archivists had further gutted them before committing them to some dark cellar, and that they would be of no value.'

No doubt due to the influx of post-war media coverage about the war crimes, Squadron Leader William Simpson, who had been Diana's friend when they were both recuperating from operations early in the war, was asked to express his thoughts on why women went into France. The following is a copy from the *Sunday Express* article in 1945:

> The interesting thing about these girls is they are not hearty and horsey young women with masculine chins. They are pretty young girls who would look demure and sweet in crinolines. Most of them are English girls who speak perfect French. Some were educated in French convents; others attended Swiss finishing schools. A few are French girls who escaped from France and agitated for a chance to go back and work underground. Cool courage, intelligence and adaptability are their most important attributes. They have to be able to pass themselves off as tough country wenches, and smart *Parisiennes*.

In 1955 when Elisabeth Nicholas was researching *Death Be Not Proud*, she managed to track down Diana's mother through Dame Irene Ward, known for fighting for unpopular causes. In the early 1950s Dame Irene herself was writing a book on the history of the FANY and had come across the story of the SOE women. In 1958 she wrote to the Foreign Secretary, John Selwyn Lloyd, and warned 'she was going to be a frightful nuisance' unless she got some answers to certain questions; one of those was 'whether Henri Dericourt, alias *Gilbert* was either working for one of our secret service organisations and put into SOE with their knowledge or had he been working for the Germans'. It was because of the questions Dame Irene asked in the House over the murdered SOE girls that the eventual history of SOE was to be written, in 1964, by Professor Foot.

Harry Rée, who spoke and wrote about his time in France during and around 1943, praised Michael Foot, who

> ... managed to write a cool and accurate book on a hot and distortable subject, in which his whole outlook was typified by the attitude he adopted towards those women agents, to whom he gave due credit, but no more. In post-war England there was a romantic image of war but ... although wars can bring adventures which stir the heart, the true nature of war is composed of innumerable personal tragedies, of grief, waste and sacrifice, wholly evil and not redeemed by glory.

At this time, around 1958, Mrs Rowden was living at Telegraph House, a tall, white house in Hampshire. Coincidentally, it had been one of a chain of semaphore stations built to convey news of the Napoleonic fleet from the Channel coast to the Admiralty. When Elizabeth Nicholas had met up with Mrs Rowden, she told her that she

> ... had been a little hurt that small recognition had been given to the glorious deeds of the band of heroines, of which her daughter was one who did not survive. She knew nothing whatsoever of Diana's work in the field, or the circumstances of her arrest. Elizabeth was amazed because in a few short weeks and without any official backing or approval, she had been able to uncover information that had been withheld from the next-of-kin of those who died.

Mrs Rowden had for 12 years [since 1945 and this was 1958] believed her daughter had failed in her wartime mission; this was the answer she had found for herself when wondering why she had been told nothing from those who came back. She knew only that Diana had died in terrible circumstances at Natzweiler; and she thought the silence could have only one meaning. That her daughter had failed.

During this visit Mrs Rowden showed Elizabeth the cocker spaniel, Wizard, given to her by Diana 'to look after you until I return'.

In October 1955 Elizabeth Nicholas met up with Harry Rée, whom she refers to as '*Stockbroker*' in her book. When she asked him why it had taken so long for Mrs Rowden to hear of her daughter's disappearance, he seemed baffled and told her that after he had escaped to Switzerland in 1943 he had sent word as soon as possible to London of Diana's and John Young's arrest. It is puzzling as to why the War Office, in the letter of December 1945 to Mrs Rowden, opted to tell her it had not learnt of her daughter's arrest until the spring of 1944.

Elizabeth kept in touch with Mrs Rowden, keeping her posted on information regarding Diana as it came to hand. This helped Diana's mother, who had been finding life extremely difficult since her daughter's death. At this time, not mentioned in Nicholas's *Death Be Not Proud*, Mrs Rowden had also had to contend with the untimely and tragic death of her youngest son, Kit, who had returned from the war unwell and who by this time had committed suicide.

'I am so happy to know that all concerned had had pleasant and kindly memories of Diana, and that she left behind such good impressions. Thank you for all you have done,' she said.

Elizabeth was thankful that the meeting had been a happy one. 'I was profoundly moved by her personality. It was the first meeting I had had with anyone connected with the women whose story I had been seeking, and I was glad that it had been a friendly one.'

The events of that November day in 1943 when Diana and John Young were arrested were such that not one of the people involved would ever forget.

In 1956, when Elizabeth Nicholas talked to the Janier-Dubry family, she was appalled to discover that they had heard not one word of news concerning Diana since the day when she had been led from their house in handcuffs. When she told them of the manner of her death in Natzweiler-Struthof, Madame Juif exclaimed: 'I went to see it a year or two ago, you know it is now a museum, a memorial to those who suffered there? It was terrible beyond all imagining; I felt ill and had to leave. Had I known that *Marcelle* had been there, I would have fainted ...'

Nicholas was able to tell them that Diana had been taken to Natzweiler only on the day of her execution, and there was reason to suggest that her months of prison had been endured in surroundings less terrible than those of that dreadful camp. Madame Juif murmured, '*Tout de meme, pauvre fille ...*'

After the arrests of Diana and Young at Clairvaux-le-lacs, the Gestapo were still searching for Raoul Janier-Dubry, and they had harassed his wife for information. She had thought quickly and told them she had no idea where her husband was. He had a mistress – and that mistress was Diana. 'I don't care about my husband or *Marcelle*. *Il m'a laisse pour cette putain.* He has left me for that whore, so what do I care? I have to accept it. I have two young children and I am pregnant with another child.'

Christiane Voha told me her mother had no choice to say this: 'The Germans must have believed her on that occasion because she did not see them again for a while.'

In speaking of that time to Elizabeth Nicholas and describing how the Germans had taken everything of value in the house, including her wedding presents, her trousseau linen, and her family heirlooms, Aimee Janier-Dubry had told her: 'What are such things when one has life?'

In that summer in 1956 in the house at Clairvaux-le-lacs some photos and newspaper cuttings were shown to Nicholas: a photograph of Diana, one of Ida Poli immediately after her return from Ravensbrück concentration camp, another of *Gabriel's* brother, and one taken by the French police of an SOE officer as he lay dying after treatment by the Gestapo, a man known to Diana. Nicholas recalled that M. Janier-Dubry senior, father of Raoul, upon being asked if he could shelter a British radio operator 'had of course been delighted' according to his daughter-in-law Edith Juif. This attitude shows the generosity of the Janier-Dubry family who knew full well the dangers involved but went ahead anyway.

They spoke about Diana with loving admiration: she was brave and gentle, honest and kind. 'She always helped me with the vegetables and in cleaning the house, said Edith Juif. '*Enfin*, one could see she was not accustomed to such work, but it was her wish to be one of us, not to add to my burdens, to be helpful. The children loved her ...' and she turned to her daughter, aged fifteen (this is Christiane Voha, who I was to meet in 2015) and said, 'You remember her, even now, *ma petite?*' Her daughter answered, 'Clearly, I shall never forget her.'

An unsolved question at the time of writing is the question of Diana's ring and cigarette holder, which I was shown and photographed when I stayed with Claude and Christiane in 2015. In *Death Be Not Proud* Elizabeth Nicholas writes: 'At the cessation of my visit I wrapped Diana's ring and cigarette holder carefully in paper and put them in my suitcase. When I returned to England I sent them to Mrs Rowden who wrote to acknowledge their arrival and said they were precious to her.'

How then, did they come back into the hands of the Janier-Dubry daughters later? Christianne told me they had never left the family, that Diana had left them in her room that night of the arrests and that they had been looked after carefully ever since.

One explanation could be that at some time Aimee Janier-Dubry might have sent them to Mrs Rowden, thinking they were rightfully hers. Then later, when Mrs Rowden, realising she did not have long to live, decided that the people who had sheltered and looked after her daughter were the ones best suited to have these precious momentos. But this is surmise on my part, a biographer who is trying to tie up the loose ends. Christiane is certain they never left her parents' home.

Elizabeth Nicholas had asked Raoul and Aimee if Diana had ever given them the impression she was afraid. They replied emphatically she had not. On the contrary: 'Sometimes they had felt her insouciance amounted to imprudence; she had, for example smoked English cigarettes when walking in the woods surrounding the sawmill. Sometimes they had talked of the Gestapo and the tortures inflicted on its prisoners; Diana had said, '"I do not think I will talk. I am not afraid of them."'

'She was of a calibre one seldom meets,' said Madame Poli.

An interesting anecdote from Nicholas' visit to Paris relates how in a café, when she asked a waiter if he remembered anything happening in the café during 1943, he replied: '*Non, personne ne se souviendrait 1943.*' No, nobody would remember 1943.

After the war John Young's brother had come to visit them and had told them of John's death in Buchenwald. It was a war many wanted to forget.

Both Vera Atkins and Maurice Buckmaster were deeply affected by the loss of their agents. It was Vera and Nigel Smith, a military historian, who, noting there was no memorial to the four agents killed at Natzweiler, undertook a campaign to persuade the French government and the *Amicale des Deportées de Natzweiler-Struthof* to install the commemorative plaque that was placed there in 1975. Vera's reports on the F Section agents' files had proved vital when they formed the basis of the Roll of Honour to the 104 dead of F Section on the memorial at Valençay.

On 21–22 June 1975 relatives of the men and women who had been killed at Natzweiler were invited to attend the thirtieth anniversary of the Liberation of the Camps of Deportation and the unveiling of the plaque. Mrs Rowden was not physically strong enough to make the journey, and in her place Rosemary, daughter of Vera, Mrs Rowden's sister, and Mark Chetwynd-Stapylton's wife Anne represented her instead.

Mark Chetwynd-Stapylton, cousin of Diana, in a letter to Rita Kramer wrote:

> The ceremony was very well conducted and was deeply moving. I sometimes think of it even now. Rosemary and I and other relatives of the murdered girls were formally introduced to Jacques Chirac, then Prime Minister of France ...
>
> The photograph of Diana from the *Daily Mail* is the same as that which adorned a photo frame in Chris' bedroom. The fact that I have kept these pieces of paper suggests perhaps that the endeavours of those girls and their eventual plight has always had a lasting effect on me; and it is not by chance that whenever I am in Knightsbridge I usually visit the church that is beside the Berkely Hotel, to pay my respects to those in SOE (Diana included) who are remembered in a plaque let into the church's outside wall facing the Berkeley.[6]

In 1958 Maurice Buckmaster was interviewed on British television by John Freeman, a shrewd journalist and one who was not going to be easily put off. Graham asked him some sticky questions: 'Mr Buckmaster, exactly how was it that *Gilbert* [Dericourt] was still able to carry on as Air Movements Officer after it had come to light that he had dealings with the Germans? Still more, how was it that after you knew that the *Prosper* circuit was blown you still sent in agents, like Noor Inayat Khan?'

In answer Buckmaster replied that 'at that stage we had no idea the circuit had been blown. It was only later we found out the truth. Noor should never have been sent into France.'

Well, surely it was up to him to send or not?

Professor Foot also contends it was a mistake to send in Noor Inayat Khan:

> She was quite unsuited to the work. She made the appalling mistake of leaving her codes and notes of transmissions lying around her flat instead of getting rid of them immediately, so when she was arrested, the Gestapo had a field day. When they captured her wireless, notebooks, etc., they made her send transmissions to London. She very correctly let them know (by code) that she was 'in hospital' – the code that meant she had been captured.

In another television programme some years later, Vera Atkins was interviewed about Henri Dericourt, and said that when she first met him she sensed that he was untrustworthy. However, when Dericourt was interviewed by Jean Overton-Fuller in the 1950s for her book *Double Webs*, he told her, 'The *Funkspiel*, the German-controlled radio game, had been kept up deliberately from London, that men had been sent out without being warned, and that they were being deliberately sacrificed for the sake of keeping it up.'

'Do you think Colonel Buckmaster knew?' Fuller asked Dericourt.

'I don't think so ... I believe that Buckmaster did not know at the time.'

14

A Day Without Sunshine

Of course we made mistakes,
And in war mistakes cost lives.
Do not think the knowledge of that
Will be with us till we die.

- Vera Atkins

Only those who brave its danger
Comprehend its mystery

- Henry Wadsworth Longfellow

As one SOE veteran was to say in the years following the Second World War:

What can one say of the women agents of SOE who faced torture and death behind enemy lines? I have no adequate words of praise for their bravery ... although I felt closer to them than most. They were attractive, feminine women mostly, in their twenties and thirties. My heart went out to them. The cover we could provide for their underground work seemed pathetically feeble. These women went into battle as heroically as any man.[1]

In the final analysis of whether women agents should or should not have been sent into France, the words which Maurice Buckmaster wrote in *They Fought Alone* resonate with me particularly as I feel they apply very much to the women like Diana who did not return

255

home. They show the affection, dedication and admiration which Buckmaster felt for his agents, and his genuine sorrow and distress for the women who lost their lives:

> The war was not restricted to men. From the purely practical point of view, women were able to move about without exciting so much suspicion as men and were therefore exceedingly useful to us as couriers. I should have been failing in my duty to the war effort if I had refused to employ them, and I should have been unfair to their abilities if I had considered them unequal to the duties which were imposed upon them. For our part, we tried by our briefing – which became more and more precise and helpful - and by all the other means within our power to protect and help them, but in the final analysis an agent had to rely on himself, or herself, upon skill, upon coolness, upon courage and, most capricious of all, upon fortune.[2]

Some exceptional men and women are marked out for glorious deeds of valour. Over the centuries war has brought out bravery in people in the face of the worst adversity. The lion retreats and the mouse roars. But Diana Rowden was no mouse, as has been proven. She was an exceptionally clear-thinking young woman, obviously well-bred, quietly spoken, calm, cultured and refined. The adage *Sans Peur* (without fear), which had stuck with her all her life, was an appropriate one. She demonstrated her lack of fear firstly in France in the months leading up to war: immediately she volunteered for the Red Cross, driving ambulances across the country, becoming involved in helping with escape routes.

It seems she never thought of herself, preferring to push the thought of danger away. It was only until the very last moment, after most Britons had long ago departed, that even she realised she had no other choice but to return to England. But even after her arrival her strong sense of duty rose to the fore, once more fuelled by the desire to return to her beloved France where hopefully she could carry on fighting the war. The desire to return was always there, always predominant.

Churchill had high hopes for clandestine resistance in occupied countries, always favouring SOE and acting as a crucial ally in its constant bureaucratic struggles with the Foreign Office and the intense rivalry between the organisation and SIS. The Prime Minister loyally defended SOE's agents. Historian David Stafford writes in *Roosevelt and Churchill* that he vetoed a plan to place SOE's agents under the control of SIS.

Lord Selborne had sent Churchill quarterly reports on SOE designed to give the best impression of the organisation and keep his approval: 'As my department works more in the twilight than in the limelight, I should like to keep you informed regularly of the progress of the brave men who serve in it.' The reports, finally released in 1992, reveal that Sir John Peck, one of Churchill's private secretaries and later British ambassador to Dublin, who handled most of the files, judged Baker Street's achievements 'impressive'. Churchill read the reports closely and demonstrated unfailing concern for the fate of individual agents. He scribbled in the margin: 'Have they been rewarded for their efforts? Does SOE know their fate when captured?'[3]

To both these questions, sadly Diana's family was deprived of the answers for some years. Diana, by a cruel twist of fate, was betrayed through no fault of her own. In the face of impossible odds she managed, in more than five months of continuous Resistance work, to stay one step of the enemy, despite the fact that the Germans knew of her existence from the very first day she landed in France. Plus, it must be remembered that she had been infiltrated into one of the most dangerous resistance areas in the country, the Jura. I am confident that if it had not been for the Germans' knowledge of her arrival, she would have somehow evaded capture and managed to survive until the end of the war.

However, it was not to be.

Should families have been told about their lost sons or daughters? This is a question which has been a moot point in many books. As mentioned in the previous chapter, it is noted in a letter written by Vera Atkins to Mrs Rowden that Diana had expressed the desire that her mother not be told until the last possible moment if anything happened to her daughter. This was to prevent unnecessary distress; after all, it was reasonable to expect if Diana had been in a prisoner-of-war camp that she would be released at the cessation of war, so Mrs Rowden would have worried needlessly. I think too much has been made of the fact that relatives were in many cases the last to know what had happened to their loved ones; from the letters on Diana's file it would seem that every effort had been made to spare Mrs Rowden distress.

Agents were not allowed, or at least were not supposed, to tell their families what they were doing. When they went on operations their next-of-kin received a short note once a month or so, which usually stated 'We continue to receive excellent news'. It would appear that Diana had indicated to her mother that she was returning to France and that she would be undertaking work behind enemy lines. She did not tell her any more than that, but it is understandable how her mother would have felt knowing her daughter was living in an occupied country like France.

However, there are still some unanswered questions. Most of these relate to how after the war, when the medals were being handed out to relatives of other SOE women, little recognition had been given to her Diana, one of the brave heroines who had not survived – Mrs Rowden had justifiably been hurt by this.

Newspapers reported almost daily on the heroic deeds of servicemen and women who had won medals for gallantry. Mrs Rowden knew nothing whatsoever of Diana's work in the field or the circumstances of her arrest. It was not until 1946 that she (and the next-of-kin of the other Natzweiler women) finally received a letter from the War Office of the circumstances surrounding their death, stating that 'they all appeared to be in good health' during their incarceration in both Fresnes and Karlsruhe prisons and during the journey to Natzweiler, and also mentioning 'that they had not been subjected to torture in Karlsruhe and Natzweiler, and that the end came upon them too suddenly to cause prolonged suffering'.

So why was Elizabeth Nicholas, in just a few weeks and without any official backing or approval, able to uncover information that had been withheld from the next-of-kin of those who died? Elizabeth Nicholas, to put it mildly, was furious that Mrs Rowden had been treated so shabbily:

Mrs Rowden had for twelve years believed her daughter had failed in her wartime mission; this was the answer she had found for herself when wondering why she had been told nothing, or had heard nothing from those who came back. She was left knowing only that Diana had died, in terrible circumstances at Natzweiler; and she thought the silence could have only one meaning. That her daughter had failed, and silence was the kindest gift authority could bestow on her. I was able to reassure her on that. I met many of those who had worked with her and held her memory in affectionate admiration.[4]

And what of the strange manner in which Mrs Rowden was informed of her daughter's arrest and ultimate death? The first letter bearing ill news was sent on 15 October 1944, saying that London had recently been out of touch with Diana, and that under the circumstances she must be considered as missing; this was sent nearly a year after Diana's arrest and more than three months after her death. Another letter was sent on 22 December and a further one again sent in April 1946, which gave details of Diana's imprisonment in Karlsruhe and her death in Natzweiler concentration camp. So the question remains: why did nobody contact Diana's mother, if only to let her know of her daughter's splendid work in the Jura?

It was a case of unfortunate and tragic circumstances that led to the arrests of Diana and John Young. Was this because of the breakdown of the *Prosper* circuit in Paris and Henri Dericourt's betrayal of the agents who landed that night in June and which ultimately led to the insertion of the false *Benoit*? In Paris, the Germans had been playing the *Funkspiel*, the radio game, with London, working back the radios of captured SOE agents, and it was because of this that they heard Baker Street would be sending an agent into the Jura to take the place of John Young upon his return to England.

And were the four women sent into France by Baker Street deliberately inserted to deceive the Germans into thinking that the invasion would come earlier than expected, in 1943 rather than 1944, knowing full well they could be going to their deaths? Andrée Borrel, Sonia Olschanesky and Vera Leigh had all worked in the *Prosper* circuit or with its contacts in and around Paris and had been known to the SD through Henri Dericourt. Diana too, it has been said but not proved, had been under SD surveillance courtesy of Dericourt.

When Francis Suttill had been captured, his arrest followed a round-up of other agents in *Prosper* which gave rise in London to suspicions of treachery, poor security and mismanagement. SIS was quickly aware of the disaster. As mentioned earlier, the personal assistant of Claude Dansey, assistant chief of SIS, later recalled how Dansey asked if he had heard the latest news: 'What news?'

'SOE's in the shit. They've bought it in France. The Germans are mopping them up all over the place.'

The accusation, if true – and it seems there was no reason not to believe this – would undoubtedly have confirmed the deep-seated suspicion of SOE by SIS and MI6. Bitter battles and petty rivalries had been played out in Whitehall from the initial inception of SOE, and which had lasted as long as the war itself. Not only was it rumoured but positively backed up that Dansey passionately hated everybody at SOE headquarters and always referred to them as 'that blasted bunch of bloody amateurs'. At best, SOE was looked upon as a lot of harmless backroom lunatics which, it was hoped, would not develop into an active nuisance; SOE retaliated by referring to SIS as 'the Bastards of Broadway', after the street where the Intelligence Service had its headquarters. However, SOE always had the support of Churchill, whose one overriding thought was to prevent Germany invading England.

In 1958, when serious accusations were made that SOE had been run in an amateurish manner and that it had consequently been infiltrated by German intelligence; that it suffered betrayals which had led to the arrests of many men and women; and that these shortcomings had been deliberately concealed, Buckmaster, indignant and outraged, responded by saying that SOE was no more amateurish than many other wartime units. He confirmed that the Germans had penetrated one important *réseau*, but only one, and that was Holland. He categorically denied all the allegations, describing as 'monstrous' that forty-seven British agents had deliberately been dropped to the Germans to distract their attention from other undercover operations.

The conspiracy theorists, of which there are quite a few – Pierre Raynaud, Jean Overton-Fuller, Elizabeth Nicholas, Larry Collins, author of *Fall from Grace,* and Robert Marshall all espouse variously the theory that SOE had deliberately sent agents into France on the premise that if caught, they would give false information about the D-Day landings, and a TV documentary on the same theme, *All the King's Men,* was produced. Professor Foot gives these theories short shrift, dismissing them as 'a good story ... a bad piece of history'.

Harry Sporborg, who had recruited Diana and who investigated Dericourt upon his return from France in February 1944, said: 'There was no doubt whatsoever in my mind that Dericourt was being employed by MI6 for functions which were outside SOE's sphere of operations.' In *Secret War* historian Nigel West also muses on the possibility of Dericourt, *l'homme qui fait le pickup*, the man who made the pickup, being a double or even a triple agent and run by SIS against the *Sichherhiedienst*.

Whatever Dericourt's faults, the fact remains that he supervised over fifty flights in and out of enemy-occupied territory and never lost an aircraft. As West states: 'Whilst one might speculate about the human cost of this success, and wonder about his involvement in the collapse of *Prosper* or the exact nature of his relationship with the SD, nothing of substance has ever emerged to tie him in with Dansey or SIS's French sections.' In his conclusion West sums up by saying there is no concrete evidence to suggest that Dansey was involved in any duplicitous dealings against SOE.[5]

Professor Foot does not doubt that Claude Dansey had the bad taste to revel in the *Prosper* debacle, but points out that that is hardly evidence that he brought it about. As far as Dericourt being a plant by SIS to follow orders from somewhere high up in London is concerned, 'this is nonsense too,' asserts Foot:

Dericourt was a *dericourtiste,* planted by the Germans and loyal to no man, only himself. He was in it mainly of course for the money and what he could get out of it and remained in it to the end ... I consider Dericourt responsible for the great disaster of the French Section in 1943 when *Prosper, Archambault* and their colleagues were arrested.[6]

Such were the conspiracy theories and serious allegations of sloppy discipline in SOE and their cover-ups by British authorities that abounded during the late 1950s and early 1960s, resulting in Professor Foot being asked to investigate and write a full official history of SOE. Too much I feel has been made of these allegations over the years in books and television programmes, to the detriment of the wonderful work done by SOE.

'Essentially, we were amateurs,' says Noreen Riols. 'We had to make up the rules as we went along.' However, MI6 agent Nigel Clive said after the war that SOE 'was unquestionably the best'.[7]

'The German authorities who gleefully spoke of the *Prosper* arrests as "our finest coup" spoke foolishly,' says Michael Foot:

Quantitively they were right; they pulled in several hundred earnest men and women who would have given them a great deal more trouble had they stayed at liberty. In the first place, for what it is worth we have to rely on Placke's word [Josef Placke, Goetz's assistant in the wireless section at Avenue Foch] 'that Dericourt was not directly concerned in the *Prosper* disaster'[8]... this stemmed from a different and simpler cause: the carelessness of the leaders. But ... undoubtedly by midsummer 1943 [at the time Diana was inserted] the enemy security services were engaged in an all-out drive against F's operations in general and this circuit in particular; in the end, as often happened, they caught up with it partly by accident and partly by design. Undoubtedly they were helped by the obscure yet important incident of the air mail; much of the agents' correspondence with London had been watched by the Gestapo, probably with Dericourt's agreement. (*SOE in France*)

However, Major Suttill's son, Francis, in *Shadows in the Fog* makes an important point: 'The evidence that I have found shows that the arrest of my father was the consequence of a series of unfortunate events, not the result of any betrayal as part of a deception plan.'

Marcel Braun, a member of the *Publican* circuit who had been placed in a cell in Fresnes along with several other *résistants*, was certain that it was Gilbert Norman who had sold them out and that there was no point in hiding anything as Norman had told them everything. Norman had assisted at the interrogation of *Prosper*, an ordeal which lasted without interruption for several days and several nights, without food or water – nor was Suttill allowed even to sit down during this period. He was severely tortured with beatings and one of his arms was broken, and Braun believed that little by little Norman completed or made up the details that the latter wished to hide. One of the German secretaries in Avenue Foch would later comment: 'They did not take to *Prosper* much, who had been very English and haughty under interrogation.'

Francis Suttill's son goes on to say: 'It appears that my father did not tell the Gestapo anything willingly, and that the few details were given under considerable pressure if they were given at all.'[9]

There is no doubt of Suttill's patriotism and integrity.

In conclusion, Michael Foot, in revising his *SOE in France*, sent a letter to Buckmaster, who passed it on to the Suttill family:

> I now have no shred of doubt left that his personal integrity, his loyalty to his friends, and his patriotism all remained absolutely intact, to the end. I am quite sure that he was no party to making or sanctioning or implementing any sort of bargain with the Germans. And everyone I met, whether among the senior survivors of the circuit, or elsewhere in F Section who had known him well, speak most warmly in praise of his character and his courage.[10]

When John Young and Diana were in the Avenue Foch, having been interrogated by either Hans Kieffer or Hugo Bleicher, and had seen John Starr comfortably sketching portraits of various German officials, very likely they would have been suspicious of what he had divulged to the Germans. Young and Diana would have been astounded as to the extent of the Germans' knowledge of SOE. Despite this, it is almost certain that Diana refused to say or confirm anything to her interrogators. It has been reported that this is so.

But one point needs remembering. 'The agents were all under sentence of death,' says Baroness Sue Ryder.

> And it was not just the German army and the Gestapo who posed this threat to their lives. Many civilians hated SOE agents and Resistance groups because their activities brought savage reprisals upon innocent people in towns and villages all over the country ... One can gain an insight into their magnificent work from looking at what happened to just a few of them, such as Diana Rowden and Vera Leigh who gave their lives yet never really received the public acclaim they deserved.

The year 1943 was an especially dangerous time for agents to be inserted into France. The country was a quagmire of agents, sub-agents, even triple agents, the Free French under de Gaulle, the Communists, the Maquis, the *Franc tireurs*, the list goes on – all living and working together in an occupied country. People who entered occupied France took their lives in their hands; they were told the chances of surviving were 50 per cent or lower, and the odds were that they would not return. War is war, after all; one lived or died. Amidst the senselessness and chaos, people can do amazing things in times of war. On my long journey, one which originally started around 2004, I have found this to be true. One would think it surprising that Diana, a poised, quiet woman, unexceptional as some might say, who essentially kept to herself, would make her country proud. She was a mouse who roared. She had no doubts about the importance of defeating Nazism. Agents like Diana pushed ahead regardless of the very obvious risks involved.

Author Rita Kramer felt it was a matter of the need for belief in what one had done – especially at the going down of the sun. *At the going down of the sun.* I have thought of these words many times while I have been writing this biography. I believe that surely it is what the agents accomplished that is more important than anything else. As Professor Foot avers:

> The value of the resistance set in motion by SOE in France proved crucial at the moment of the invasion and afterwards, and what matters is that there were these people who were willing to chance their own lives to protect a way of life, what they saw as a world worth fighting for. After the war we saw the plan Germany had for England. Think what life would have been like for us if they had won.

Lisa Graf, the political prisoner in Karlsruhe who was friendly with Diana and the other women agents, said tellingly: 'I thought at the time when I saw those girls, they are not going to come back. And so I thought, I will fix them all now in my mind. I remember her [Odette's] face. If I think now I do not see the faces of the others, you know.'

And there are others who would always remember Diana – people like the Janier-Dubrys, the people of the Jura Resistance, and the Clerc family, who always carried Diana in their hearts. They would never forget her.

Elizabeth Nicholas's description of Diana given earlier from their schooldays is surely one of the clearest and most far-sighted:

> ... one of the most diffident, most reticent people I had ever met ... She was, I thought sixteen years later, too mature for us. We

were still schoolgirls in grubby white blouses concerned with games and feuds and ha-ha jokes. She was already adult, and withdrawn from our diversions; none of us, I think, ever knew her.

And there it is. *She was of it, but never part of it ... none of us ever knew her.* Bob Maloubier, her fellow trainee in Party 27Y, felt the same: 'She kept to herself, she was with us but remote.' I have often wondered if, after her father died, Diana played a significant role in the mothering of her two brothers. She may have had responsibilities thrown on her young shoulders at too early an age. If that is true, then it is no wonder she loved her care-free existence in the south of France. It was in that country that she could be a child without any cares. But it was not to last. Returning to England, a move she hated, she went straight to the Manor House school, with its strict rules, then to the Sorbonne to obtain her diplomas. However, very soon with the advent of war she was in the middle of a country invaded and split in two, where she pitched in to nurse and help Allied airmen in escaping. Her duties never ceased. For two years she lived dangerously, before finally escaping to England. Almost straightaway she was thrown into the turmoil of a country under siege from the Germans, not occupied but under the pressure of invasion with all the anxieties that came with it. She thought longingly of returning to France. In her two years there she had seen much and it had instilled in her the belief that she had to return to 'do her bit', as she told her mother. Nothing deflected her from this purpose.

'Perhaps, even then,' wrote Elizabeth Nicholas, 'the seeds of the courage that was to ripen in war were already in her, and were unconsciously made manifest to us. And yet I remembered her with great clarity, though we had met only occasionally after she left school.'[11]

Diana was a free spirit, a fact that William Simpson, the scarred RAF pilot whom Diana befriended when they were both convalescing, noticed. Maybe that was why I could find no evidence of Diana having had a romantic involvement. Is it too presumptuous to speculate that had she survived the war she may never have married?

We will never know. An article which mentioned Diana asked if she had been used by London Control as a decoy, therefore leading to her execution. This was never given credibility by Bill Simpson, who considered Diana to be good material after meeting her.

Some writers have commented on Diana's French, that it may not have been up to standard. This is not so. Yvonne Clerc told me Diana's French had been excellent, although '*elle parlait avec un léger accent anglais*'. And in a letter to her brother-in-law in Melbourne, Mrs Rowden wrote that 'Diana spoke French like a native'. In speaking of their French teacher at the Manor House, Elizabeth Nicholas wrote: 'Unlike the rest of us, Diana had been spared much of Madame Mathieu's vitriolic temper.' Would SOE have sent a woman with barely passable French into enemy-occupied France as an agent-courier, an occupation where she would be severely tested over and over again?

However, a passage in Peter Churchill's book *Spirit in the Cage* describes her as 'patently English'. Why did SOE send such a woman who looked so obviously English to act as a courier, a dangerous occupation in an area such as the Jura? It was essential that any agent sent into France should be accepted unquestionably as a Frenchwoman. However, the French people I have discussed this with, such as the Janier-Dubrys and Yvonne Clerc, have all said that although Diana did look English she spoke excellent French, and that it did not matter that her English appearance or her slight accent was noticed by the French themselves. Many Germans could not speak French, and those who did would probably not have been able to detect a slight accent.

It must also be remembered that 1943, the year Diana was inserted into France, was a vitally important year to the Allies with the invasion imminent, therefore there was a pressing need for French-speaking agents.

Maurice Buckmaster was thought by some to have been a little naïve for a secret service chief, and to have lacked the ruthlessness that one might have expected. But no one ever questioned his dedication to the job: he was acutely aware of the importance and value of his agents and he cared about them deeply.

The Janier-Dubrys have clear memories of Diana. Claude Janier-Dubry remembers Diana coming into the sawmill factory where she was playing with her sister Christiane to pick her up. 'I have very clear memories of her shoes which were beautiful. I must have been hurt and was unable to walk. Another memory is of her smoking with a cigarette holder.'

Regarding *l'affaire Benoit*, they knew nothing of the false agent – neither where he had come from, nor where he went. But as for the real *Benoit,* M. Juif possessed a cutting dated January 1955 which said that the French authorities were trying to secure the extradition of the man named by the Juifs, against whom they wished to lay charges. The cutting explained that these charges were in connection with his wartime activities; he had gone first to Canada after the Liberation, and then, when extradition proceedings started, he had taken flight and travelled to somewhere in South America. He has never been brought to justice.

Today, seventy-five years after the war, the true story of Maugenet is still not clear. Some people claim there was no false *Benoit*: the two were one and the same. It was at first thought, by Elizabeth Nicholas in 1956, that the genuine *Benoit* had acted against his will, that he must have revealed his contacts and his rendezvous to the Germans. How else had they known to take him to Lons, and from there how had they traced Diana and Gabriel to the sawmill at Clairvaux, unless he had spoken? Others thought at the time that the first *Benoit* may have been tortured. From documents released in the years since the war by historians such as Michael Foot, it is known that the two men were in fact very different in looks – they could not possibly be mistaken. What if the real *Benoit*, Maugenet, had not been tortured at all? There may have been no need for torture. The Janier-Dubrys are inclined to think this is so. Nicholas thought it possible that *Benoit* was shocked by his immediate arrest and rendered utterly demoralised by the discovery that London had made arrangements for his reception in France with a German-controlled W/T, and from then had done precisely what the Germans asked of him. Later it was reliably reported that he was on excellent terms with the Gestapo.

There is a third possibility. I am in possession of a document relating to the arrests of Gabriel and Paulette, entitled 'Top Secret – Report on Judex 2'.

The full story of the arrest of GABRIEL and PAULETTE seems to be as follows. The sources of information are:

SCHNEIDER, Gestapo Interpreter and now head of Securite Militaire at Lons-le-Saunier (and a great personal friend of GABRIEL and PEDRO).

The Poli, Juif and Janier Dubry families at CLAIRAUX.

The 'real' BENOIT (who is almost certainly our Captain MAUGENET), together with a 'false' BENOIT, was brought to LONS-le-SAUNIER by the Gestapo Commissaire Special from the Rue CHAUSSET, Paris. They had with them presumably as guard, two members of the P.P.F.

At Lons the 'real' BENOIT gave his Canadienne to the false BENOIT.

Descripions of the two men are as follows:

Real BENOIT:
Age: 40–45.
Height: 1m 60.
Dark hair, small moustache; sometimes wore glasses.
Said to have been a Canadian officer and to have done the Syrian campaign.
Had a glass-case with action messages in.
Spoke English to GABRIEL.
Stated he had been landed by Lysander near NANTES on the night of the 15/16 November 1943.

False BENOIT:
An Alsatian.
Speaks German, French and English.
Height: 1 m 60
Chestnut hair, no moustache.
Sometimes wore glasses.
Had seen GABRIEL in a bar in London and knew him.
Had been in France for eleven months.
Employed at the Rue CHAUSSET.
Knew PAULETTE.

To the above descriptions, given by SCHNEIDER, the POLI family added the following details concerning the 'false' BENOIT. He had very bad, black teeth in front; he had a habit of jerking his head to put his hair back in place he had very brilliant penetrating eyes.

The 'false' BENOIT arrived in CLAIRVAUX at 7.15 hours, wearing a Canadienne and carrying a light brown crocodile-skin briefcase. At 7.35 he arrived at the PAULY house with PAULETTE. He was the bearer of a letter from GABRIEL's wife, in which she referred to the birth of a small nephew, stated that she had a septic knee, and had finished working with the BBC, but was still living in London. GABRIEL was written in very simple script (presumably Miss MORRIS's) on the outside of the letter.

He returned a somewhat evasive reply to GABRIEL's question 'What do they think of me in London?' (GABRIEL had threatened resignation unless materials arrived), said 'Je m'appelle JACQUES, and stated his intention of going down to LONS-le-SAUNIER, where he had left his suitcase with explosives in them.

At 9,00 hours he left for LONS-le-SAUNIER with RAOUL (son-in-law of the family).

Thereupon GABRIEL went off on his bicycle 'no-one knows where', but was back in the house at 18.20 hours, when PAULETTE entered 'blancho' and BENOIT 'sans regarder' followed by the Gestapo, firing their revolvers. GABRIEL and PAULETTE were arrested and taken away.

Thereupon Madame JUIF hid the crystals, only just in time apparently as the 'false' BENOIT returned an hour later, armed with mitraillette and revolver and threatened her with death unless she revealed the whereabouts of the set and crystals.

At the end of all this only POLI's wife was taken away.

When GABRIEL was brought in to LONS-le-SAUNIER that evening, the 'real' BENOIT looked through the key-hole and recognized him. He then came into the room and GABRIEL was asked if he recognized him: he replied that he did.

Three days later, PEDRO arrived at POLI's house to make enquiries.

This report cannot be taken at face value; there are many errors and one can only add it to the other suppositions. There may have been two *Benoits* that evening, but in discussions with the Janier-Dubry family they say there was just the one.

After his acquittal Dericourt confessed to Jean Overton-Fuller that he had given away three men, one of whom was Albert Maugenet. He had to do 'monstrous things,' he admitted, in order to keep up his end of the dangerous game he played, but he was 'no monster.' This is overlooking the facts of the chicken farm which he bought and paid for, as well as of his wife's expensive fur coat, reportedly worth a huge amount, that was given to him by the Germans in exchange for information about the flight carrying Maugenet and the others. However, Overton-Fuller maintained that the Germans didn't need Dericourt to tell them about the Maugenet flight: arrangements had been made for it on Pickersgill's captured radio set by the German Placke. All evidence points to the fact that it really was an impersonator who went to Lons-le-Saunier in place of the real Maugenet.

Noreen Riols spoke to me about some of the characters in this story, people like Harry Rée who was a great friend of Francis Cammaerts. 'I remember very well him saying to me, "I looked around and found a daughter waiting for me when I got home." He had left England when his wife was about seven months pregnant, and it had been arranged that at the time of the birth if it was a girl a message would come over the *message personnels*, "Clementine looks like my father," and he heard those same words.'

She continued:

Harry was a very highly strung man. He could not sit still for two seconds. He was like a bowl of soap suds, and could collapse almost immediately. He was a very nice person; I liked him enormously.

Now Vera Atkins was very British in her outlook and accent. She had very piercing blue eyes and was a very elegant woman; she would wear very simple immaculate clothes and she smoked 'Craven A' cigarettes out of a long cigarette holder. An amazing woman and with certain quirks. She refused to go back to the office in anything other than a taxi. Bob Maloubier said she flirted with him. Vera, who always gave the impression of being cold and straitlaced, had many lovers, one of whom was the German ambassador to Romania, Count Friedrich Werner von der Schulenburg, a family friend. The Count was secretly anti-Nazi and after the abortive attempt on Hitler's life in 1944, the count was executed along with many others who had been involved in the plot.

Noreen was terrified of Vera. 'I was so afraid of her but did not dare call her anything other than Miss Atkins. There was no doubt she was very fond of her agents, but she had her favourites.'

And who were her favourites? 'Definitely Violette [Szabo]. She was really beautiful and spoke with a real Cockney accent.'

'Vera and Buck remained friends right up to the end, to the day Buck died.'[12]

Elizabeth Nicholas makes an interesting observation that John Starr and Hugo Bleicher had removed once and for all the role of the agent from the romanticized realms of cops and robbers, revealing it for what it was: a sad journey through a territory of fear and darkness amid great loneliness. It is fair to say (her account was written in 1958) that to find the whole truth about what happened in Occupied France is impossible. The French Resistance was 'hard, strong, indestructible,' says Nicholas. 'We cannot judge the achievements of the French Section by purely military standards, nor should we judge them against the background of the massive hordes that were deployed by the Allies in 1944. We should judge them against the dangers of 1940, and 1941, of the days when our backs were to the wall and victory a distant concept of faith only.'

Yvonne Clerc never forgot Diana. To Elizabeth Nicholas she spoke of Diana as a daughter, a sister: her memory was real and strong and very much alive, and the love she felt for her was still true and undiluted. 'Nothing had been forgotten, nothing.' These sentiments were plain to see when I visited Madame Clerc in 2015, exactly one hundred years since Diana was born. As we spoke of those times in the war and all that Diana had done in the Resistance, and of the arrests, Yvonne told of the sadness of waiting for her when the war was over, when hostilities ceased once and for all and when her husband finally came home. She must have wondered what had become of her lovely English friend: had she been liberated from prison, and if she had, how long would it be until she visited them again?

Yvonne passed me a photo. It was of Diana. In sepia, it was possibly taken when she was a few years younger. I passed it to Claude Janier-Dubry, who shivered as if a ghost had brushed by her. Although the photo is not in colour, one can almost see the blue of her eyes and the reddish, wavy hair. She is wearing earrings in the shape of flowers and a locket around her neck. She looks self-assured and slightly pensive, as if she knows what her future will hold.

Then Yvonne gave me a letter. Straightaway I recognised Mrs Rowden's writing. Yvonne spoke slowly, her eyes far away: 'After the war was finally over, we hoped that somehow we would get word that Diana was safe. We hoped, you know – we hoped that somehow she had survived. She was a young, strong woman, so we went on hoping. After all, several people had come back from the camps. *Tout de même* ... but as time went on we started to think something was wrong. She had always said she would return to France when it was over. And then, one day a long time later a letter arrived. It was from the *mere de Diana*.' Mrs Rowden's letter reads as following:

Dear Madame Clerc,

I wish to express my thanks for your kindness to my daughter who spent her last days close to you. It is a consolation to know that she was with true friends who were good to her. She deserved this, being always so good with other people.

We were very close and my loss is a terrible tragedy for me, but I like to think that she was able to do what she wanted – fighting against the Nazis with wonderful people like you and fighting for our two countries.

Please excuse my mistakes.

Warm regards and best wishes and thank you again for everything you did.

Christian Rowden

When Diana left the Clercs and went into hiding, she left the photo of herself behind. It is thought she did this in case she did not come back, in which case the Clercs would have something to remember her by. I remember also what Christiane and Claude Janier-Dubry had told me – she had left behind a ruby ring and a cigarette holder on the day she had been arrested. 'They are not going to take these things,' she had told Aimee Janier-Dubry. And for the first time I wondered if Diana had a premonition she might not survive.

Historian Max Hastings in *The Secret War* makes no apology when writing about whether captured agents talked or not:

Almost every prisoner of any nationality gave away a little or much, with or without undergoing torture. Controllers expected only that their field officers and agents should withhold names for a minimum of twenty-four or forty-eight hours, to enable meetings to be cancelled, contacts to flee … Captured agents were usually offered a 50 per cent chance of life if they talked, and such bargains were sometimes kept. The broad truth about spies of all nationalities who fell into enemy hands was that they were kept alive as long as they could serve a purpose, and shot when their usefulness expired.

There was a high demand for agents in 1943 as it was a critical time in the war. France remained Baker Street's most active and successful theatre. It proved relatively easy to insert agents by light aircraft in the north and by parachute further afield. Between 1941 and 1944, the RAF flew 320 Lysander sorties, of which 210 were successful, landing 440 passengers and evacuating 630 at a cost of only six pilots killed. A majority of all Allied agents captured by the Germans in Europe were victims of betrayal. Oluf Réed-Olsen wrote of his experience as a British spy in Norway: 'One was most afraid of one's own people; I think all agents, saboteurs and other "visitors" in Norway will agree this was so.' This would have been the case in France as in all German occupied countries.

Max Hastings is sure that a majority of all Allied agents captured by the Germans in Europe were victims of betrayal: 'As in the case of an Englishman, Harold Cole, a deserter from his army unit, taking with him the Mess funds. It was discovered he had been working for the Germans for months. MI9 considered him responsible for fifty deaths of members of the "Pat" Line and their connections.'

Was patriotism one of the main reasons why people joined SOE? Or was there perhaps a need to escape a boring existence, a bad marriage or relationship? Was there a romantic desire to fight or, in extreme cases, to die for one's country? In the early days, SOE recruited people from the old boys' network, until they were forced to look elsewhere later in the war and the networks became crowded. Those with the best prospect of survival on SOE operations were the most ruthless and untrusting: 'But, however strongly their instructors discouraged it, there was also a romantic buccaneering streak about the organisation that brought into its ranks many men and women who would never have become professional spies for SIS.'[13]

'It was not enough to be patriotic, or even to be bilingual,' says Hastings. 'People had to speak like a native. One had to have the ability to blend into the background. This is where being a woman came in handy. It was not enough to be courageous. An agent had to be cautious, to be able to keep one's mouth shut. Francis Cammearts made the perfect agent, and Tony Brooks. And, I think, Diana Rowden, despite looking typically English.'[14]

Hastings is of the opinion that too much post-war attention has focused upon the deeds of SOE's British agents, who hazarded only their own young lives in the cause of a great and indisputably romantic adventure, and too little upon the peoples of Europe, of all ages and both sexes, who joined one of hundreds of Resistance networks. Their contributions should be judged much more by the magnitude of their stakes and their sacrifices than by the military achievements, or lack of them. For all SOE's extravagances and follies, it became the most effective British secret operations organisation of the war, and justified Churchill's leap of imagination that inspired its creation.

In the past year I have been lucky to make contact with Victoria Boyle, a cousin of Diana and whose mother, Rosemary Chetwynd-Stapylton, was the daughter of Mrs Rowden's sister, Vera. Victoria was able to fill in many of the gaps in this story about Diana and her family:

When I was growing up I was devoted to Aunt Chris. However, she was quite a formidable woman. She had very definite political views and didn't take kindly to any political figure disagreeing with her point of view. Perhaps it had something to do with what happened during the war, the tragic loss of Diana, and her youngest Kit who came back from the war psychologically damaged. She loved dogs, particularly the spaniel Wizard, the one Diana gave her to look after her. I can remember her always being in bed and after Wizard had passed away, another spaniel, Kirsty, lying on her stomach. He would lie there all day and woe betide anyone who tried to move him.

After the war France had a mu
who served at de Gaulle's Int
returning to France just after
fought for the Resistance!' Th
the last moment or when it was
been won he referred to as '*naɉ*

Buckmaster told Elizabeth
officers had been recruited by
were no records, that everyb
to keep up with paper, and tl
unit. I felt then as I do now, t
himself to me as a very hard n
was indeed so.'[16]

Buckmaster also made the
in French Section, France was
birth, most had lived the grea
some had been in France in
the Occupation for varying
'To put yourself in their pla
must imagine yourself droppir
France was not a foreign cou
they were.'

In researching this biograp
and numerous files, spoken ai
world, including writers and l
films, television programmes ar
thousands of miles from my
Germany and France in pursu
know Diana quite well. Howe
that is the lack of any evidenc
or lover. Perhaps an opportun
have been a case of 'in the futu
told anyone. She was a very pi
restrictions on my research.
Diana, was unable to help me.
in England. I asked Christiane
with Harry Rée, remembering
to greet him, a broad smile oi
Switzerland. 'Oh, Harry, oh F

Diana's younger brother, Kit, who had been repatriated and returned home from the war ill, had committed suicide not long after the war ended. One can only imagine the effect this tragedy had on Mrs Rowden.

It was rumoured that the boat *Sans Peur*, which Diana and her brothers sailed in the south of France and loved so much, had actually belonged to Jacques Cousteau. Victoria has no knowledge as to what happened to the boat.

We talked about Vincenzo, the Italian retainer who stayed with Mrs Rowden. 'Towards the end of his life his mind seemed to wander,' says Victoria, 'and he could be found sitting outside wearing gumboots and two pairs of pjamas. But he was a kindly soul and absolutely devoted to Aunt Chris who said very little about Diana. If somebody mentioned her name there was just this vague muttering in answer.'

Mrs Rowden had suffered from heart disease for 'as long as I knew her and eventually she had to go into a nursing home. I think, but am not sure, Vincenzo pre-deceased her. The last time I went to visit her I held her hand with one hand and my newborn child in the other. I wanted to be able to let her know that it would be a case of "right then, carry on".'

After Mrs Rowden's death in 1979, Victoria and her mother Rosemary were cleaning out Telegraph House and came across photos of some Germans, 'the ones who had put the four girls to death at Natzweiler, and there was a great line with the words "DEAD" written across them. It still makes me sick to think of it. We ripped the photos into little pieces and burnt them.'

Mrs Rowden's oldest son, Maurice, inherited Telegraph House. He died in 2003. Every effort had been made to contact him when his mother was dying, and in the end her solicitor made contact 'but Maurice didn't want to know. He had cut himself off from all the family. It was understood that he blamed his mother for the death of his younger brother, Kit, who wasn't the same when he came home, invalided out of the army.'

'Why would he think it was his mother's fault?' I asked Victoria, but she had no idea. 'It was never talked about. He just didn't want any contact with us. It was so sad. I have often wondered if he ever married, had children. To think Aunt Chris could have had grandchildren whom she never knew about.'

and replied: 'Oh, no, I don't think so. After all, he had just become a father.'

It matters little. Diana had been happy in what she was doing; her life was very full, and there would have been no time to dwell on the future. She managed to pack so much into her young life. When the war was finally over she would have returned to France, the country she loved. She not only implied this to the Clercs but also to the Janier-Dubrys. As her mother said: 'Diana would have found some way of returning to France. She was determined to go back ...'[17]

In May 2015 my good friend in England, Elspeth Forbes-Robertson, took me to Beaulieu. It was a warm, sunny spring day and the cherry trees were in full bloom. At the site could be found an oval memorial to the fallen agents of SOE set into a wall with their names written in gold. Sat on a seat beneath an oak tree where the sun warmed my face, I had pause to reflect on a very full three weeks, travelling around England and France, and thoughts crowded my mind: the generosity of the people in the Jura like the Janier-Dubry sisters, who extended the warm hand of friendship to a woman they scarcely knew; the day spent with Yvonne Clerc and her daughter in St Amour; the service at Valençay where I laid a poppy at the foot of Diana's photo; Tangmere aerodrome, the museum, and the cottage that was the last port of call for agents before they left England; and lastly, Boarmans, a remote but picture-perfect country estate in the woods, where Diana did the last part of her training.

Finally I had come to Beaulieu, the place where Diana and the party of 27Y trained, with its church in the twelfth-century abbey where the smell of history permeated through everything. I turned my face up to the sun and thought of Mrs Rowden. Did she come here to sit and remember?

That May in the Jura was beautiful. Purple mountains looked down on to little cobblestone villages; everywhere the roads were lined with trees, their pink and white blossoms scattered across the way. When I stayed with Claude Janier-Dubry and her sister Christiane, I walked the same long road as Diana had once done – the Route Lons-le-Saunier and the streets of Clairvaux-le-lacs – all the time thinking of her taking these same roads on her bicycle in 1943, delivering messages to other *résistants* and living with the constant fear of discovery. The factory and the Swiss-style house where Diana and John Young lived during those tumultuous days no longer existed. On the site instead there stood a small *supermarche*, the *Atak,* surrounded by pretty trees. Diana was everywhere. I thought: this is where she once walked, this is where she rode her bicycle, delivered her messages. Claude lives in the house her parents, Raoul and Aimee, built some years after the war. It is a house full of memories; photographs of her parents, her own family, of the children around the time when Diana stayed with them. 'This is my brother,' she said to me. 'He was the child Diana did not see. And this is Aunt Ida. When she came back from the camp in May 1945 she weighed only *trente-sept kilos*. We were all so excited to see her after such a long time. My father and my grandparents collected her from Paris in a friend's car as Papa's car had been confiscated by the Germans.'

The war affected people like the Janier-Dubrys, the Polis and the Juifs for a very long time. Ida Juif had a son, Jacques, who was born after the war. 'At that time Ida and her husband were living close to the German border,' said Christiane Voha. 'He was forced to learn German at school, even in Clairvaux. Jacques had a German penfriend who sometimes came to stay with the Polis. My mother, Aimee, on hearing the child speak German would put her head in her hands and weep. She couldn't bear the boy speaking German. And of course she remembered the *Kapo* and the horror of the deportation and the arrestations.'

Christiane's own son was born on 19 November, the anniversary of the *mission tragique*. 'It was not a good omen,' said Christiane.

In many ways Diana was a complex character, a contradiction; outwardly shy, poised, but strong as a lion, an excellent linguist, a remarkable shot, and a good cook. There is no doubt she loved her family – she was very close to her mother and her two brothers and they shared a special bond. But there was a certain reticence about her. Bob Maloubier, her fellow trainee in group 27Y, said she kept to herself. He found her diffident, yet Mrs Rowden described her daughter as 'so gay, she packed so much into her life, sailing a boat with reckless skill, catching and gutting fish'.[18] Elizabeth Nicholas could never reconcile this person with the shy, withdrawn teenager of her school days. I also find it difficult to reconcile the two Dianas, but think the explanation is a simple one. It is not uncommon for shy people to display a different side of their personality in certain circumstances, and war would certainly do that.

Diana was always polite, with beautiful manners, and was very proud of her Scottish heritage. She loved children and, to use an old-fashioned term, she was 'a lady'. Madame Rhaithouze could see 'she was not used to menial tasks but pitched in anyway'. Ida Poli said she was of a calibre one meets seldom. There was also the lasting gesture of leaving her photo behind with Yvonne Clerc, who had told her not to do so because it was dangerous. 'We will never know if she left it on purpose or if she just forgot to take it with her. We both felt she had a premonition that she would be caught.'

After the war Maurice Buckmaster spoke of the qualities of some of the women agents, including Diana:

Some of the young woman agents like Noor Inayat Khan, although unworldly and dreamy, were idealistic and very brave and mostly unprepared for a complex world of traitors and informers. And because they were not immediately captured this would have given them a reassurance that all was well. That some of these agents were able to do what they did, such as Francis Cammearts, George Starr, Krystyna Skarbek and Diana Rowden, who in a short period of time, did wonderful work in the Jura, and who, by no fault of her own, was in the end captured and imprisoned, was remarkable. Diana, working in a remote and mountainous area in France, could not be protected against betrayal.

It is important to remember that the dead deserve honouring and that SOE's effort was not made in vain. Buckmaster continually praised its efforts, backed up by Eisenhower who was able to say that 'the operations of SOE together with those of the Maquis, with whom they were so closely associated, had shortened the war in Europe by nine months.'[19] If it is true that the war in Europe was shortened by nine months, SOE needs no further testimonial.

Some of their achievements were remarkable. The bombing of the heavy water plant in Norway and missions in Greece, such as the blowing up of the Gorgopotamos and Asopos viaducts which cut off supplies to the Germans for some months, could be classed as some of SOE's most formidable achievements.

Of the 104 SOE deaths in France and Germany, eighty-five men and women died in concentration camps, mainly by execution. In Ravensbrück concentration camp for women, eleven women agents were executed and two died in the camps – Cecily Lefort in Ravensbrück and Yvonne Rudellat in Belsen. One died of meningitis, Muriel Byck. Forty-one women agents were sent into France as well as the one who was already in France, Sonia Olschanesky. Only eight returned.

Three girls shared the distinction of being the first WAAFs to land in France, all in June 1943. They were Diana Rowden, Cecily Lefort and Noor Inayat Khan.

In the sitting room of the Special Forces Club in London hangs a watercolour by Brian Stonehouse of Diana, Vera Leigh, Andrée Borrel and Sonia Olschanezky, their heads bowed as they walk down the *Lagerstrasse* on their way to the crematorium at Natzweiler; it is profound in its simplicity and the economy with which the impending doom of the women is apparent. The first girl is tall with dyed blond hair, Andrée. There follows a small girl with dark hair, Sonia. Then there is Diana, easily distinguishable with her tartan ribbon in her fair hair. She is wearing a grey jacket and skirt. The last woman is Vera. The women are walking in single file, their heads to the ground as if they cannot bear to see what is around them.

I am struck by their bravery, their steadfastness. The painting is positioned between black-and-white photographs of the four girls: Andrée on the left, the central watercolour in the middle, then Diana, Vera and lastly Sonia. A German *Hauptman* wearing a peaked cap walks in front of the girls, and a German soldier brings up the rear. The painting is on loan to the Club by the executors of the Stonehouse estate.

Stonehouse has managed to capture the tension, the fear in the women's hearts. They must have had an inkling of what was in store, despite being told they were going to do agricultural work in the camp. Why didn't they turn and run? Better to be shot than the alternative. The prisoners could not help them – nobody could.

Positioned on the walls of the staircases at the Special Forces Club are more black-and-white photos in black frames of all the SOE agents. These are the studio photos taken before leaving on their various missions. Some agents bear slight smiles, others are grave. All have that certain look of people in wartime, a mixture of courage and slight anxiety. They had their whole lives ahead of them; some were married, many had children. They had a life to return to, the prospect of a good life in peacetime in which they could hold up their heads and know that what they had done had made a difference.

It would seem Diana inherited her strength of character from her mother, who throughout her long life showed remarkable courage and strength when faced with tragedy. No doubt the despair for all three of her children which she carried around with her must have threatened to overwhelm her at times. In later years, with the departure of her last living child, Maurice, from her life the last link with her children would have been severed. She had endured much: the death of her only daughter in circumstances most of us would find impossible to cope with, followed by the suicide of her youngest son, Kit, and Maurice's alienation from the whole family. Whatever argument he had with his mother, it would seem he judged her too harshly for Kit's suicide. It was no wonder Mrs Rowden took to her bed, blaming the reason on her bad heart. As her nephew Mark Chetwynd-Stapylton said in summary: 'A sad family, the Rowdens.'

Incredibly, Mrs Rowden's heart, which had not been good during the war, beat on for a number of years until, after being cared for a long time by Vincenzo, she went into a rest home in Surrey. She died on 14 April 1979.

I will leave the last words to Diana's mother, who knew her daughter more than anybody else. She summed up Diana's character perfectly: 'Diana crowded more into her twenty-nine years of life than do many people living twice or three times as long. She loved life, and every moment was to her an adventure. She was gay, vital, selfless, and self-reliant.'

These words say it all. I wish I had met her.

There were mistakes, of course. There always are in a battle. And you can't help thinking about the men who died because of them. They might have been saved. But then, there would have been other mistakes and other men would have died. The mistakes are not so important now except when they provided lessons for the future. The important thing is not to forget the dead.
- C. Hibbert, *The Battle of Arnhem*
(London 1962)

Appendices

The following is from a recruiting leaflet, honest in laying out the stark reality.
'Men who come to the Maquis to fight live badly, in precarious fashion, with food hard to find. They will be absolutely cut off from their families for the duration; the enemy does not apply the rules of war to them; they cannot be assured any pay; every effort will be made to help their families, but it is impossible to give any guarantee in this manner; all correspondence is forbidden.

Bring two shirts, two pairs of underpants, two pairs of woollen socks; a light sweater, a scarf, a heavy sweater, a woollen blanket, an extra a pair of shoes, shoelaces, needles, thread, buttons, safety pins, soap, a canteen, a knife and fork, a torch, a compass, a weapon if possible, and also a sleeping bag if possible. Wear a warm suit, a beret, a raincoat, a good pair of hobnailed boots.'

THE DEMISE OF THE SOE

Winston Churchill was urged to keep Britain's secret espionage unit going after the Second World War to counter 'the Russian menace', files released by the National Archives show.

But he inadvertently signed the death warrant of the Special Operations Executive (SOE) by delaying a decision until after the 1945 general election which was won by Labour under Clement Attlee.

Lord Selbourne, who, as Minister of economic warfare, was head of the service, argued against putting it under the control of the Foreign Office, which wanted to merge it with the SIS. He said that to do so would be 'madness' and that giving the Foreign Office control of the most secret of Britain's services would be like 'putting an Abbess in charge of a brothel.'

Files at the National Archives show that Lord Selborne kept arguing with Churchill to keep SOE going after the war. In May, 1945, two months before the election, he said it could be instrumental in containing the emerging Soviet threat and dealing with what he described as the 'smouldering volcanoes' of the Middle East.

Churchill postponed a decision, writing, 'after the election' in his files. Lord Selbourne continued his campaign with Attlee, but the new Prime Minister dissolved the SOE.

MESSAGES CONCERNING PAULETTE'S PICK-UP

11 October 1943

Confirming my telephone conversation with D/FP, you will be picking up our agent **PAULETTE.**

The necessary contact is as follows:

Madame Thierry at Bakers shop at Valentigney 7 kms south of Montbeliard by bus. 'Ask for Madam or Michel at side door through porte cochere: "Did Marcelle pass this morning?" Reply: 'No, but I will go and look for her.'

We have told our organiser responsible for PAULETTE that she will be picked up in the next fortnight.

Cipher Tel to Berne   21.10.43

Your   2389

1. Your Para 1 have given instructions to pick up PAULETTE at address given by you. Imperative she remains at that address and does not REPEAT does not REPEAT not join Gabriel
2. Your para 2.   Well done. Keep us posted.
3. Your Para 3. Regret constant bad weather prevented all operations your area. hoping for better luck next moon
4. Your para 4. Nievre contact noted. Regret impossible send organiser this moon. Will contact hold good for November using same password and can you give postbox where organiser could deliver messages to be passed to us via Berne.
5. Answer soonest.

0230 22.10.43 MLC Origin F Approved by J.

Cipher Tel To Berne   21.10.43
(Taken from Harry Rée's file)
Cipher tele from Berne
Desp 1132 18.10.43

Following from Cesar dated 11th
1. Paulette has gone off and joined Gabriel
2. Peugeot affair proceeding well. 9000 volt transformers moldy
3. Await parachute operation urgently
4. Bothey found everything O.K. in Nieve
5. Please confirm whether you will send somebody this month.

Cipher Tel From Berne

IMMEDIATE
Following from C E S A R delayed en route.
   Reference my telegram 2389 Para 1. In view of P A U L E T T E ' S action during my absence please contact her directly via G A B R I E L instead of as per my telegram 2326 PARA 4

Top-secret Commando Order issued from Hitler's HQ:

From now on, all opponents engaged in so-called commando operations in Europe or Africa, even when it is outwardly a manner of soldiers in uniform or demolition parties with or without weapons, are to be exterminated to the last man in battle or in flight. In these cases, it is immaterial whether they are landed for their operations by ship, or aeroplane, or descent by parachute. Even should these individuals, on being discovered make as if to surrender all quarter is to be denied on principle.

And a supplementary Directive:

I have been compelled to issue strict orders for the destruction of enemy sabotage troops and to declare non-compliance severely punishable ... it must be made clear to the enemy that all sabotage troops will be exterminated, without exception, to the last man. That means that their chances of escaping with their lives is nil. Under no circumstances can they be expected to be treated according to the rules of the Geneva Convention. If it should be necessary for reasons of interrogation to initially spare one man or two then they are to be shot mmediately after interrogation. This order is intended for commanders only and must not under any circumstances fall into enemy hands.

Be near me when my light is low,
When the blood creeps, and the nerves prick
And tingle; and the heart is sick,
And all the wheels of being slow.
Be near me when the sensuous frame

Is rack'd with pangs that conquer trust;
And time, a maniac scattering dust,
And life, a fury slinging flame.

Be near me when my faith is dry,
And men the flies of latter spring,
That lay their eggs, and sting and sing,
And weave their petty cells and die.

Be near me when I fade away,
To point the term of human strife,
And on the low dark verge of life
The twilight of eternal day.

In Memoriam, Alfred, Lord Tennyson

Notes

PART ONE

Prologue
1. Janier-Dubry papers.

Chapter One
1. Elizabeth Nicholas *Death Be Not Proud*.
2. Mark Chetwynd-Stapleton papers. Letter from him to author Rita Kramer. Mark was the son of Sir Alfred Edward Pease, 2nd Battalion, and Emily Elizabeth Smith. He died on 1 July 1995.
3. Gillian Tindall, *Three Houses, Many Lives*.
4. Ibid.

Chapter Two
1. Mary S. Lovell, *The Mitford Girls*.
2. Christabel Bielenberg, *The Road Ahead*.
3. Nancy Wake, *The White Mouse*.
4. John Rowden, Melbourne, Australia.
5. Rowden family papers.
6. Noel Barber, *The Week That France Fell*.
7. Mrs Rowden's private papers.
8. Irene Nemirovsky, *Suite Francaise*.
9. Rowden's letter to her brother-in-law in Melbourne.

Chapter Three
1. Yvonne Clerc, *Résistant in the Jura*.

Chapter Four
1. M. R. D Foot, *SOE 1940–46*.

2. Ibid.
3. Ibid.
4. Max Hastings, *Secret War*.
5. Ibid.
6. Ibid.
7. David Stafford, *Churchill and Secret Service*.
8. Ibid.
9. Donald Hamilton-Hill, SOE *Assignment*.
10. Maurice Buckmaster, *They Fought Alone*.
11. Maurice Buckmaster, personal file.
12. Noreen Riols, interview with author.
13. *Between Silk and Cyanide*, Leo Marks.
14. M. R. D. Foot, *SOE In France*.
15. Ibid.
16. M. R. D. Foot, *Confessions of an SOE Historian*.
17. Vera Atkins, IWM interview Sound Archives.
18. Yvonne Baseden, SOE agent.
19. Francis Cammaerts, *A Pacifist at War*.
20. M. R. D. Foot, *SOE in France*.
21. David Stafford, *Britain and European Resistance*.
22. Peter Wilkinson and Joan Bright Astley, *Gubbins and SOE*.
23. Squadron Leader William Simpson, *One of our Pilots is Safe*.
24. *Daily Mail*.
25. Diana's personal file.
26. Maurice Buckmaster, *They Fought Alone*.
27. Max Hastings, *Secret War*.
28. In Diana's case this was done before she saw Jepson and would account for the gap between the initial interview and going before the selection board.
29. Jepson was still writing at the age of ninety with Boris Karloff and Alec Guiness as his friends.
30. Reconstructed from Rowden family archives.
31. Maurice Buckmaster, *They Fought Alone*.
32. M. R. D. Foot, *SOE 1940–46*.
33. Rowden family papers and conversatons with Diana's cousins.

Chapter Five
1. Diana's P.F.
2. Rowden family papers. Recollections of Victoria Boyle and William Simpson.
3. Buckmaster, *They Fought Alone*.
4. Ibid.
5. Ibid.
6. Henri Diacono.
7. Captain Paul Raymond Tessier was arrested one week after landing in France. Died 22 August 1944.
8. George Millar, *Maquis*.
9. Guido Zembsch-Shreve, *Pierre Lalande: Special Agent*.

10. In reality the Sten was not all it was cracked up to be. It jammed often, at the worst moments in combat. A case in point is that of Sir Tasker Watkins, VC, the only officer left in his company. Lt Watkins in the Welsh Regiment had been fighting his way across a cornfield in Northern France when he was cut down by German guns. His weapon, the Sten, at the crucial moment, jammed. Undaunted he hurled it at the German manning the post then shot him with his pistol.
11. Carolyn Seymour-Jones, She Landed by Moonlight.
12. Diana's P.F.
13. Michael Foot, *SOE in France.*
14. Cyril Cunningham, *Beaulieu: The Finishing School for Agents.*
15. Philippe de Vomecourt, *Who Lived to See the Day.*
16. Richard Heslop, *Xavier.*
17. Diana's P.F.
18. Ibid.
19. George Millar, *Maquis.*
20. Ibid.
21. Correspondence between Christian Rowden and John Rowden after the war.
22. David Khan, *The Code Breakers.*

Chapter Six
1. M. R. D Foot, *SOE in France.*
2. Hugh Verity, *We Landed by Moonlight.*
3. Ibid.
4. Ibid.
5. *Secret War,* BBC documentary.
6. Ibid.
7. George Millar, Maquis.
8. Hugh Verity, *We Landed by Moonlight.*
9. Ibid.
10. Squadron Leader Geoffrey Rothwell, DFC & Bar, *Légion d'Honneur, Croix de Guerre 1940 & Palme,* Order of Leopold II & Palme.
11. Pierre Raynaud's P.F.
12. Susan Ottaway, *Sisters, Secrets and Sacrifice.* According to Maurice Southgate, 'Cecily was the wrong type for the work. She drew attention to herself by her behaviour ... her laugh could be heard a mile away.' She survived in this role for only three months and after her arrest was taken to Ravensbrück, where she died some time in early 1945.
13. *The German Penetration of SOE,* Jean Overton-Fuller.
14. Leo Marks, *Between Silk and Cyanide.*
15. Maurice Buckmaster, *They Fought Alone.*
16. Andrée Borrel was to die at Natzweiler.
17. *Shadows in the Fog,* Francis J Suttill.
18. Maurice Buckmaster, *They Fought Alone.*
19. David Stafford, *Churchill and Secret Service.*
20. Maurice Buckmaster, *They Fought Alone.*

21. Michael Foot, *SOE in France.*
22. Noreen Riols, *Ministry of Ag. and Fish.*
23. Ibid.
24. Ibid.
25. Maurice Buckmaster, *They Fought Alone.*

PART TWO

Chapter Seven
1. Rowden family archives.
2. Harry Rée papers.
3. de Baissac interrogation, 21–23 August 1943.
4. A postwar speech by Harry Rée.
5. Yvonne Clerc in conversation with author.
6. Harry Rée private papers.
7. Ray Jenkins, *A Pacifist at War.*
8. George Millar, *Maquis.*
9. M. R. D. Foot, *SOE in France.*
10. Francis Cammaerts [Need to know type of source]
11. Jean Overton-Fuller, *The Star Affair.*
12. Yvonne Clerc to author.
13. Christiane Janier-Dubry. [Need to know a type of source]
14. Janier-Dubry family conversation with author.
15. Ibid.

Chapter Eight
1. E. H. Cookridge, *They Came from the Sky.*
2. After the war Dericourt was tried by a French court and found not guilty.
3. Hugh Verity, *We Landed by Moonlight.*
4. Ibid.
5. The two Maugenets were very different in looks. See end of chapter.
6. E. H. Cookridge, *They Came from the Sky.*
7. Christiane Voha in conversation with the author.
8. Ibid.
9. Paper on 'German penetration of SOE', top secret, late 1945.

Chapter Nine
1. Jean Overton-Fuller, *The Starr Affair.*
2. Ibid.
3. George Millar.
4. Ibid.
5. Jean Overton-Fuller, *The Starr Affair.*
6. Vera Atkins in BBC documentary *Secret War.*

7. Brossellette did not immediately die, although most of his bones were broken, but died later in hospital.
8. Nora Baker – alias Noor Inayat Khan.
9. Jean Overton-Fuller, *The Starr Affair*.
10. Max Hastings, *The Secret War*.
11. Letter from Vogt to Jean Overton-Fuller.
12. Rita Kramer, *Flames in the Field*.
13. Elizabeth Nicholas, *Death Be Not Proud*.
14. Sarah Helm, *A Life in Secrets*.
15. Ibid.
16. Testimony from Odette Hallowes to author Liane Jones.

Chapter Ten
1. Jerrard Tickell, *Odette*.
2. Sarah Helm, *A Life in Secrets*.
3. Ibid.
4. Ibid.

Chapter Eleven
1. Sarah Helm, *A Life in Secrets*.
2. Floris Bakels, *Angels from Heaven*.
3. Ibid.

Chapter Thirteen
1. Jean Overton-Fuller *Double Webs*.
2. This is mentioned in several books on SOE.
3. Maurice Buckmaster.
4. Hugh Verity, *We Landed by Moonlight*.
5. Vera was referring to Henri Dericourt.
6 Letter to Rita Kramer from Mark Chetwynd-Stapylton.

Chapter Fourteen
1. Anonymous but probably Maurice Buckmaster.
2. Maurice Buckmaster, *They Fought Alone*.
3. F. H. Hinsley, *British Intelligence in the Second World War*, vol ii, pp. 14–15.
4. Elizabeth Nicholas, *Death Be Not Proud*.
5. Nigel West, *Secret War*.
6. *SOE in France*. It has been reported, but never confirmed that Dericourt died in a plane crash in south-east Asia in which he was the pilot.
7. Max Hastings, *The Secret War*, p. 272.
8. Placke Interrogation in 'Dericourt', P.F. 10 April 1946.
9. Francis Suttill, *Shadows in the Fog*.
10. Ibid.
11. Elizabeth Nicholas, *Death Be Not Proud*.
12. Interview with Noreen Riols, 2015.

13. Max Hastings, *Das Reich*.
14. Ibid.
15. Conversation between Victoria Boyle and author.
16. Elizabeth Nicholas, *Death Be Not Proud*.
17. Conversation with author and John Rowden.
18. Conversation between Elizabeth Nicholas and Mrs Rowden.
19. *They Fought Alone*, Maurice Buckmaster.

Bibliography

Bakels, Floris, *Angels from Heaven* (St Edmondsbury Press) 1977

Bailey, Rosemary, *Love and War in the Pyrenees* (Weidenfeld & Nicholson) 2008

Barber, Noel, *The Week France Fell* (Stein & Day) 1976

Beevor, J.G., *SOE Recollections and Reflections 1940-45* (The Bodley Head Ltd) 1981

Bertram, Barbara, *French Resistance in Sussex* (Barnworks Publishing) 1995

Bielenberg, Christabel, *The Past is Myself* (Corgi Books) 1970

Bielenberg, Christabel, *The Road Ahead* (Bantam Press) 1992

Binney, Marcus, *Secret War Heroes* Hodder & Stoughton 2005

Bleicher Hugo, Edited by Ian Colvin *Colonel Henri's Story* (William Kimber) 1968

Buckmaster, Maurice, *They Fought Alone* (Odhams Press Limited) 1958

Buckmaster, Maurice, *Specially Employed* (The Batchworth Press) 1952

Bailey, Roderick, *Forgotten Voices of the Secret War* (Ebury Press) 200

Churchill, Peter, *Of Their Own Choice* (Hodder and Stoughton) 1952

Churchill, Peter, *Duel of Wits* (Hodder and Stoughton) 1953

Collins, Larry, *Fall From Grace* (Collins) 1986

Cookridge, E. H., *They Came from the Sky* (Corgi Books) 1976

Cookridge, E. H., *Inside S.O.E.* (Arthur Barker Ltd) 1966

Cowburn, Benjamin, *No Cloak, No Dagger* (Jarrolds Publishers) 1960

Cunningham, Cyril, *Beaulieu, The Finishing School for Agents* (Pen & Sword) 1998

De Vomecourt, Philippe, *Who Lived to see the Day* (Hutchinson) 1961

Escott, Beryl E., *Mission Improbable* (Patrick Stephens Ltd) 1991

Fitzsimons, Peter, *Nancy Wake* (Harper Collins) 2001

Foot, M.R.D., *SOE In France* (Her Majesty's Stationery Office) 1966

Foot, M.R.D., *SOE: The Special Operations Executive 1940-46* (British Broadcasting Corporation) 1984

Foot, M.R.D., *Confessions of an SOE Historian* (Pen & Sword) 2008

Hastings, Max, *Das Reich* (Michael Joseph Limited) 1981

Hastings, Max, *Secret War* (Harper Collins) 2015

Hamilton-Hill, Donald, *SOE Assignment* (New English Library) 1975

Bibliography

Helm, Sarah, *A Life in Secrets* (Little, Brown) 2005
Heslop, Richard, *Xavier (*Rupert Hart-Davis Ltd) 1970
Hinsley F. H., *British Intelligence in the Second World War* (Stationery Office Books) 1993
Howarth, Patrick, *Undercover* (Phoenix Press) 2000
Jenkins, Ray, *A Pacifist at War* (Hutchinson London) 2009
Jones, Liane, *A Quiet Courage* (Bantam Press) 1990
Kemp, Anthony, *The Secret Hunters* (Michael O'Mara Books Limited) 1986
Kent, Stewart & Nicholas, N., *Agent Michael Trotobas and SOE in Northern France* (Pen & Sword) 2015
Kramer, Rita, *Flames in the Field* (Michael Joseph) 1995
Lovell, Mary S., *The Mitford Girls* (Little, Brown) 2001
Mackenzie, William, *The Secret History of SOE* (St Ermin's Press) 2000
Marks, Leo, *Between Silk and Cyanide* (Harper Collins) 1998
Marshall, Robert, *All the King's Men* (Fontana Collins) 1988
Millar, George, *Maquis* (William Heinemann) 1945
Millar, George, *Road to Resistance* (The Bodley Head) 1979
Miller, Russell, *Behind the Lines* (Pimlico) 2002
Hamilton-Hill, Donald, *SOE Assignment* (New English Library) 1975
Nemirovsky, Irene, *Suite Francaise* (Chatto & Windus) 2006
Nicholas, Elizabeth, *Death Be Not Proud* (Cresset Press) 1958
O'Connor, Bernard, *RAF Tempsford* (Amberley) 2010
O'Connor, Bernard, *Churchill's Angels* (Amberley) 2012
Ottaway, Susan, *Sisters, Secrets and Sacrifice* (Pen & Sword) 2013
Overton-Fuller, Jean, *Secret Agent* (Pan Books) 1961
Overton-Fuller, Jean, *The Starr Affair* (Victor Gollancz Ltd) 1954
Overton-Fuller, Jean, *The German Penetration of SOE* (George Mann) 1975
Overton-Fuller, Jean, *Double Webs* (Putnam) 1958
Riols, Noreen, *Ministry of Ag and Fish* (Macmillan) 2013
Simpson, William, *I Burned my Fingers* (Hamish Hamilton)
Simpson, William, *One of our Pilots is Safe* (Hamish Hamilton) 1945
Stafford, David, *Churchill & Secret Service* (Overlook Books) 1998
Stafford, David, *British and European Resistance* (Thistle Publishing) 2013
Stafford, David, *Secret Agent* (BBC Worldwide Limited) 2000
Stafford, David, *Ten Days to D-Day* (Little, Brown) 2003
Stevenson, William, *Spymistress* (Arcade Publishing) 2007
Suttill, Francis, *Shadows in the Fog: The True Story of Major Suttill and the Prosper French Resistance Network* (The History Press) 2014
Tickell, Jerrard, *Moon Squadron* (Allan Wingate) 1956
Tindall, Gillian, *Three Houses, Many Lives* (Chatto & Windus) 2012
Verity, Hugh, *We Landed by Moonlight* (Ian Allan Ltd) 1978
Wake, Nancy, *The White Mouse* (The Macmillan Company of Australia) 1985
Webb, Anthony M., *The Natzweiler Trial* (William Hodge and Company) 1949
Werth, Leon, *33 Jours* (Melville House) 2015
West, Nigel, *Secret War, The Story of SOE* (Hodder and Stoughton) 1993
Zembsch-Schreve, Guido, *Pierre Lalande, Special Agent* (Leo Cooper) 1996

Index

Index